CHANEL'S WAR

CHANEL'S WAR

ESCAPE FROM FRANCE

RICHARD WALLACE

For
Jacqueline Marion, Helen, Linnet, Tracy,
and
Jacqueline Hélène

Jacket quote courtesy of chanel-muggeridge.co.uk.

First published 2025

The History Press
97 St George's Place, Cheltenham,
Gloucestershire, GL50 3QB
www.thehistorypress.co.uk

© Richard Wallace, 2025

The right of Richard Wallace to be identified as the Author
of this work has been asserted in accordance with the
Copyright, Designs and Patents Act 1988.

All rights reserved. No part of this book may be reprinted
or reproduced or utilised in any form or by any electronic,
mechanical or other means, now known or hereafter invented,
including photocopying and recording, or in any information
storage or retrieval system, without the permission in writing
from the Publishers.

British Library Cataloguing in Publication Data.
A catalogue record for this book is available from the British Library.

ISBN 978 1 80399 979 1

Typesetting and origination by The History Press
Printed and bound in Great Britain by TJ Books, Padstow, Cornwall.

The History Press proudly supports

Trees for LYfe

www.treesforlife.org.uk

EU Authorised Representative: Easy Access System Europe
Mustamäe tee 50, 10621 Tallinn, Estonia
gpst.request@easproject.com

CONTENTS

Timeline of Key Events Covered by *Chanel's War*   6
Introduction: Atelier No. 5   13

1. The Blood-Dimmed Tide   29
2. *Les Fifis*   41
3. A Knock on the Door   53
4. Hollywood and a Diamond Duke   60
5. Saint Mugg   69
6. Your German Friend   78
7. Spatz   89
8. Agent F-7124   99
9. The Property of Jews   113
10. Dear Winston   137
11. Not Your Finest Hour?   146
12. Don't Lose a Minute   155
13. *Gang des Tractions Avant*   162
14. Who Has Seen Coco?   174
15. Zombie   181
16. Mademoiselle Only Drinks Champagne   192
17. Bottoms up!   207
18. Fiasco   216
Postscript: Shadows Deep and Long   225

Acknowledgements   230
Notes   231
Select Bibliography   242
Index   250

TIMELINE OF KEY EVENTS COVERED BY *CHANEL'S WAR*

1939

France declares war on Nazi Germany (3 September).

Chanel closes Maison CHANEL but keeps the perfume business running. Her lover (and a later *Résistance* leader), Pierre Reverdy, tells her war is a 'time to hide, lie low and keep quiet'.[1]

1940

The German Luftwaffe bombs Paris (3 June).

The Wertheimer perfume factory in Pantin, the suburb of Paris where CHANEL No. 5 is manufactured, is destroyed by German bombing.

As the German army approaches, Chanel flees and heads to the small village of Corbères-Abères in the Pyrénées to stay with her nephew, André Palasse, and his family. She later learns André has been interned in a German prisoner of war (POW) camp.

Paris is declared an open city by the French government as it attempts to regroup in Bordeaux (13 June).

German troops enter Paris, beginning four years of brutal occupation (14 June).

France signs an armistice with Germany, dividing the country into two zones: an occupied zone administered by the Nazis (known as the *Zone Occupée*) in the northern and western part of the country, and the *Zone Libre* (Free Zone) in the south (22 June).

Maréchal Philippe Pétain becomes Head of the French State, based in the Free Zone spa town of Vichy (10 July).

Chanel sets off for Vichy, 434km away from Corbères-Abères, to obtain papers for André's release. Her lawyer, René Chambrun, advises her to return to Paris and seek out a sympathetic Nazi powerbroker to help her and secure her safety in the city.

Recognising the writing was on the wall for Jews and Jewish businesses in Europe, the Wertheimer brothers 'sell' Société des Parfums CHANEL to an aircraft manufacturer from Bordeaux, Félix Amiot, without consulting Chanel. The deal stipulates Amiot would hold the perfume business in trust for the Wertheimers.

Chanel returns to Paris and resumes her residency at the Hôtel Ritz on Place Vendôme with the help of her new friend and lover, Baron Hans Günther von Dincklage, a German aristocrat and embassy official first recruited by the *Abwehr* (German military intelligence) in 1919 as agent F-8680.

Pierre and Paul Wertheimer and their families arrive in New York and immediately set up a company to continue manufacturing their cash cow, CHANEL No. 5, in America.

A representative of the Wertheimers, Greg Thomas, retrieves the precious No. 5 formula from Félix Amiot and buys supplies of No. 5 ingredients from the Mul family, exclusive suppliers of the perfume since its creation in 1921.

1941

Greg Thomas returns to New York with his precious cargo of No. 5 ingredients.

Von Dincklage introduces Chanel to his *Abwehr* boss, Hermann Niebuhr, who tells her about the Wertheimer business arrangements (i.e. the Amiot Société des Parfums CHANEL deal and the New York perfume factory).

After intense lobbying by Niebuhr, the Nazi department responsible for the confiscation and disposal of Jewish-owned assets appoints

Georges Madou as provisional administrator of Parfums CHANEL (8 February).

Chanel, von Dincklage, the French traitor Baron Louis de Vaufreland, and Niebuhr conceive a plan to demonstrate how Chanel's English political contacts could be useful to the Nazis. In return for her cooperation and complicity, Niebuhr promises to help with André's release and the return of Parfums CHANEL to her.

To speed things up, Chanel personally writes to Madou claiming that Parfums CHANEL 'is still the property of Jews' and had been legally 'abandoned' by the owners[2] (5 May).

Dr Kurt Blanke, Head of the Entjudung (the elimination of Jewish influence), informs Chanel there is nothing he can do to legally wrest control of Parfums CHANEL from Félix Amiot, and the case is closed.

Chanel and the Spanish-speaking Vaufreland travel to neutral Spain by overnight train on an *Abwehr* mission (5 August).

Although Chanel's mission was unsuccessful, the *Abwehr* is satisfied with her commitment and release André. Chanel is also given an official *Abwehr* agent number, F-7124, and the code name Westminster.

1942

Chanel begins the manufacture of rogue fragrances under the brand name Mademoiselle Chanel. These rogue products included a No. 1, a No. 2, a No. 3, and a No. 31.

1943

Chanel and von Dincklage travel to Berlin as guests of SS General Walter Schellenberg, Reichsführer Heinrich Himmler's intelligence chief.

Chanel, von Dincklage, and Vera Lombardi travel to Madrid for a Schellenberg operation code named Modellhut (Model Hat). But after they arrive and check into the Hôtel Ritz, the bizarre plan quickly unravels and descends into farce (17 December).

1944

Chanel vacates her suite at the Hôtel Ritz on Place Vendôme, after the failed 20 July assassination attempt on Hitler, when the Gestapo begins rounding up suspects hiding in the hotel.

Résistance uprising in Paris (19 August).

Paris is liberated by the Allies (25 August).

Chanel, Major Muggeridge of MI6, and Muggeridge's lover dine at 31 rue Cambon (25 August).

Chanel is interrogated at the headquarters of the French Forces of the Interior (FFI) on the Île de la Cité but is released hours later through the intervention of *Résistance* leader Pierre Reverdy. A few days later she arrives unscathed at the chic Hôtel Beau-Rivage in Switzerland (September).

1945

Former Vichy official Paul Morand interviews Chanel in Switzerland for a prospective biography.

1946

Von Dincklage is finally granted Swiss entry. He and Chanel resume the stylish and well-upholstered lifestyle they enjoyed during the war.

A French court issues an urgent warrant to bring Chanel to France for questioning. A presiding member of the court, Judge Roger Serre, orders French police and border officers to escort the wanted Chanel back to Paris (16 April).

1947

The Wertheimers agree to pay Chanel almost US$400,000 in back royalties and 2 per cent of world sales (the equivalent of US$25 million a year in modern currency) of No. 5 plus the rights to produce her own scents (but without the numeral 5) from Switzerland.

Judge Serre interrogates Chanel's nephew, André Palasse (20 November).

1948

Chanel begins live cell therapy designed to arrest the ageing process, practised by Swiss surgeon Dr Paul Niehans at Clinique La Prairie.

Chanel appears before Judge Fernand Leclercq at the Court of Justice in Paris to answer questions first requested of her two years earlier (4 June).

1950

Chanel attends her old friend Misia Sert's funeral in Paris (October).

1952

Parisian-based journalist and editor Michel Déon spends a year with Chanel writing her biography.

1953

Total amnesty (French Law No. 53–681) for certain crimes committed during the Second World War comes into effect, paving the way for Chanel's return to Paris.

The Wertheimers agree to finance Chanel's return to haute couture.

The New York Times announces Chanel's first show after fifteen years will occur on Friday, 5 February 1954 in Paris.

1954

Pierre Wertheimer negotiates a new deal with Chanel: the Wertheimers will finance the Maison's headquarters on rue Cambon, the remuneration of her staff, any expenses associated with her collections, her personal expenditures, and all her taxes for the duration of her life in exchange for total ownership of the brand.

1854

INTRODUCTION: ATELIER NO. 5

At precisely 3 p.m. on Saturday, 9 January 1971 the monstre sacré of the fashion world,[1] Mademoiselle Gabrielle 'Coco' Chanel, left her splendid third-floor suite at 31 rue Cambon in Paris and descended its famous mirrored spiral staircase.

Chanel's working routine hardly varied from year to year, following the same strict lines and rigid ethos she imparted to her clothes. The journalist George W. Herald, witnessing her method in the mid-1960s, described the effect she had on those in her working orbit.[2] As soon as she entered Maison CHANEL's fitting room, known as 'Atelier No. 5', everyone inside the salon immediately stopped what they were doing and held their breath. The tiny 5ft 3in, 45kg couturière casually smiled and nodded as she moved across the floor, her signature two-tone slingback shoes rhythmically clacking against the floorboards like castanets.

In 1931 Chanel was described as:

> ... little-boned, well-shouldered, slim, not tall; with small juvenile features which her diffident gestures, her decided manner, make seem intriguingly precocious. Her eyes are luscious, the color of sweet dates; her hair is short, curly, and brown; her voice low.[3]

Now, at 87, she is 'small, dark and simian'[4] but still has the walk and supple figure of a girl (topped off in those days by a severe bob of jet-black hair, which many thought was a wig sewn into the hatband of her signature straw boater to hide her bald spots). It is a look she has been cultivating for over seventy years. 'Cut off my head, and I'm thirteen,'⁵ she once remarked to Truman Capote. To Carmel Snow of *Harper's Bazaar*, she was more brazen: '... when she urges you, as she frequently does, to squeeze her buttocks, you find they're as hard as a cement ball.'⁶

But, of course, she is no ordinary girl. She is the girl who can suck the air out of a room and render everyone in it speechless without trying. Such reverence is expected, never demanded, always offered, like an acknowledged token of gratitude served up by a nervous supplicant on a silver salver. Mademoiselle has become so accustomed to the sensation, she barely registers the effect.

Though it is the weekend, Chanel is wearing her uniform: a pastel bouclé tweed suit accented with soft purple braids, an Arabian three-string pearl necklace, and sparkling bracelets. When she died, her wardrobe contained just three suits, two of which (the pastel one and another with a small pattern) she had worn for the last three years. A brand-new white suit dating from August 1969 completed her personal collection.⁷

At the rear of the room, half a dozen sleek, young house models sit awkwardly on chairs covered in white dust cloths, like pupils waiting to recite their homework. Most of them have been made up to mimic Chanel's look in the 1950s, with earrings, thickly drawn black eyebrows, and broadly painted red mouths.

In the silence, everyone waits for Mademoiselle to settle and compose herself.

As she has done almost every day since she emerged from exile in 1954, Chanel drapes a pair of dainty dressmakers' scissors around her neck and takes a seat on a gilded chair (visitors thought it looked more like a throne than a humble chair). On the floor of the Parisian studio are boxes full of dressmaking paraphernalia, and on another chair lies a pair of thick piano-black spectacles, one of a number that have been scattered strategically around the building to ensure Chanel always has one within reach. Around her, poised like racehorses nudging the wire at the start of a race, are the heads (called *premiers*) of the nine workshops (*ateliers*) that perform little miracles for Maison CHANEL.

The dangerous game begins. Everyone breathes a little.

The first outfit from the new collection to be shown in under a month's time is presented to her (Chanel's fetish number was five, and she invariably debuted her collections on 5 February and August every year). It is a basic black cocktail dress. Chanel calls the model over to check that everything is sitting right. She quickly pulls an arm off the shoulder, dismantles the collar with her scissors, and repositions everything on the outfit in a different way. Then she hacks off an ornament and declares to one of the *premiers* the material is superfluous and should be thrown away like fat off the bone.

Another outfit is presented.

Chanel snips the stitches of an armhole with her scissors and uses long bead-headed pins to reposition it point by point, sticking them in with determined thrusts like a frustrated assassin. Her face is tense. Spotting another suspected bulge, she grasps it with her fingers and tears it this way and that. The models are used to the rough treatment, swaying with Mademoiselle's cut and thrusts like limp dancing partners.

The rejected 'fatty' material from the black cocktail dress is discreetly stowed away in one of the dressmaking boxes. Chanel stretches out on the floor to see whether the new dress falls properly, turns onto her back, pulls the hem towards her, and then accepts the hand of a *premier* to get back up when she is satisfied.

Things are not going well. She doesn't like anything she sees. The waist is too big on one and the back is too bare on the other. Chanel's clothes always have a small shoulder, a high waist, and short sleeves. She drapes fabric over her models and cuts it away like a gardener trimming a hedge. The fabric is always off-grain, so it naturally hugs the figure, making a woman look alluring while the narrow shoulder makes her look smaller.

The hacking and tearing and ripping continues.

A neutral cardigan jacket without a collar is presented with patch pockets and gold buttons. The edges are finished in navy-blue braid. Traditionally, the back of a CHANEL jacket has one seam that runs straight down the middle. Her jackets are straight and structured and a bit boxy, with silk linings and slim cuffs that sit high on the shoulder. A gold chain is sewn into the hem so they hang perfectly from the shoulders.

But something is wrong with this one – or at least not quite right. Chanel tilts her head and grimaces.

The *premiers* are biting their lips and taking copious notes. There is a hint of gently rising hysteria in the cold, austere room. Armpits are itchy. Chanel lights a Camel cigarette (she routinely favoured Gitanes before the war, only switching to the American brand after it) and inserts it into a long, golden cigarette holder. She smokes and does not exhale. The house models are trying to keep calm and quiet, but after every violent alteration by Mademoiselle, her teeth clenching the ebonite mouthpiece of the cigarette holder, they are becoming more and more nervous, highly strung and emaciated as they always are.

She plays with the jacket for what seems like hours, tugging and pinning the narrowly cut sleeves, elongating the arms, and flattering the curve of the body. In between drags of her cigarette, she says it should be comfortable enough for the model to raise her hands above her head without feeling constrained by the fabric. She moves on to a delicious fur-collared jacket in pale wool lined with a Japanese silk print. After it gets the full Chanel treatment, it's the turn of a cream jacket trimmed with black braid.

Everyone is exhausted. Finally, she gives up and retreats upstairs to her apartment, with a handful of *premiers* and models (or 'mannequins' as she likes to call them) for final touches to some of the garments that have made it to an advanced stage. She is given a variety of necklaces, flowers, brooches, chains, and belts to pick from. A hat is offered, a twist on the straw boater she first sold over sixty years ago. She pulls it straight down over a model's head until it's secure over the brow. The fitting is eventually over when she says, 'Now ... there you are ... it's not so tacky, is it? Not too bad, don't you think? So go ahead.'[8]

The model moves to a podium between the precious coromandel screens as instructed and poses one last time for Mademoiselle to be sure everything is perfect.

The aim is to show as many dresses as possible on the day the new collection is unveiled. From over 100 potential outfits, only sixty to seventy normally make the cut (before the Second World War it was reported she designed about 400 frocks for each of her February and August collections).[9] The eliminated outfits are discarded without pity or remorse. Chanel is ruthless. Some of the *premiers* quietly cry after she leaves the room for the evening drive in her silver Rolls-Royce, dabbing their eyes with linen castoffs. Chanel works on living models, unlike other Parisian dressmakers, who prefer using sketches and patterns in their workrooms:

> Fashion is like sculpture, I must feel with my hands how the clothes fit on the body ... On paper one can cheat, stretch the torso, draw out the legs. I don't sell paper, I sell dresses ... I am the last of my kind. I will have no successors.[10]

It is a process she has used since the earliest days of Maison CHANEL, as described in a *New Yorker* profile of her in 1931:

> Some of the dressmakers who have passed through art or trade schools sketch their designs first, others of more practical training go straight for the scissors and cloth. Chanel cannot sketch and doesn't like to sew. Apparently she describes what she wants to a *première,* who then turns up with the rough form, which Chanel invariably finds all wrong. As she has a sound theory that no one can tell what a dress looks like either on paper or on a cutting table, or in anything but the material for which it was intended, the model is put on a mannequin and the model and the mannequin may then go through as many as thirty destructive fittings, which may last only half the night or the better part of a week. Also, if the material is costly, the fittings may go through the better part of a bolt of velours or lame [*sic*]. However, to such textiles Chanel is cold. She says the only fabrics which take color perfectly are wool and cotton, especially cheap cotton—one of the many professional views held by her which have pained her rivals.[11]

For Chanel, fashion was a business, not an art form: 'We don't work from genius, we're tradespeople. We don't hang clothes in galleries to be seen, we sell them.'[12]

And when things don't sell, Mademoiselle could be waspish. Jackie Rogers, a former CHANEL house model, recounted the day when:

> ... Princess Paola of Belgium came to see a private showing of the whole collection. We all streamed out, one after another, modeling the latest designs, but in the end the Princess bought nothing. Chanel

was furious and came down the stairs screaming, 'Give me the little French woman with the *argent dans le sac*!' ('money in her bag')[13]

The dresses she sells are deceptive in their simplicity and elegance. It is the workmanship that separates them from the cheap copies that sell for a fraction of a finished CHANEL. Extreme care is applied to every eyelet, pocket, seam, and button. It takes at least 150 hours to make one dress. Often, the finer details in her work are hard to see, except for those with a trained eye and a tactile understanding of understated luxury.

But such perfection has a price and, like Enzo Ferrari, who only consented to sell street cars in order to keep his racing cars on the track, Chanel had to rely on worldwide sales of CHANEL No. 5 perfume and other side products to compensate for the huge annual losses of her haute couture business.

She doesn't care. The only thing she cares about is complete strangers raking up spurious details of her past. It is the one thing she does not tolerate. But she is eternally thankful no one can get it right, not even her. Everything, like the fabrics of her dresses, can be manipulated, torn out, reconstituted, put back together again in a completely different way from the original and still be true to the first intent. So long as it hangs properly, fits well, and works, it will pass the test of time and be copied and certified as the embodiment of an acknowledged fact.

For years, American producers tried to bring her life story to the stage. The first was Alan Lerner (co-writer of *My Fair Lady*) in 1960. He told her he was going to write a musical comedy about her when he went to see Mademoiselle in her black-and-white house in Lausanne. Chanel was shocked but pretended not to care. A comedy?

She knew her life was more tragic than comedic. It was, like everyone's, littered with bad memories she would rather forget, some of them still life threatening. Black spots of repressed pain, she called them, encroaching shadows in the sunshine. It was just too much to bear thinking about, this trivialising of her life's journey and accomplishments. Typical of these Americans to think everything of note in a person's life amounts to nothing more than a collection of superficial, hunky-dory Broadway moments to be shared with all and sundry for a measly dollar at a time. She gave Lerner a good lunch and he trudged back to the US empty-handed (in 1969 Lerner got his wish, with Katharine Hepburn in the title role of *Coco*, a short-lived Broadway musical which the real Coco refused to see in protest at the producers' decision not to cast Audrey Hepburn in the title role).

Unlike her clothes, the Chanel story is messy, complicated, devious, and unstructured. She is like the scheming, vindictive Marquise de Merteuil in Pierre Choderlos de Laclos's *Les Liaisons Dangereuses*, who resorted to inventing herself and 'ways of escape no one has ever thought of before':[14]

> When I came out into society, I was fifteen. I already knew that the role I was condemned to, namely to keep quiet and do what I was told, gave me the perfect opportunity to listen and observe. Not to what people told me, which naturally was of no interest, but to whatever it was they were trying to hide. I practiced detachment. I learned how to look cheerful while, under the table, I stuck a fork into the back of my hand. I became a virtuoso of deceit. It wasn't pleasure I was after, it was knowledge. I consulted the strictest moralists to learn how to appear, philosophers to find out what to think, and novelists to see what I could get away with. And in the end, I distilled everything to one wonderfully simple principle: win or die.[15]

Her need to destroy, to manipulate, to torture herself, her models, and her friends was a constant feature of her life, never more so than when she returned to the Ritz from her evening drive on Saturday, 9 January 1971.

Usually after the sedate 10–12km promenade around the left and right banks of the city, she would stop off at Angelina. Anton Rumpelmayer, a Bratislava native, ran the chic Parisian patisserie on rue de Rivoli and, at her preferred table of No. 45, Chanel would order a sugary croissant with dark chocolate and either a double espresso or a cup of green tea, or her favourite hot *chocolat l'Africain*, a blend of cocoa beans mixed with whole milk that's whipped, mixed, and brewed for almost two and a half hours.

But tonight Mademoiselle was tired, fidgety, and restless from the disappointing fitting earlier in the day. She opted to go straight up to her white, sixth-floor bedroom suite overlooking Place Vendôme at the Hôtel Ritz, where she could be attended to by her maid, Céline (Chanel insisted on calling her Jeanne). It was much smaller than the 188m² second-floor suite she once occupied in 1937. (This suite, 302, is now known at the Ritz as the 'Coco Chanel Salon'.) Only very special friends were allowed to see her there as opposed to the legendary apartment atop rue Cambon, which served as a kind of not-so *privée* reception/office/entertaining space for clients.

Chanel had been at the Ritz since 1934, when her first suite consisted of a sitting room with a wood-burning fireplace and a small bedroom. From the hotel's back entrance, she crossed the street to her rue Cambon salon at noon every day to avoid passing the rival Maison Schiaparelli boutique at Place Vendôme. One of the salon's *vendeuses* was always on lookout and would say, 'She's coming! She's coming!', ensuring everyone was alerted and attentive. Mademoiselle then entered Maison CHANEL and climbed the stairs, speaking in guttural French to the sales girls on her way to her private apartment. Some of the girls were there because they did not speak French but they could speak English or German or Italian. To those who struggled to keep up with her, she'd wave away their insecurities about what little French they knew. 'Just speak it quickly, then it doesn't matter,' she'd tell them in croaky English.[16]

On 9 January Chanel had a troubled, sleepless night.

The octogenarian's habit of sleepwalking had intensified with age. Several times in the months preceding her death, Céline discovered her naked in her room, holding a pair of scissors, stabbing and ripping up her pyjamas, reducing them to useless scraps on the carpet. The maid had to lock her in her room most nights for her own safety and confiscate her beloved scissors from their place on the bedside table. Chanel used them every night to cut the pills away from their foil covering before injecting herself with Sedol, a form of morphine introduced to her by Misia Sert. Chanel had relied upon the drug since 1935 (after the death of her last great love, Paul Iribe) to help her sleep. Her friend Claude Delay described her reliance this way: 'Her injection was a substitute for love …

Sedol was her last defence against the night – the ultimate and solitary penetration.'¹⁷

Chanel took off her make-up with the corner of a towel dipped in cream, washed herself underneath, then took a bottle of cold water from a small refrigerator to her bedside table. As usual, Mademoiselle was attended to by her faithful and adoring retinue of helpers: the butler, François Mironnet; the maid, Céline; and a secretary, Lilou Grumbach. Sometimes, if the weather was dreary or Mademoiselle seemed restless and fidgety, François would remove his white gloves and sit beside Chanel while she ate something in the suite to keep her company, or else he played cards silently and purposely with Lilou in a room close by Mademoiselle's while she fell asleep.

The following morning, a Sunday, she was so disconsolate she remained in bed. At 1 p.m. Claude Delay visited her at the Ritz and saw her sitting at her dressing table applying make-up, painstakingly drawing on dark brows and scarlet lipstick while inspecting her appearance in the mirror:

> I often found her alone, sitting at her dressing-table, gazing down into the garden, looking at the chestnut trees. She was still so slender, thin as a girl in her white pyjamas. 'One shouldn't live alone,' she'd say. 'It's a mistake. I used to think I had to make my life on my own, but I was wrong.'¹⁸

After Chanel swallowed a glass of sugar and water with a Noprin capsule (a mild sedative used for headaches and backaches), they left together for lunch at Chanel's regular table downstairs, separated as usual from the other diners by a vast space: 'Monsieur Ritz bowed. Coco ordered her famous unsalted ham to start with, followed by a minute steak with boiled potatoes, a melon for desert [sic], and the customary well-chilled Riesling.'¹⁹

Hours after everyone had left the room, the two women eventually went for Chanel's habitual afternoon drive:

> She put on her coat of tweed lined with kalgan (lamb's wool). 'It's ten years old,' she said. Washable beige gloves, open at the wrist. The Cadillac drove up the Champs-Élysées, crammed with

a gloomy crowd, and took us on 'her' drive: round the racecourse in a mist pierced by a blinding sun ... we came back past Trocadéro ... the Place de la Concorde.[20]

When the car returned them to the Ritz, the sun had already set, and an icy, iridescent moon filled the bruised sky. Getting out as Delay said goodbye, Chanel announced with a weary smile she would be working at rue Cambon the next day.

Mademoiselle returned to her sixth-floor bedroom and found Céline waiting for her. She said she was tired, so very tired, and wanted to lie down on the bed fully clothed. Céline nodded and apprehensively left her alone. Around 8.30 p.m., Chanel asked Céline to open the window as she was struggling to breathe and then began frantically lunging at phantoms and demons only she could see, screaming, 'They're killing me ... they'll have killed me.'[21] Céline and Lilou went to Chanel's bedside to calm her down while she struggled and groped for her Sedol injection. Céline eventually broke the stubborn phial, and Mademoiselle stabbed the quivering syringe into her hip. 'You see,' she said defiantly, 'this is how one dies.'[22]

They were her last recorded words.

Or were they?

According to Oriole Cullen, curator of the September 2023 Victoria & Albert (V&A) Museum's exhibition 'Gabrielle Chanel. Fashion Manifesto', on that night she did ask Céline to open the window of her suite at the Ritz because she couldn't breathe, but then calmly took her usual night-time sedative and died in her sleep.[23]

Even in death, Chanel exists as a contradiction of time, space, and memory (James Brady, correspondent of *Women's Wear Daily*, described her as 'a biased mass of contradictions'.)[24] Whatever the circumstances of her death, the next morning her shrivelled dead body lay on her bed at the Ritz. Céline had dressed her in the suit she wore every day with a white blouse and tucked her hands beneath the linen sheets. A linen handkerchief was tied under her chin to keep it in place. In the cold January light, she looked very small, like a serious little girl solemnly participating in her first holy communion.

Jackie Rogers, the one-time Chanel house model who became very close to Mademoiselle in the 1960s, blamed her rapid decline on her secretary, Lilou:

> I was devastated when I found out she had died alone with only Lilou at her side. Later, it was discovered that all of her jewels were missing, and they still have not been found to this day. I have always wondered why Lilou took so much abuse from Chanel. She was always very possessive of Chanel; she was more than a secretary and assistant to her. She had also managed to keep everyone away from Mademoiselle, including me, and now I think I know why. The few times that I saw Chanel in her last years things were always difficult because of Lilou. I even tried to arrange a reconciliation … but was constantly told that now wasn't the right time, and it sadly never was.[25]

The years of surviving through every kind of impossible situation were finally over for Coco Chanel. Her ruthless drive to succeed, her uncanny instincts on what needed to be done at any given moment, and her ability to reinvent herself at any given time were at an end, burned out by old age, drugs, and the ravages of unrepressed ambition.

Chanel was the supreme survivor. Throughout her life she always did what she had to do in order to ensure this survival. These things were done without question, without remorse, without coercion. It was the only way she knew, and it had served her well.

For Chanel, survival meant escape: escape from poverty, escape from ignorance, escape from ridicule, escape from conformity, escape from rejection, escape from reality, escape from love, escape from servitude, escape from anonymity, escape from gratitude, escape from dependence, escape from persecution, and escape from fact:

> As a neighboring countryman said of Chanel by way of explaining her great success: 'In the first place, she's Auvergnate; in the second, she has the endurance of a greyhound; and third'—he added with an appropriate note of respect—'she has the true affection for money.'[26]

This affection came to her at the age of 12 when she realised: '... without money, you are nothing, that with money you can do anything ... I would say to myself over and over, "Money is the key to freedom."'[27]

Chanel used money to escape from everything that tied her down, that repressed her burning determination to succeed, to win whatever the cost. Her life was an audacious performance, a masterpiece of illusion. She deceived everyone, especially herself. She was on the verge of going under repeatedly, disappearing without a trace at any time, all the time. She was unafraid of anyone. She would not be ignored. The diminutive, dusky waif played dangerous games with dangerous people and benefited from the experience, becoming stronger and more resilient as a result. And rich, richer than she ever imagined she would be during those icy cold nights in Aubazine when she cried herself silently to sleep ... so rich the money began melting into the background like wallpaper one ceases to notice.

Chanel viscerally needed to be where the action was, where decisions were made, where the right people with the power to make the right things happen for her congregated, because the life she wanted could only be earned this way, and she knew, above everything else, the right things didn't happen to you in exile. Only inconsequential things flourished on the periphery. If you wanted to survive, to succeed in the snake pit, you had to be at the centre where the winners lived, performed, killed, and passed on their secrets to others waiting silently in the shadows for the chance to perform. And when it's your turn, you must perform or else become nothing to nobody.

She had such ambition that fellow addict Truman Capote described it being clearly visible in the taut stem of her neck:

> ... one thinks of a plant, an old hardy perennial still pushing toward, though now a touch parched by, the sun of success that, for those talented inconsolable primed with desire and fueled with ego and whose relentless energy propels the engine that hauls along the lethargic rest of us, invariably flourishes in the frigid sky of ambition.[28]

And yet Chanel's greatest performance, her greatest escape, her greatest achievement in escaping certain death at the hands of her countrymen when Paris was liberated from the Nazis in August 1944, she kept quietly to herself, ensuring as much as she could that no possible record of the details continued to exist. For eighty years after the end of the Second World War, this incredible feat of courage, luck, and ingenuity in the midst of incredible danger has never been fully explained or revealed, deliberately shrouded in disinformation and secrecy by family, friends, wary governments, risk-averse business partners, and fellow collaborators.

A mere seven years after her death, the following nonsense appeared: 'She retired in 1939 after years of personal tumult that had included a well publicized love affair with the Duke of Westminster.'[29]

Then nothing, a blanked-out period of fifteen years, until 'she made a comeback in 1954 and again her fashions became popular, especially in the United States'.[30]

This black hole persisted into the twenty-first century.

During the 2011 release of Hal Vaughan's book *Sleeping with the Enemy: Coco Chanel's Secret War*, the CHANEL organisation dismissed unsavoury claims about its founder's Nazi affiliations and activities during the Second World War in the following manner: 'More than 57 books have been written about Gabrielle (Coco) Chanel. To decide for yourself, we would encourage you to consult some of the more serious ones.'[31]

The CHANEL organisation's position, that no one knows for sure exactly what she did during the war and these activities will always remain a mystery, was reinforced by the French establishment. In an interview with *The New Yorker* to coincide with the release of his book, Vaughan had this to say:

> The work of Robert Paxton (historian, author of the pioneering 1972 book on French collaboration, Vichy France: Old Guard and New Order 1940-1944) never quite rubbed off on our memory of Chanel—and for a simple reason. She is essentially a hard-currency machine. Chanel is an icon, an idol in France—never mind the details of her life, her anti-Semitism, her dealings with the Nazis. Interestingly enough, I should mention that the French have not bought my book—at least not yet. It's coming out in America and in Britain and in Germany. It's been translated in

[*sic*] Portuguese and translated into Dutch. But the French have yet to buy the book.³²

The problem facing researchers like Hal Vaughan is that, as Chanel's besotted biographer Isée St John Knowles put it, many testimonies have been amputated over the years, sometimes by illustrious biographers and historians. There are still untapped sources, but they remain in private collections, and 'the private hands in which they lie are resolutely opposed to divulging them for fear of damaging Chanel's image'.³³

In a bid to end the debate once and for all about her wartime activities, Knowles wrote a querulous book with the cooperation of Chanel's adoring great-niece, the late Gabrielle Palasse-Labrunie, entitled *Coco Chanel, cette femme libre qui défia les tyrans* (*Coco Chanel, the freedom-loving woman who defied the tyrans of her day*). The book claimed to reveal, for the first time, Chanel's own unpublished account of her war, as she recounted it orally to the artist Limouse from 1941 to 1951. Limouse, in turn, conveyed these memories, which became his memories to Knowles. Needless to say, Knowles was wholeheartedly on her side, and his life's mission was to clear her name of any wrongdoing.

It is a pattern we find in many Chanel biographies. A willingness to accept her word when we know she enjoyed making mischief with her life as if it were a garment that could be hacked and altered until it looked perfect, just right for a particular moment on a particular day for a particular purpose. As four-term British prime minister William E. Gladstone once observed, 'The first essential for a Prime Minister is to be a good butcher.'³⁴

Chanel was a good butcher. She hacked and she cut the bits of her life that didn't fit, were of little use, or weren't worthy of her esteem.

As regards this particular examination of a fascinating and neglected period of her life, the aim is to uncover what really happened to Chanel between 1939 and 1954. To reveal what ended up on the atelier's floor, so to speak – what she thought she had swept away and dumped into obscurity forever.

What is the real story behind this gaping black hole in Chanel's official history? In my view, the real story is not that she escaped from

Paris and certain death in 1944 (who wouldn't have tried to do that, given her situation?). The real story is how, and the audacious means she employed to pull it off.

It is a mystery that has never, until now, been examined coldly with the aid of new information and a certain degree of imagination. The mystery occurred when Nazi Germany was still fighting madly for survival, massacring civilians and indiscriminately deporting people to concentration camps. France itself was a country burning for revenge. In Paris, roaming gangs of violent thugs gorged themselves on the red-hot desire to get even with collaborators. Hollow-eyed families pined for the chance to inflict devastating wounds on those who had survived the horrors of the war on a full belly and a soft bed while others lived on rats, or were gleefully tortured, their children's lives randomly decimated by evil.

As one eyewitness later wrote:

> The truth is that under the German occupation everyone who did not go underground or abroad was in some degree a collaborator and could be plausibly accused as such. The barber who cropped the bullet heads of German soldiers, the greengrocer who sold them fruit, the waiter who served them meals, the whore who went to bed with them, the entertainer who sang to them, the clown who made them laugh, were all collaborating. I felt desperately sorry for the individuals who were picked on for this soi-disant crime, especially when, as sometimes happened, I actually saw the pack going after their victim – shaving the head of some wretched girl, hunting down a German soldier who had got left behind, carrying some gibbering, trembling creature off to prison.[35]

Chanel's escape was no mean feat. She did not simply jump into her chauffeur-driven Cadillac and arrive unscathed in Switzerland as the majority of Chanel biographies and websites claim. And she could not have done it without direct help.

In the same vein, Chanel's so-called exile in Switzerland has been routinely described over the years as a murky period when she lived off the immense royalties generated by the products of her brand in a kind of serene coma of indifference. Nothing can be further from this 'truth'. She not only lived in constant fear of being assassinated by French fanatics throughout this time, but she was also constantly scheming to get back into the game of haute couture.

Chanel the person, however, would have been unimpressed by any public airing of these revelations during her lifetime. The facts were her business, no one else's. If pressed, she'd certainly resist any further elaboration, twisting her mouth and shrugging her shoulders in that Gallic way of hers, adroitly passing the whole thing off as something one just did in the prevailing circumstances. One of many people who did, she might add. One simply had no choice in the matter. None.

Like the Marquise de Merteuil, for Chanel it was yet another compulsory choice in a string of compulsory choices of either winning or dying (and she had no intention of ever dying).

'Why was that so unusual?' she might ask a misty-eyed interviewer as she imperiously reclined across one of her supple chaises longues, her dense black eyes boring into her interrogator's thick skull like tracer bullets.

Why indeed?

1

THE BLOOD-DIMMED TIDE

A few days after Paris was officially liberated on Friday, 25 August 1944, with white ash floating in the air from the thousands of incriminating documents burned by the Germans in the days preceding it, Coco Chanel received a confident knock on the door of her private suite at 31 rue Cambon.

She had been expecting this intervention. It was just over four years since the Germans approached the city in June 1940. At the time, she had packed all her belongings into several trunks and left them in the Hôtel Ritz's reinforced cellars before heading for the Pyrénées.

Now, history was repeating itself.

Four years ago, the bits of ash that covered the city were the work of French bureaucrats burning everything that couldn't be transported into their cars, heading south to what they thought was the relative safety of the provinces. Chanel was back in Paris a couple of months later, on an important personal mission, but by then the Ritz, including her suite with a view of Place Vendôme, had been dispassionately appropriated for the use of senior German military officials and prominent Nazis, who included Reich Marshal Hermann Göring.

Chanel wasn't the only one to flee the French capital in June 1940. The last of the convoys carrying the Louvre's masterpieces had left, snaking their way into secret cavities of the French hinterland. Even her great nemesis, Elsa Schiaparelli, had joined the exodus. This was nine months after Schiap and several other leading fashion designers like Molyneux and Lanvin decided to keep their businesses going while Chanel decided to close hers as the German crisis intensified.

François Coty, a formidable rival of Chanel in the perfume industry, took an idiosyncratic approach to the crisis: he established a far-right movement that attracted 80,000 followers in Paris alone.[1]

Perhaps they were all spooked by the German Kommandatura's threat, as issued to Lucien Lelong, who led the Chambre Syndicale de la Couture in 1940: French haute couture designers and workers numbering over 13,000 artisans, without exception, would be immediately transported to Berlin and Vienna as the new fashion capitals of a new Europe. Lelong's response was terse and defiant: 'You can impose what you will by force, but Paris's haute couture is not transferable, either en bloc or bit by bit. It exists in Paris or it does not exist at all.'[2]

Nevertheless, the reality of German occupation was that haute fashion was hardly affordable or even accessible, so the Kommandatur's threat was more a case of belligerent posturing than a real intention. Most of Europe had stopped purchasing new clothes from 1939 onwards, but in France during the occupation, new clothes, like everything else in France, became a commodity that was strictly rationed. The allowance for women during the entire war amounted to two dresses, two aprons or blouses, one mackintosh, two pairs of winter gloves, one winter coat, three blouses, two overalls, three pairs of underpants, six pairs of stockings, six handkerchiefs, and one pair of flat shoes.[3]

In response, most women turned to sewing and adapting other materials for everyday use, like wood for shoes, rayon (a textile fibre made from wood cellulose) for clothes, and torn, discarded parachute fabric to make men's shirts. Winter clothes were quilted with cotton wool. By 1942, extreme measures were being taken: gussets, box pleats, or half-belts were banned on men's suits and overcoats, and double-breasted waistcoats and knickerbockers were also banned. Trousers were allowed only one pocket, and trouser cuffs were forbidden. Children were no longer allowed to wear sailor collars, and boys had to wear short trousers until the age of 15. Of course, the French were quick to find ingenious solutions to such intractable problems:

> Can't find stockings in the shops? No problem, women could resort to stitching or dyeing their legs with walnut oil (not forgetting the

thin black line for the seam) ... there were even ready-made kits for this. Large bags were theoretically forbidden; however, carrier bags (some made from the superb cashmere scarves so many had inherited) were worn across the shoulders, very useful for stuffing products bought in shops whenever supplies came in, and if possible, double-bottomed bags, so that documents or other secret messages could be safely transported.[4]

Between 3 and 14 June, three-quarters of Parisians left the city as soon as they could. Photographs of the exodus show congested roadways with vehicles, bicycles, and homemade carts stacked high with hurriedly collected belongings. The panic affected everyone, from wealthy individuals and small business owners to families, itinerant workers, municipal employees, and the elderly. The mass evacuation was chaotic, with many frantically attempting to reach relatives in the provinces, homes in the country, or simply fleeing the advancing, menacing Germans.

Municipal administrators who lived in towns and cities in the way of this flood of refugees often couldn't handle the number of people passing through. In Chartres, Jean Moulin, prefect of Eure-et-Loir, stayed at his desk throughout the onslaught and tried everything he could to feed the vast deluge of citizens evacuating the Paris area. The experience left him distraught and physically devastated. At its peak, 2 million men, women, and children left Paris during the course of a few days, leaving the city almost deserted. They joined 6 million other traumatised French citizens on roads leading anywhere but back from where they came from. This significant and unprecedented movement of people heading south and west grew so substantial, it was likened to a biblical event, earning the name *Le Exodus*.

How did ordinary French citizens cope with such an upheaval? As the Oxford historian Robert Gildea put it in *Marianne in Chains*, his 2002 study of occupied France, they muddled through as best they could: 'One of the most marked consequences of the Occupation was the narrowing of horizons. Frightened by the unfamiliarity and unpredictability of the new order, people fell back on their families, their churches, their trades, their villages, towns and pays.'[5]

France shrank back to an almost feudal mindset, curling up into an embryonic ball of self-preservation to withstand the daily indignity of unimaginable suffering at the hands of its detested occupiers. People hunkered down. The Republic's *liberté, égalité, fraternité* (liberty, equality, fraternity) was ousted by the Pétain Vichy regime's mantra of *travail, famille, patrie* (work, family, fatherland).

But that's not to say there weren't moments of grudging enlightenment for a select few, like the young novelist/philosopher Albert Camus: 'Why is it that knowing how to remain alone in Paris for a year in a miserable room teaches a man more than a hundred literary salons and forty years' experience of "Parisian life"?'[6]

Wracked with chronic tuberculosis, Camus wrote these words in his notebook sometime between March and May 1940 while he was finishing a 30,000-word first draft of the novel he was calling *Un Étranger* at what used to be the Hôtel du Poirier on the rue Ravignan. The little hotel sat on cobblestones with a little fountain on one of Montmartre's buttes, or hills. It could only be reached by a set of steep steps and was right next to the Bateau-Lavoir, a rickety labyrinthine hovel full of artist workshops where Picasso painted *Les Demoiselles d'Avignon* in 1907.

Once his draft was finished, Camus left the gloomy Hôtel du Poirier for the Madison, a far more reputable and convivial hotel nearer the heart of Paris. Domiciled at the Madison, he observed through his window the growing lines of the biggest displacement of people in French history: dense streams of citizens and animals moving along the Boulevard Saint-Germain towards the Place de l'Odéon, then heading south to the Porte d'Italie, one of the ancient gates of the city. This mass evacuation had a desperate consequence, creating a dangerous vacuum in which all kinds of nefarious criminal enterprises, both organised and un-organised, were able to fester and flourish. None was more hideous than the exploits of Paris's worst-ever serial killer: the venal Marcel André Henri Félix Petiot, aka Dr Satan.[7]

During the early days of the German occupation, Petiot served as a doctor who provided fraudulent disability statements for French citizens conscripted to forced labour camps in Germany. But Petiot's most profitable work, his speciality, during this time involved the cruel and vindictive supply of false, and at times entirely fabricated and non-existent, escape routes out of France. He feigned possession of a reliable and established method for smuggling individuals sought by the Nazis or the Vichy government to safety, charging the desperate and unsuspecting a fee of 25,000 francs. Under the alias 'Dr Eugène', he was assisted by three accomplices who steered victims to him, often Jews, *Résistance* fighters, and out-of-favour businessmen. Once the destiny of these victims was in his control, he would inform them they needed an inoculation for entry into the receiving country. All part of the service, of course, whereupon he injected them with cyanide, collected all their valuables, and disposed of their remains.

Petiot first dumped the bodies in the Seine river, but when a plethora of dead bodies floated to the surface after a storm, he later burned or submerged them in noxious quicklime to destroy them. After a while, even his horrific exploits caught up with him when neighbours told the police in March 1944 the area always smelt suspiciously bad, as if someone was making illegal alcohol, and that Petiot's house chimney was constantly emitting clouds of dirty, smelly smoke at all hours of the day. Wary of a rampant chimney fire, the police passed the buck to the local fire department, who arrived to find a coal stove on fire in the basement of Petiot's house at 21 rue le Sueur. They also discovered dead bodies in the stove, strewn across the basement, along with assorted reeking body parts in canvas bags and in a quicklime pit in the backyard. Petiot's victims' suitcases, clothes, and other mundane small items filled the remaining space in the basement.

Following the *Libération* of Paris, Petiot used several disguises and noms de plume to evade capture. He even posed as an unlikely captain in command of French counter-espionage activities and a civilian convenor of Allied prisoner interrogations! Incredibly, working under the alias 'Valeri', he was also drafted by the authorities to assist in the manhunt for himself. Such luck couldn't last and Petiot was detained one night at a Paris Métro station while carrying a German weapon, 31,700 francs in new notes, and fifty sets of flawless official identity papers. In 1946 Petiot went on trial. He confessed to murdering nineteen of the alleged twenty-seven victims found in his basement but, in his defence, claimed they were either Germans or collaborators and he was doing the French state a service. In total he was alleged to have killed sixty-three so-called enemies of the state around Paris. Petiot was guillotined on 25 May 1946.

Mirroring Petiot's venality and corruption was the infamous Paris gangster Henri Lafont who, from his sinister establishment at 93 rue Lauriston, collaborated extensively with the Germans in a vicious orgy of violence, mayhem, and torture. In exchange for his efforts and the use of his men, the Nazis turned a blind eye to his more notorious caprices and acts of terror, bestowing numerous benefits and unique privileges to maintain his allegiance.

It was through the willing connivance of French citizens like Lafont that the Nazis successfully reinforced their position in France using a small number of troops and elderly reservists, despite the growing influence and impact of the *Résistance*. Beneath the façade of its clean, orderly, and elegant appearance, the so-called free city of occupied Paris was one of the most deceptively unsafe and dangerous places for a person to survive during the Second World War, precisely because of this closely controlled, thin veneer of glamour.

The orchid-loving Lafont was the embodiment of this new kind of terror, a cynical venality not seen in France since the Revolution of 1789. Together with his bestial policeman sidekick, Pierre Bonny, they worked a gang that included the former captain of France's 1930 World Cup football team (Alex Villaplane who, on 13 July 1930, led France in their first World Cup match when they beat Mexico 4–1), an Algerian who ran the famous French Connection heroin smuggling ring, and France's first public enemy number one.

By 1944 Lafont was the most powerful Frenchman in Paris, able to pressure senior SS officers into releasing prisoners, bully collaborators, and remain completely unfazed by the most senior, ruthless Nazi officers in the capital. Lafont was among the most viscerally hated men in Paris when his petrified German protectors abandoned him and the city as the Allies approached. Unlike Petiot, he was executed by firing squad along with Bonny, Villaplane, and five others at Fort de Montrouge on the perimeter of the city on 26 December 1944, tied to a stake without a blind, a cigarette defiantly clamped between his lips.

The French were not completely subdued during the early days of the occupation. The *Résistance* movement needed a catalyst to mobilise a sense of defiance that could be replicated throughout the country by seemingly ordinary men and women. It finally received it when French indignation was at breaking point a year after Germany's invasion, and one incident among many in August 1941 distilled its essence.

As with most French towns and cities, the Germans had ruthlessly plundered Versailles, requisitioning houses, food, weapons, cars, and anything that wasn't bolted down. Every civic building was branded with enormous fluttering red pennants scorched with hideous black swastikas. They frequently marched up and down the streets and recruited mesmerised children for Nazi youth groups. Another ploy was inducting itinerants into the Legion of French Volunteers Against Bolshevism, a collaborationist militia. Ceremonies marking the occasion were usually grand affairs attended by not only German officials but Vichy leaders, including the leading French political collaborationist Pierre Laval.

For many citizens, the sight of young Frenchmen dressed in enemy uniforms was distressing and shameful, beyond the pale. In the audience at one ceremony in Versailles on 27 August was Paul Collette, a veteran of the First World War and the Battle of Dunkirk. Pulling out a pistol, Collette fired five bullets and injured five people including Marcel Déat, a prominent collaborationist, and Laval, who was saved by a lucky cufflink.[8] Collette spent the rest of the war in prison but his futile gesture had roused pent-up feelings of disgust, especially among the young, against French citizens who continued to follow Vichy directives, listen to Radio Paris or, even worse, joined collaborationist movements that became accomplices of the local militia.

It was not until 1995 that newly elected President Jacques Chirac finally broke French society's taboo of silence, admitting 'the French government had given support to the criminal madness of the occupiers'.[9] In the twenty-first century, French President Emmanuel Macron spoke on his country's role in the genocide of French Jews in July 2017, denouncing his far-right politicians who regularly dismissed the Vichy government: 'It is convenient to see the Vichy regime as born of nothingness, returned to nothingness. Yes, it's convenient, but it is false. We cannot build pride upon a lie.'[10]

Libération from daily atrocities (the Petiot and Lafont cases were the most sensational of a plethora of heinous crimes committed by the French against their fellow citizens either for profit or survival) was a long time coming and a long, hard slog in achieving. France experienced immense devastation during the conflict, with approximately 75,000 lives lost and 550,000 tonnes of bombs dropped on their land, making it the second most bombed nation on the Western Front after Germany.[11] An Allied invasion was always a question of when and not if, and both sides, Parisians and their Nazi occupiers, knew about its imminent approach in the tense weeks prior to D-Day.

How the various sides responded, and the measures they took in light of such intelligence, differed as their respective situations changed.

For the Germans, the privately held belief their Western defences would eventually be overrun by the Allies accelerated their focus on three major activities that consumed their remaining time in Paris: the annihilation of the city, reviving a stalled plot to assassinate Adolf Hitler, and most horrendously of all, finalising the mass deportation of Jews to concentration camps and rounding up suspected French *Résistance* agents still at large in the city.

German vulnerability to an Allied invasion through areas of France and the Low Countries during 1944 was largely due to the abysmal quality and lacklustre attitude of their troops stationed there: since 1941, these troops had been recuperating German divisions burned out from the Russian Front. The French coastline was defended by a slender contingent of these garrisoned troops, from which the most capable and proficient had been sent east to win an unwinnable war. But, as rumours of a western front gained ground after 1943, more German units were transferred there from other fronts to bolster these garrisons. By the end of May 1944, some fifty-eight German divisions, out of nearly 300, were stationed in France, Belgium, and the Netherlands.[12]

The veteran 68-year-old Field Marshal Gerd von Rundstedt commanded all German armed forces in the West, comprising two army groups: Army Group B, led by Germany's most famous field marshal,

Erwin Rommel, was based in northern France and the Netherlands; and Army Group G was deployed within southern France. Despite his deteriorating mental state, even Hitler recognised that repelling a Western invasion was Nazi Germany's last chance to recapture the initiative: 'Once defeated the enemy will never again try to invade ... the whole outcome of the war depends on each man fighting in the West, and that means the fate of the Reich as well!'[13]

To the despair of the German High Command, the army's response to the landings on 6 June was characterised by sluggishness and confusion. The ongoing adverse weather conditions not only complicated the decision-making process for Supreme Allied Commander Dwight D. Eisenhower; it also caught the Germans by surprise. In the absence of any perceived immediate threat, Rommel travelled to Germany to visit his wife while numerous senior commanders were also absent from their posts, catching up on personal business. The success of the Allied deception plan, Operation Fortitude, led the Germans to believe that Normandy was a feint and the primary Allied landings would occur later in the Pas de Calais region. The impact of Fortitude exceeded Allied expectations and resulted in the delay of numerous valuable German units from repelling the Allied landings in Normandy until July.

On D-Day, however, German forces stationed along the coast did surprisingly manage to execute their duties to the best of their abilities. The seasoned 352nd Infantry Division successfully inflicted significant casualties on American forces assaulting the Omaha beachhead. In other locations, numerous bunkers and artillery positions withstood the initial Allied aerial and naval bombardment, resisting the full brunt of the Allied onslaught for several hours. But these vigorous German countermeasures could not be sustained.

By the time the Allies were advancing rapidly towards Paris in July, twenty-five out of thirty-eight German divisions had been completely annihilated. The remainder had been reduced to fragmented, scattered debris. The Germans incurred a total of 290,000 losses in Normandy: 23,000 fatalities, 67,000 injuries, and an additional 200,000 missing or captured. Approximately 2,000 vastly superior German tanks had been allocated to Panzer divisions on the battlefield but scarcely seventy tanks survived the conflict.[14]

As the scale of Germany's capitulation increased, von Rundstedt implored Hitler to pursue a peace agreement with the Allies. Hitler promptly replaced him with General Günther von Kluge.

The effect of the Allied successes and von Rundstedt's dismissal on a section of German officers billeted in Paris was decisive. A plot to assassinate Hitler,[15] which had lain dormant since March 1944, was suddenly revived in early July when the principal instigator, Oberst Claus von Stauffenberg, was manoeuvred into the position of Chief of Staff to General Friedrich Fromm at Reserve Army headquarters situated on the rapidly deteriorating Bendlerstraße in central Berlin. This role allowed von Stauffenberg to attend Hitler's military meetings at the Wolfsschanze compound in East Prussia and the Führer's Berchtesgaden retreat in Bavaria, thereby providing him with an opportunity to kill him with either a bomb or a pistol.

In Paris, led by General Carl-Heinrich von Stülpnagel, the German military commander of occupied France, and Generalleutnant Hans Speidel, Rommel's chief of staff, plus a cluster of high-ranking officers, were persuaded by the conspirators to assume direct control of Paris following Hitler's death and negotiate an immediate armistice with the advancing Allied forces.

Senior German officers were concentrated at Paris's best hotels during the occupation. The Ritz was known as 'Luftwaffe central station', though it later expanded its clientele to the other branches of the German war machine. The Meurice and Lutetia were known as base camps for the *Abwehr* (German military intelligence), while Hôtel Le Bristol remained one of the few not to be requisitioned by the Nazis.

According to Tilar J. Mazzeo's study of wartime activities at the Ritz, *The Hotel on Place Vendôme: Life, Death, and Betrayal at the Hotel Ritz in Paris*, the hotel's barman, Frank Meier, passed notes from Speidel and von Stülpnagel to other conspirators as they planned the French end of the 20 July plot. Mazzeo says these plans were partially hatched in Meier's bar while the principals were enjoying his cocktails.[16] Meier was the perfect courier for the Nazis as he ran a notorious gambling operation out of the hotel and his activities were made under the guise of placing bets. It was one of a series of two-way bets by Meier, which ultimately cost him his job: with the

Allies closing in, he asked some of his clients to pay their tabs into his private London bank account. When this was discovered after *Libération* he promptly disappeared, popping up later in the south of France and dying in 1947.

Following the plot's failure, von Stülpnagel fled the city and tried to kill himself. Failing that task, he was eventually captured and hanged in Berlin. Speidel was jailed by the Gestapo before escaping and surrendering to French forces in Germany. In Paris, the Gestapo rounded up, tortured, and executed over 1,000 conspirators.

The carnage paved the way for the appointment of General Dietrich von Choltitz as von Stülpnagel's successor. The general took command in Paris on 8 August 1944 with instructions personally delivered by Hitler to destroy all religious and historic monuments when ordered. To leave no doubt in the general's mind, the directive was re-issued and reinforced via cable, instructing von Choltitz to reduce the capital to rubble and ruins at Hitler's choosing.

In his 1951 memoir *Is Paris Burning?*[17] von Choltitz claimed he spared the 2,000-year-old city by disobeying the Führer's so-called Nero Decree[18] because he knew Hitler was crazy. Von Choltitz's version of history was reiterated by his son in an interview with the UK *Daily Telegraph* in 2004. The general's son, Timo, said:

> If he saved only Notre Dame, that would be enough reason for the French to be grateful. But he could have done a lot more. France officially refuses to this day to accept it and insists that the Resistance liberated Paris with 2,000 guns against the German army. To official France, my father was a swine, but every educated French person knows what he did for them. I am very proud of his memory.[19]

In 2014 French historian Lionel Dardenne, from the Museum of Order of the Liberation, which commemorates *Résistance* fighters, proposed an alternative theory: the city endured due to the reduced strategic significance assigned to it by Allied commanders and because it surrendered early, before any devastation could occur. Dardenne maintains: 'For many who know the story of the uprising well, [Von Choltitz's] account is absolute self-serving fantasy. He portrays himself as the saviour of the city, but the truth is he couldn't have destroyed it.'[20]

Von Choltitz had neither 'the men, material nor air support to level the city',[21] assistant curator Dardenne said. Also, von Choltitz was a compliant career soldier who had participated 'in the levelling of cities like Rotterdam and Sevastopol, and was not sentimental about destruction'.[22] Von Choltitz was released from Allied incarceration in 1947, and in 1956 discreetly visited his old wartime headquarters at the Hôtel Meurice, asking to see his former opulent suite and operations centre. After spending no more than fifteen minutes in his wartime quarters, Choltitz left.[23] Perhaps he was there to retrieve something he had hidden?

Despite the Nazi general's alternate take on history and the 2014 release of the Franco-German film *Diplomacy*, which depicts von Choltitz negotiating with Raoul Nordling, a Swedish diplomat and friend of the *Résistance*, to save the capital from Hitler's maniacal orders, Dardenne is unconvinced: 'He's created a legend for himself. People make a place for themselves in history either by saving or destroying. He decided his myth would be that he saved the city. It's totally false. The story was entirely made up. Yes, Nordling discussed saving some prisoners ... but that's it.'[24]

Whatever the veracity of von Choltitz's story, other nefarious activities in the name of mopping up loose ends were implemented in Paris by the Gestapo as the Allies approached, rendering it an even more (if that was possible) dangerous place to be without protection.

2

LES FIFIS

While Chanel was holed up during the war in a comfortable suite at the Ritz, another notable tenant resided there at the same time: a New York-born former actress named Blanche Auzello, whose Jewish heritage and perilous endeavours for the *Résistance* remained concealed during the German occupation. In contrast to Chanel's concealed occupation exploits, Auzello's story was one of a thousand stories that played out across Paris as the Allies closed in and the Nazis went berserk, unleashing the most heinous and vindictive sides of their remote grasp of humanity on shell-shocked Parisians. Blanche's tragedy was that someone, perhaps another resident at the Ritz where she was well liked and cared for, sold her out.

Informers in Paris were rife. No one knew who to trust. Betrayal was another form of survival, because the betrayed never came back. If they did, they were irreparably damaged. Thousands were involved in the process including, ironically, the people who loved you the most. Betrayal was the easiest act to perform for the most hideous of consequences. It was also the easiest act of perfidy for an individual to conceal.

Blanche Auzello (née Rubenstein) was the spouse of Claude Auzello, the long-serving managing director of the Ritz, who previously held the position of assistant manager at Claridges in London and was a recipient of the *Légion d'honneur* during the First World War. In June 1944, she and fellow *Résistance* member Lily Kharmayeff were audaciously dining at Maxim's, the fashionable restaurant that was a favourite with the Nazi elite, when she was apprehended by the Gestapo.[1] Chained to a dozen other individuals with ankle restraints, she was taken by truck to Fresnes, the notorious prison on the fringes of Paris, infamous for being the initial destination on the way east to German labour and concentration camps. She received a soiled robe and wooden clogs to wear and was forcibly placed into a room where her *Résistance* companion, Lily, stood against a wall, her wrists and feet restrained by metal shackles. As she attempted to embrace her, Lily was swiftly and brutally removed from the room by the guards.

The two women would never see each other again.

For the first time since the war began, Blanche was visibly scared and feared for her life. It was a different kind of danger she was now feeling, not like the adrenalin rush of attending to a severely injured Royal Air Force gunner, concealing him near the Ritz in Paris during the daytime, and transporting him to a waiting barge on the Seine while masquerading as a German nurse accompanying a young Nazi soldier. It was also different from the time when Lily's lover asked her to transfer microfilm, showing secret German artillery positions around the Atlantic coastline, to a French railway employee.

Those were adventures. This time she was well and truly at the mercy of people who were so mercurial, they could take out their pistols on a whim and shoot you without ever knowing fully why they did it, except, perhaps, that they just felt like it. She could hardly swallow she was so sick with fear and dread. She was shaking. This was no longer a game. This was her life.

Thankfully, a few hours into her internment she realised her adopted Catholic identity remained intact when a priest was shown into her cell and offered to pray with her. Blanche had forged her American passport twenty years earlier to avoid any potential impact of her Jewish origins on her husband's career. She altered her last name to Ross, modified her birthplace to Cleveland, converted to Catholicism, and reduced her age by four years. One night, she received a package of her preferred brand of cigarettes from a guard, which produced muted laughter from her cell mates. It meant Claude had visited the prison but, in contrast to the other imprisoned wives, she had not been permitted to see him. Blanche regarded this detail as an ominous sign of things to come.

Following her display of affection towards Lily, Blanche was dragged into solitary confinement and was only let out of her tiny cell for interrogations. Day after day, for hours on end, a plethora of allegations were directed at her: she had sheltered dangerous adversaries of the Reich; she had assisted known fugitives and participated in overt acts of terrorism; she was a filthy high-class whore whose husband hired her out to German officers for intelligence gathering.

Unable to get anywhere with this line of attack, her interrogators focused on her relationship with Lily: is she a Russian agent? Is she a Jew? A betrayer? A ballet dancer? What exactly does she do for a living? Blanche was assured if she disclosed the truth about Lily, she would be liberated the following day. But Blanche would only reveal that she and Lily had become friends on a yacht travelling from Egypt to France in the 1930s.

The days without interrogations were far worse. She witnessed shootings, tormented screams, guards laughingly mopping up riverbeds of congealed blood. She was eventually moved to an even smaller cell than her previous one, where there was no room to even lie down. Food and water were delivered randomly. Sleeping was impossible. She experienced intermittent bouts of delirium and violent, sweaty tremors. This lasted for days. One morning, despite her madness and emaciation, she noticed unusual activity in the prison. She heard shouting, scuffling, loud bangs, and screeching trucks leaving the courtyard. Maybe the Germans were evacuating?

Before she could grasp the possibilities of the commotion, she was again pulled in for questioning. Incredibly, amidst the chaos and palpable sense of danger all around them, the guards began assaulting her with questions about Lily again. Getting no response, she was beaten and tortured. Other interrogators came and went. It was never-ending. She was drenched in her own filth. Unable to take anymore, delirious, perhaps hoping for a quick death, she confessed to being a Jew and having a fake American passport.

The exasperated and increasingly nervous guards cautioned her that if she persisted in this ridiculous manner, they would shoot her. At that point, another guard entered the room announcing the final truck was about to leave. His voice was barely audible above the noise produced by the anguished creature Blanche had transformed into. She was struck in the head to quieten her down but when she continued to howl and scream and wail uncontrollably, one of the guards unclipped his revolver and pointed it at her head. Another guard, perhaps anxious to escape the place and bring this nonsensical interrogation to an end, stepped in front of him shaking his head and tapping his temple, signifying that Blanche was obviously insane. The men left her on the ground, her body compressed into a ball like a mound of excrement.

But the door of the cell was now open like all the other cells, and once Blanche was aware of the silence, she left the prison barefoot and made her way towards the Ritz 19km away. A fellow *Résistance* agent recognised her and called the hotel. Claude had difficulty recognising her. She had lost over 20kg and her ravaged, tortured body was covered in sores and welted scars. She had also lost most of her hair and what remained was frizzy and frazzled like singed wisps of cotton thread. There was no sign of Lily Kharmayeff when Blanche returned to Fresnes after it was safe a few days later.

Blanche was 'lucky'. Jacqueline Fleury-Marié, just 20 years old was not.

On 15 August 1944 the train she and other female *Résistance* suspects were herded into disappeared into the night. After seven days and seven nights, the women were forced out of the cattle cars at the point of a gun, with the sick and elderly thrown onto the ground. Female guards of the SS with vicious dogs on chains greeted the new arrivals. Jacqueline later wrote in her 2019 memoirs *Résistante*:

> Disoriented, frightened, arranged in our lines of five by five, we hit the road. Our convoy stretches out in columns of miserable limping women, tormented by hunger and worse still, by thirst. We pass through a large village with pretty houses. The streets are deserted, but behind the curtains, we can see the silhouettes of inhabitants watching us. We are reduced to zombies. Since our departure from Fresnes we have not stopped descending down the scale of humanity. When we left France, we were still female prisoners, now we are like animals on our way to the slaughterhouse.[2]

Before long, Jacqueline and the rest of the train arrived at the gate of a large camp. They encountered bizarre women, bald, emaciated, dressed in oversized striped gowns: 'At that moment, we still have some illusions. But they won't last long.'[3]

On 21 August 1944, Jacqueline and her *compagnons* had arrived at the edge of the Baltic Sea. Forced to shed their belongings and clothes in exchange for striped gowns and shoes ten sizes too big, Jacqueline and the others looked at each other and nearly laughed. 'Have we just entered the antechamber of madness?'[4]

Jacqueline had just entered the Nazi concentration camp for women at Ravensbrück.

By mid-August 1944, Paris was on the verge of *Libération* even though the Allies considered it a non-essential military target that should be circumvented for other, more pressing priorities. However, General de Gaulle, the leader of the Provisional Government of the French Republic, naturally thought otherwise and campaigned vehemently for its symbolic importance to his people: Paris must at all costs be liberated by French soldiers. He got his way. The city and its citizens, both French and German, were on high alert.

Things escalated at breakneck speed. The momentum was unstoppable. On 10 August, the national military committee of the *Francs-tireurs et Partisans* (FTP) issued an order for insurrection. On 11 August, railway workers in the Paris region called a strike that quickly spread unchecked as the top echelon of the French Forces of the Interior (FFI) in Paris, led by Colonel Rol-Tanguy, took the precaution of relocating to the slimy subterranean chambers beneath Place Denfert-Rochereau. On 15 August, after an exceptionally hot and sticky day, the *Confédération Générale du Travail* (CGT) union bit the bullet and initiated a general strike.[5] These moves forced collaborating elements within the discredited Paris police to mobilise a substantial force of armed personnel in anticipation of trouble and to send a clear signal that any more threats of civil disobedience would not be tolerated. It didn't work. Postal workers initiated a strike that was quickly joined by press workers and Métro personnel.

Unbelievably, as Paris succumbed to the fervour of *Libération*, the final German trains fanatically departed from the Pantin goods yards next to *Gare L'Est*, doggedly transporting last-minute deportees to camps inside and around Nazi Germany.

In one instance, the Gestapo forced a large contingent of Allied airmen into cattle carriages attached to one of the numerous trains that also carried people such as Jacqueline Fleury-Marié. The oppressive heat and humidity of July intensified the suffering of the 168 airmen who had been compelled to march for three hours without respite from Fresnes prison to the awaiting cattle train. Assured by the tetchy guards that they were en route to a POW camp operated by the Luftwaffe, the aviators were confined in enclosures that were designed for forty individuals or eight cattle. Instead, the Gestapo confined ninety-five men inside a single vehicle. First Lieutenant Joseph Frank 'Joe' Moser of the United States Army Air Force recalled the hideous arrangements:

> The only ventilation was provided by openings about one foot high and three feet wide near the top and at each end of the car. Barbed wire was stretched across these small openings to discourage anyone from thinking they might fit through. Two five-gallon buckets had been pushed into the car with us. One had water and it was to be our water supply. The other was empty, and it would be our toilet.[6]

Captured members of the French *Résistance* shared the train with these men. Like the other last trains that left Pantin, the ultimate destination of Moser and his associates was not a Stalag Luft; it was Buchenwald, the SS-operated concentration camp located near Weimar, Germany. Upon arriving at this evil place, the SS shaved their heads, doused them in disinfectant, and petulantly gestured at the chimneys inside the camp spewing out dense black smoke as their only means of escape.

Across Paris, *Résistance* men and women constructed makeshift barriers out of anything that could be moved while the police transformed Paris police headquarters into a fortress. Violent confrontations ensued between the Germans and the FFI. A cursory ceasefire was declared on 20 August, but the agreement was soon violated and vicious street fighting recommenced. The inadequately armed *Résistance* fighters confronted 20,000 German soldiers roaming the city bolstered by tanks and field mortars under the command of General von Choltitz in the fight of their lives.[7] German aircraft mercilessly strafed them during the day. Casualties mounted.

Faced with this overwhelming disadvantage, de Gaulle insisted Eisenhower release the French 2nd Armoured Division (2e DB), commanded by General Leclerc, so it could march immediately on

Paris. On 21 August, a messenger dispatched by *Résistance* commander Henri Rol-Tanguy successfully made it across German lines to alert Leclerc that Allied involvement was absolutely imperative to preventing more carnage in the Parisian rebellion. Rough statistics later compiled by the Paris police revealed that during the initial four days of the uprising, the majority of casualties were *Résistance* fighters: 483 fatalities and approximately 1,200 injuries.[8] Most of these clashes had occurred in working-class communities.

On 22 August, while General von Choltitz's forces attempted to re-establish control over the city, General Eisenhower finally ordered the 2e DB and the US 4th Infantry Division to ready their troops for an assault on the French capital. In the evening of that day, a Piper light aircraft flown by Captain Callet of the 2e DB flew over the city and his observer, Lieutenant Mantoux, dropped a sparse message from Leclerc on weighted paper that fluttered into the courtyard of police headquarters: 'Stand firm, we're on our way.'[9]

The morning after this information drop, the 2e DB, supported on its right flank by the US 4th Division, marched on Paris.

Inside the city the situation was tense. A spark was needed. The Germans soon provided it. An armoured unit, not under von Choltitz's direction, imperiously positioned itself at the Champs-Élysées near the Grand Palais, where it immediately came under fire from Paris police. The Germans promptly dispatched two miniature unmanned 'Goliath' tanks, each equipped with 50kg of explosives, directly towards the Grand Palais. When these explosives were detonated, the shock waves were so intense that ancient structures trembled and the sound echoed angrily throughout Paris. Lions, tigers, and horses performing at a nearby Swedish circus stampeded and fled the scene, along with a herd of disgruntled prostitutes locked in the Palais for their safety by the police who bolted when released.

With frenzied wild animals adding to the mayhem of Parisians stalking German units and German snipers shooting at will, von Choltitz attempted to calm things down by issuing a public statement. He requisitioned a Luftwaffe aeroplane and scattered thousands of hastily drafted leaflets over the city like confetti, urging Parisians to cease firing at von Choltitz's troops in return for peace. It was ignored. Also on that day, 23 August, Hitler issued an ultimatum to Field Marshal Walther

Model and von Choltitz, insisting Paris either be vigorously defended or destroyed without delay. It too was ignored.

A more pressing problem was the growing shortage of food and deprivation of basic living conditions. The city's gas supplies ceased to exist, and electricity was rationed to only a few hours a day, which in turn had a detrimental effect on the city's water supply, which relied on creaking pumping stations for power. Parisians, sensing it was now or never, came out into the streets to help the *Résistance*. The *Résistance* newspaper *Combat* captured the resurgent mood for action when it wrote: 'The Paris that is fighting this evening wants to command tomorrow. Not for the sake of power, but for justice; not for the sake of politics, but for morality; not for the sake of dominating the country, but for its greatness.'[10]

Meanwhile, the communist newspaper *L'Humanité* kept up its remorseless appeal for unfettered violence: 'Attack is the best form of defense. Harass the enemy. Not a single Hun should leave insurgent Paris alive.'[11]

At dawn on 25 August, with the *Résistance* running out of ammunition, the Allies finally entered the city by the Porte de Saint-Cloud, Porte d'Orléans, Porte de Gentilly, and the Porte d'Italie. The breakthrough was reported by *Time* magazine's chief war correspondent, Charles Christian Wertenbaker. Wertenbaker's open-topped jeep followed General Leclerc's armoured car as French forces entered the city through the Porte d'Orléans, a harrowing manoeuvre photographed by Robert Capa for *Life*. Wertenbaker wrote:

> The streets were full of people—Resistance groups armed with any old rifles, white-clad doctors and nurses carrying stretchers, and citizens old and young who, in spite of the danger, could not stay at home on this day. They gathered in crowds wherever something was happening, and everywhere something was happening. One crowd gathered around a German officer kneeling in the street praying for his life. A Resistance group was determined to shoot him on the spot, but three marines of the French Division got him free and took him prisoner ... the Germans raised the white flag. Then, as French Resistance forces went to take their surrender, they opened fire again. French tanks came up and forced a second

surrender. The two German commanders were taken out and shot in the street.[12]

At around 4 p.m., von Choltitz surrendered at the Hôtel Meurice, headquarters of the Militärbefehlshaber in Frankreich (the German high military command in France) before signing the official surrender at the Paris Police Prefecture and a ceasefire agreement at General Leclerc's command post at the Gare Montparnasse.

It was over.

The liberation of Paris resulted in over 1,000 casualties among the FFI. It is estimated that 800 to 1,000 *Résistance* fighters were killed, with an additional 1,500 sustaining serious wounds. There were 582 civilian fatalities, and 2,000 injuries reported; 156 soldiers of the 2e DB were killed and 225 were wounded. German forces suffered 3,200 fatalities while 12,800 of their personnel were captured.[13]

From this rubble of blood and guts, a new phoenix arose, according to one eyewitness:

> ... a myth that had been created, whereby Paris was liberated by French patriots to the unanimous delight of its population, apart from a few mauvais sujets (bad sorts) who were faithfully dealt with. Eisenhower gave this myth a great push forward when he publicly stated that the French Resistance was the equivalent of putting into the field some twenty divisions – that is, rather more than the British contribution to the Normandy landings.[14]

Growing 'like a coral reef, gaining accretions all the time',[15] this myth found its apogee in Marcel Ophuls's film *Le Chagrin et la Pitie*.

In reality, the euphoria of *Libération* ignited a further outpouring of revenge and retribution. The *épuration sauvage*, the pursuit of Nazi collaborators, was well underway before the Allies rolled into the streets of Paris. After *Libération*, however, it intensified to an abnormal degree.

François Rouquet and Fabrice Virgili's 2018 book, *Les Françaises, les Français et l'Épuration* ('The French and the purge'), is a detailed study of the French need to punish or attack all those considered to have betrayed their country and their fellow citizens. It was almost a time-honoured tradition, harking back to the 1789 Revolution when Maximilien Robespierre spoke these words at the trial of Louis XVI on 3 December 1792:

> Peoples do not judge in the same way as courts of law; they do not hand down sentences, they throw thunderbolts; they do not condemn kings, they drop them back into the void; and this justice is worth just as much as that of the courts.

Unlike 1792, the average Frenchman believed that traitors were punishable under Article 75 of the Penal Code.[16] Unfortunately, this misunderstood provision was also used to excuse monstrous acts of depravity worthy of the Gestapo.

Marauding gangs of FFI thugs enthusiastically took up the cause of 'purification', combing the more affluent arrondissements for women denounced by friends and neighbours for having 'horizontal' liaisons with Germans. When identified, whether the accusations were spurious or not, these women (estimated in excess of 20,000[17]) were publicly humiliated, stripped of their clothes, their heads shaved, their bodies smeared with tar, branded with swastikas, and ignominiously paraded around towns and taunted, stoned, kicked, punched, spat upon, and in some cases publicly executed. Black marketeers (*profiteurs de guerre*) were also targeted, as were hoarders of essentials such as butter, eggs, and cheese.

The word 'collaborator' had a particularly notorious, toxic association for the French during the Second Word War, born out of a particularly insidious moment in French history:

> On 30 October 1940, six days after meeting with Adolf Hitler in the railway station at Montoire, Philippe Pétain announced on French radio that 'a collaboration has been envisioned between our two countries.' Since then, 'collaboration' has been the word by which we denigrate political cooperation with an occupying force.[18]

Philosophical and moral definitions of collaboration (what types of actions should be considered collaborationist and what types of evidence were credible) were luxuries put to one side in the zealous rush for revenge. Where did the neutral act of 'accommodation' end and overt 'collaboration' begin? Deliberating the nuances was never a priority of the FFI.

Participating in covert Nazi activities such as aiding the enemy, denouncing fellow citizens for blood money, involvement in organised Jewish round-ups and deportations, profiteering from the black market, and promoting Nazi ideology were pure acts of collaboration, without question. But what if you were a humble waiter at the Ritz? Would doing your job by serving a table of German officers be considered collaborationist behaviour? Were you a collabo if the only option to feed your children was to accommodate a German soldier with access to food? Was the madam of the One-Two-Two Club a collabo when she was instructed to open her brothel only to German officers, or were any of the other madams of over thirty brothels used solely for the pleasure of German soldiers collabos?

Not that the French authorities didn't try to define what was in and what was out. On 15 March 1944, the *Conseil National de la Résistance* (National Council of Resistance, or CNR) explicitly restated the offences it would use to evaluate suspected collabos:

Taking part in a collaborationist organisation
Taking part in propaganda
Denunciation
Any form of zeal in favour of the Germans
Black market activities[19]

It was a rather loose attempt, and no doubt it was arrived at after many weeks of agonising debate. One of the ways the CNR attempted to figure out a workable solution was for ordinary citizens to ask themselves the question: were they working with Germans or Nazis? If the answer was the latter, they most likely collaborated. If the former was genuine (e.g. waiting on a table of German soldiers), it might be more difficult to prove collabo intentions.

Such subtle and suave administrative distinctions were lost in the maelstrom of revenge and depravity before de Gaulle's administration could establish some kind of order in September 1944. In that month, citizens were appointed to oversee judicial tribunals, official detention centres, internment camps, and prisons where suspected collabos could be held while their guilt was either established or dismissed.

But inevitably, cruelly, and illegally, a certain degree of damage had already been inflicted. Police prefects estimated that up to 6,000 illegal executions occurred prior to the *Libération* of France, with an additional 4,000 occurring afterwards (based on assessments made in 1948 and 1952).[20] From 1944 to 1951, French courts sentenced 6,763 individuals to death for treason and other offences, with 3,910 of these sentences issued in absentia.[21] A total of 791 legal executions were conducted. However, the crime of *indignité nationale* was the most prevalent sentence meted out to French men and women investigated for collaboration, resulting in the loss of citizenship rights for 49,723 individuals.[22]

In the days after *Libération*, many apprehensive French citizens like Coco Chanel waited inside their fancy suites and lavish right bank apartments, expecting to hear at any time the dreaded knock (mimicking Gestapo and French police tactics used during the occupation) from an ad hoc delegation of the dreaded FFI that Chanel sardonically referred to as *Les Fifis*.

It is doubtful she took comfort from the treatment meted out by the FFI to other notables such as Maurice Chevalier, Jean Cocteau, Sasha Guitry, and Serge Lifar, or another superstar of French society, the actress Arletty, who was arrested on a charge of treason for her overt relationship with a German Luftwaffe officer, Hans-Jürgen Soehring. Arletty's alleged commentary on her acquiescence, 'My heart is French but my ass is international'[23] (*Si mon cœur est français, mon cul, lui, est international*), spread like wildfire through French society and probably saved her from being paraded through the streets. Instead, the authorities dealt with her quietly, sentencing her to eighteen months imprisonment, the majority of which was served discreetly in a privately owned château.

It didn't take long for the dreaded knock to occur on Chanel's door at 31 rue Cambon. Gesturing at her maid, Germaine Domenger, and her butler, Léon, to continue their duties, Chanel took a deep breath, coolly smoothed the lines of her simple navy-blue dress, and opened the door to her sumptuous apartment atop Maison CHANEL.

3

A KNOCK ON THE DOOR

Despite her calm pretence, Chanel was terrified before she opened the door and only marginally less terrified when she saw who it was.

At least it wasn't the mercurial, monstrous *Fifis*.

Instead, standing before her was a smiling, immaculately groomed and uniformed British army major, fresh from Victor Rothschild's mansion on the Avenue Marigny. He was accompanied by an old friend of hers.

Both were expected for dinner.

As the young major moved through the open door, Chanel couldn't resist an opening salvo. Regarding his pressed seams, clean shirt, and close shave, she remarked he obviously was new to Paris. Tucking his hat under his armpit, the major's face creased with laughter and he returned his hostess's fire with greasy charm: obviously on such an occasion one has to make an effort for the greatest couturière still living in Paris. Chanel acknowledged the effortless parry with a nod and motioned the couple to a deep sofa upholstered in Spanish suede.

And so Major Malcolm Muggeridge of MI6, 'with a sense of being on duty as well as pleasure bent',[1] gingerly entered the relative safety of Chanel's 'lavish haute-couture and perfume emporium'.[2]

Indeed, it was lavishly furnished. The claustrophobic, gilt-riddled clutter of the apartment was meant to be intimidating. Though Muggeridge was accustomed to being regularly entertained in the salons of the super-rich, he was nonetheless confronted by a pot-pourri of treasures that dazzled the eye and smothered the senses. Almost every wall was lined with floor-to-ceiling bookshelves filled with thick leather-bound books (*probably never opened*, Muggeridge thought). Antique camellia-etched coromandel-lacquered screens, either pressed against walls or strategically positioned at the entrance, divided the interiors (she had a famous aversion to doors, relying on these elegant screens to segregate spaces). Gold Venetian lions (her zodiac sign was Leo) and elaborate, exquisitely engraved cigarette boxes were scattered over an ornate wooden desk worn from decades of use; a golden hand sculpture from Giacometti, extravagant custom-made crystal chandeliers, and metal Chinese horses were other expensive props dotted here and there.

Since the 1920s:

> Chanel's taste has run to Coromandel screens and chinoiseries, mirrors, masses of fine period furniture and precious items ... Her fancy for gilt and painted furniture Chanel explains by saying that it reminds her of merry-go-rounds at country fairs, of which she is fond. It is here, amidst gold and lacquer, and usually only when urged to it now, that Chanel gives her small parties, at which she acts like a guest.³

Thankfully the windows were open, and he accepted a frosted glass of chilled champagne before flopping on the vast suede sofa, the colour and texture of wet sand on the beach at Deauville.

He was a little disappointed, he later confessed, to be at rue Cambon and not at his hostess's more risqué apartment at the infamous Hôtel Ritz on Place Vendôme. Chanel had shrewdly vacated her apartment there after the failed 20 July assassination attempt on Hitler, when the Gestapo went into overdrive and began rounding up suspects hiding in the major hotels. Another of her considerations was not wanting to be holed up there when the Allies liberated Paris. It would not have been a good look, even though everyone knew that was where she'd been sleeping for the past four years.

Muggeridge was certainly aware of the significance of these specially allocated Ritz apartments and wished to understand first-hand why they had been so mythologised (or demonised depending on who you spoke to) by ordinary Parisians.

The fact the Ritz's Privatgast (private guest) section was strictly reserved for officially sanctioned friends of the Reich and vigorously policed by guards (as specified in the following dictate) might have had something do with its mystique: 'On orders from Berlin the

Ritz was reserved exclusively for the temporary accommodation of high-ranking personalities. The Ritz Hotel occupies a supreme and exceptional place among the hotels requisitioned.'[4]

The Ausländers (non-Germans) allowed to stay there constituted a who's who of Nazi sympathisers, Nazi appeasers and, in Chanel's case, Nazi remoras (a fish, sometimes called a suckerfish, that attaches itself to a larger fish like a shark, snacking on scraps of meals, bacteria, and waste matter from the larger creature). Chanel's gifted rooms (227–228) were near Fern Bedaux's (243, 244, 245), the elegant wife of fascist arms dealer Charles Bedaux – the couple who lent their luxurious country home, Château de Candé, to the Duke and Duchess of Windsor for their wedding in 1937. On the same floor were the Dubonnet family and Mme Marie-Louis Ritz, wife of the hotel's founder, César Ritz. Reich Marshal Göring occupied the Royal Suite when he was in town (apparently Blanche Auzello told Chanel that Göring suddenly appeared one day clutching an exquisite, diamond-studded marshall's baton specially designed and made for him by Cartier.)[5]

Anyone entering or exiting the hotel had to be assessed by sentries stationed around the clock at the sandbagged entrances, checking passports and identity papers. There were also strict orders regarding the dress and deportment of German guests (Ausländers had to be invited): 'No weapons of any sort were allowed inside the establishment … manners had to be perfectly correct and no subaltern (junior) officer was allowed.'[6]

Of course, the food was sumptuous. At a time when Göring mandated that French citizens were to survive on 1,200 calories per day (an amount that constituted half of the average person's necessary caloric intake) and the elderly on 850 calories, one German officer observed: 'In times like these, to eat well and eat a lot gives a feeling of power.'[7] Lunch at the Ritz consisted of grapefruit, filet of sole cooked in a dry German wine, or roast chicken with fried potatoes, fresh peas, and asparagus with hollandaise sauce. Fresh fruit rounded off the feast.

The meal Chanel had prepared for Muggeridge and her old friend that hot, stifling evening in September 1944 was to be no less sumptuous.

Why did Chanel consent to see a British intelligence officer a few days after *Libération*, despite (according to Muggeridge) having no 'cause for serious anxiety'?[8] After all, she had already:

... successfully withstood the first epuration assault at the time of the Libération by one of those majestically simple strokes which made Napoleon so successful a general; she just put an announcement in the window of her emporium that scent was free for GIs, who thereupon queued up to get their bottles of Chanel No. 5, and would have been outraged if the French police had touched a hair of her head.[9]

It was a spectacularly successful tactic with soldiers of all nationalities, even the French, queuing for hours on end to get their free Paris souvenir. Those who couldn't speak French merely held up five fingers and were rewarded. For Muggeridge, the tactic had less to do with generosity than it had to do with buying time and space for protection during the chaos, as he expressed in his 1972 memoir, *Chronicles of Wasted Time*: 'Having thus gained a breathing space, she proceeded to look for help *a gauche et a droite* ...'[10]

It was classic Chanel, figuring out a way to survive through another extreme, life-threatening circumstance. It helped that she was inured, perhaps even addicted, to extreme sensations throughout her life, having lived through several extremely tragic situations already. It was another unique challenge, another case of win or die. She already had the tools, acquired from an early age, that she could use to navigate through such difficulties, as her friend Charles-Roux noted:

Yes she was rich. But with her, no precaution was silly and no profit negligible, and however rich she might be she took everything that came her way, like those peasant women who will throw nothing away in times of defeat or invasion but hoard it all, saving the bread and old bones from one month to the next. Gabrielle definitely belonged to that breed and was, we may as well confess it, a miser.[11]

Muggeridge had been briefed on Chanel's special qualities and her 'case':

At the Boulevard Suchet (where the French Services Speciaux were based), I heard much talk, mostly cynical and facetious, about the different grades and categories of ennuies then being endured, and gleaned a good deal of information on the subject, of varying degrees and reliability; not least about the famous Mme Coco Chanel.¹²

Through a mixture of wading through her bulky French Services Speciaux file and verbal encounters with Services Speciaux informants, Muggeridge also arrived at the conclusion that Chanel, the spotless fashion icon and force of nature, was largely a facetious invention.

It wasn't a hard verdict to reach.

Gabrielle Bonheur Chanel was born in an ordinary train compartment on a scorching hot day. Her mother, Eugénie Jeanne Devolle, was on her way to meet her father, Auvergnat wine trader Henri Chanel, in Saumur. The birth date was documented in Saumur town hall as 19 August 1883. The infant's surname was misspelt, likely due to a clerical error, and so the world's most famous fashion designer officially died as Gabrielle Chasnel due to an error on her French birth certificate. Of all the things in her life Chanel sought to erase, confuse, conceal, and alter, she never sought to correct the name on her birth certificate as that would have confirmed her illegitimacy and impoverished status.¹³ Another version of the story has her born in a hospice for the poor in Saumur, at a charity run by the Sisters of Providence. Subsequently unearthed records show her unwed 21-year-old mother, Jeanne, and her street-hawker father, Henri-Albert, eventually married a few years later. Things were tough from the outset, and they lived an itinerant life, bouncing from one squalid hovel to another.

Gabrielle was the youngest of four sisters or the second eldest of three. There were also two brothers (another boy, Augustin, died at 6 months). When she was 6 or 12, her mother died. In 1931 the official story was: 'Her childhood was obscure, healthy, bucolic. She was one of four motherless little Auvergnate sisters reared on the land by an aunt who did what she could for them, including, fortunately for one, seeing that they learned how to sew.'¹⁴

Another story has the widower Chanel deciding to lodge the girls with two aunts and hiring out the two remaining boys to a farmer.

He then supposedly left for either South or North America, never to be seen or heard of again.

The aunts, the ladies Devolles, occupied a pretty farm near Issoire, in the heart of Auvergne. They are described as two old maids dressed habitually in black who rarely left their grey-stone cottage. They sat in a dark living room with closed windows, knitting all day, and found it extremely tiresome and tedious to keep the boisterous Chanel girls entertained after school. According to charming accounts in early Chanel biographies, the aunts reared horses for the army and the Chanel girls were involved in their training. Gabrielle even became an outstanding horsewoman by the age of 10! But as she grew older, her aunts struggled to manage her increasingly restless and demanding behaviour.

In reality, the poverty of the Devolles household was grinding and relentless.

Again, she and her two sisters were given away, this time to the stone-cold Cistercian monastery in the town of Aubazine founded in the twelfth century and maintained by the Sisters of the Congregation of the Sacred Heart of Mary. Again, she was abandoned and alone, dumped five hours south of Paris in one of the least-visited regions of France. She was 12. The nuns in their black habits could not control her either. She would not be tamed. It was apparent to everyone this rather peculiar, withdrawn child was only waiting for an excuse or an occasion to escape the suffocating narrowness of French provincial life. Meantime, she learned to sew.

Through various twists and turns and brushes with rich, aristocratic men such as the debonair Étienne Balsan, who helped her along the way and spruced up her manners in the process (but not her peasant cunning), she underwent a kind of metamorphosis and wound up on the margins of more affluent circles. Re-branded from 18 onwards as 'Coco' (a nickname derived either from the ditty she sang as a circus showgirl, the shorthand version of the French word *cocotte*, or the mounds of cocaine she and her set were rumoured to devour at parties), she later met the great love her life: the polo-playing English shipping tycoon Arthur Capel.

A tall, suntanned man, it was Capel (known as 'Boy' in Parisian society) who financed her first millinery shop in Paris at 21 rue

Cambon. He also set her up in a fine apartment overlooking the Seine and bought her a blue Rolls-Royce with a chauffeur. The shop did not survive. In March 1914, she relocated to Deauville and tried again, this time with her sister. They opened a boutique alongside the opulent Hôtel Normandie, again using Capel's money. This time, after many years of trial and error, her business began to grow and gain popularity with rich holiday makers. In July 1916, now back in Paris, she took over a draughty four-room apartment at the fashionable rue Cambon that was badly in need of repair and opened the fashion *maison* that still exists today. She also created around this time les Tissus CHANEL to reproduce high-quality fabrics.

Chanel's first haute couture collection was presented at 5 p.m. on 5 August 1916, announcing to the world the age of laced female bondage, stiff whalebone corsets, dyed ostrich feathers, and frilly lace petticoats was over, and the age of easy-to-wear, comfortable, sleek sportswear in breathable natural fabrics was now available and within reach for thousands of Parisian women. The CHANEL silhouette was boyish: a sinewy, thin figure with broad shoulders, slim hips, and a hardly noticeable bosom.[15] The look and her business took off. After the sudden death of Capel in 1919 she moved to 31 rue Cambon.

Up to this point, Chanel's French Services Speciaux file was rather flimsy. Between 1919 and 1944, however, the file was thickened by witness and surveillance reports normally accorded to radical politicians, enemies of the state, or foreigners of interest who could be useful in furthering the economic ties of the host country. It is a measure of Chanel's growing influence and stature in between-the-wars France that she merited such attention, and this is what struck Muggeridge the most as he trawled its contents. This was no mere couturière; this was a unique force of nature that even the highest levels of French society insisted on keeping tabs on.

Nevertheless, Muggeridge was shrewd enough to guess the file contained only a fraction of Chanel's official and unofficial history. For the rest of the Chanel story, and details of her legendary allure, which would have been deemed bureaucratically irrelevant but so important to his understanding of the Chanel phenomenon, he had to rely on the first-hand accounts and recollections of his nervous dinner partner that night at rue Cambon.

4

HOLLYWOOD AND A DIAMOND DUKE

Muggeridge would have been amused to learn that Chanel's exalted position in pre-Second World War French society was largely precipitated and cemented by two daring but flukey innovations of her own making.

The first concerned her hair.

One night after returning to rue Cambon from a holiday in the French Riviera, her gas heater exploded. Looking at her singed long black hair in the bathroom mirror, she impulsively took a pair of scissors (Chanel's go-to instrument when she was stressed or restless) and cut off her long, thick tresses.

A few evenings later Coco decided to go to the opera. It was a pivotal moment. As soon as she entered her box, escorted by three extremely handsome polo players, hundreds of *lorgnettes* (opera glasses with long handles) turned towards her in astonishment. Wearing a simple black dress and three faultless strings of pearls around her neck, her skin beautifully caressed by the rich Mediterranean sun and her hair cropped short like a boy, her chic look upended every vital rule and convention of female beauty that was accepted in those days. She looked strong, vital, and confident. When she arrived at her salon the next morning, visibly exhilarated by the impact of her night at the opera, her excited models wanted to follow her lead, so she trimmed their hair into short fringes with her scissors. The daring bob cut became the look of the age.

Chanel, however, gave her friend Claude Delay a different version of the radical haircut's genesis: 'I'd never been to the Opera before. I had a white dress made by my own modistes. My hair, which came down below my waist, was done up round my head in three braids – all that mass set straight upon that thin body.'[1]

Like every other Parisian, she had so much hair, it was:

> ... crushing me to death ... There was a gas burner in the bathroom. I turned on the hot tap to wash my hands again, the water wasn't hot, so I fiddled with the pilot-light and the whole thing exploded. My white dress was covered in soot, my hair – the less said, the better. I only had to wash my face again – I didn't use make-up. In those days only the cocottes used make-up and were elegant. The women of the bourgeoisie weren't groomed – and they wore hats that flopped all over the place, with birds' nests and butterflies ... I took a pair of scissors and cut one braid off. The hair sprang out at once all round my face. In those days I had hair like sable.[2]

She then cut off another braid and, pleased with the outcome, told her crying maid to cut them all off:

> I slipped on a black dress I had, crossed over in front – what a marvellous thing, youth – and caught in at the waist, with a sort of minaret on top ... When I got back that evening the maid had washed my hair and my braids were waiting for me in the bathroom like three dead bodies.[3]

The second innovation concerned her nose.

Coco Chanel had a visceral horror of other people's odour. It was an aversion she could never shake. It made her physically sick if there was an smell in her presence that troubled her, especially perspiration on unwashed clothes. If someone gave her flowers, she was adamant she could smell the hands of the person who had picked them.[4] Her most gracious compliment to a woman was to say she smelled 'clean'. Even while living at the Hôtel Ritz at Place Vendôme after her return to Paris in 1954, she stipulated, like a rock star, that a number of empty tables had to separate Mademoiselle's table from other diners when she was dining there. Eating with the smell of other people's food was a 'horror!'[5]

If the restaurant was too full, she would stay in her natural shantung pyjamas and towelling mules, a silk muslin scarf over her hair, and eat her lunch in her suite: '... the Krug well chilled, the asparagus served à la vinaigrette – "No sauce mousseline, it's all flour." Toast melba in a folded napkin, purée of new potatoes and peas. A little Gorgonzola and Gruyere, and "good strong coffee."'[6]

In early 1921, Chanel was invited to Ernest Beaux's extraordinary perfume laboratory at La Bocca, near Cannes. The Moscow-born Beaux, once the Russian Tsar's official perfumer, put ten sample bottles in front of her and declared he believed he had finally found what Mademoiselle had specified. Chanel dutifully pressed her snub nose to each flagon and upon completing her task, indicated the fifth bottle was the one she desired. Another version has Beaux presenting her with bottles labelled 1 to 5 and 20 to 24. Apparently, in this version, she first plumped for number 22 but when it didn't sell, she resorted to number 5.[7]

Most perfumes at that time and before comprised extracts of patchouli, moschus, rosewood, geranium, bergamot citron, violets, roses, orange blossom, and opoponax. But flagon No. 5 contained a new element.

During his service in northern Finland during the First World War, the sensitive Monsieur Beaux couldn't help but notice that the lakes and rivers emitted a refreshing scent during the midnight sun. Returning from the war, he couldn't get that scintillating smell of freshness out of his mind and wanted to replicate it artificially if he could. In doing so he returned to Finland multiple times to compare his concoctions to the natural scents, and after three trips he felt he had it. He had managed to recreate the scent of Finnish snow regions by combining aldehyde ($CH_8\ CHO$) with essences of wood, violet, and jasmine derived from Grasse in southern France.

This creation was sample No. 5.

In 1924 Chanel had it mass-produced by the firm A Bourjois & Cie (manufacturers of Poudre de Riz Bourjois and assorted beauty products) in rectangular flasks with the bland inscription 'CHANEL No. 5'. She became a multimillionaire within two years thanks to the commercial acumen of Bourjois owners Paul and Pierre Wertheimer. The Alsatian-Jewish Wertheimers had created a worldwide distribution network that catapulted No. 5 to every corner of the world. In Paris they bought Galeries Lafayette, the huge department store on Boulevard Haussmann, and stocked it with Bourjois products. By 1931 she had become so rich she had to hide it and was admired for her financial tenacity:

> ... perhaps the closest estimate of her financial genius is contained in a statement accredited to the banking house of Rothschild, a European establishment discerning enough to have made a fortune even out of the Battle of Waterloo: 'Mademoiselle Chanel,' they are reported as solemnly saying, 'knows how to make a safe twenty per cent.'[8]

Chanel, in contrast to the popular misconception she promoted, was an astute businesswoman and a good hater. Despite the fact that they had made her rich, for her entire life, she maintained a wary loathing-hate-loathing relationship with the Wertheimers, especially Pierre (he was 'the bandit who screwed me'[9]). She was convinced they secretly exploited her, embezzled her money, robbed her of millions of American dollars annually. Four years after signing an agreement with Chanel that gave her a 10 per cent share in Les Perfumes Chanel S.A. and the profits from worldwide sales of No. 5, the Wertheimers specifically engaged a lawyer just to deal with the tetchy couturière.

Chanel's sharpest competition during the decade preceding the German occupation of Paris in June 1940 came from the designers Jean Patou and Elsa Schiaparelli. Of the two, 'Schiap', as she was affectionately called by her clients, was the most dangerous. Chanel first regarded her new competitor with only cursory attention. Maison CHANEL had been established for two decades, whereas Schiaparelli, at 35, was a novice in the industry. Upon any mention of Schiap's name in social circles, she would waspishly respond, 'Oh, you mean that Italian artist who sells knitted things?'[10]

This was an allusion to Schiap's sensational figure-hugging knitted sweaters. The Schiaparelli silhouette was the antitheses of CHANEL. Where CHANEL compressed, Schiaparelli expanded. The bosom was accentuated rather than flattened. Even the Schiaparelli house perfume, called 'Shocking', of course, was sold in tactile curvy bottles resembling breasts. Chanel couldn't stand it. There's a possibly apocryphal story that one afternoon, a close friend of hers, the Duchess of Ayen, visited her wearing a Schiaparelli blouse. The alpha couturière immediately stood up and impulsively grabbed the blouse from her friend's shoulders, shouting it didn't even fit her. The competition had not only caught up with CHANEL; it had wounded its omniscient creator. Salvador Dalí summed up the changing of the guard:

> The thirties were not Chanel's period. Her style had sprung from World War I and, just like myself, she had been one of the symbols of the postwar era. In contrast, Elsa Schiaparelli, with her cynical concept of fashion, her hunter's hats, and parachute costumes, was heralding the advent of World War II.[11]

It wasn't all doom and gloom. There was still sufficient sunshine to make money and have fun. Acquiring property in the 1920s and '30s was part of the fun. Chanel had come a long way in a short space of time, and the list of real estate she acquired stretched to a 1719 town house just off the Place de la Concorde; a small, moated, old Norman manor at Mesnil-Guillaume, near Lisieux; a chic modern villa she built and furnished in beige at Roquebrune on the Riviera; and a furnished flat in Venice.[12]

Also in the 1930s, Chanel began designing clothes for Hollywood. At the height of the Great Depression, Samuel Goldwyn attempted to entice her with an offer of a million dollars (about US$14 million in today's money) to design clothes for his movie stars. Despite her well-known distaste for Jews, Chanel took the cool million from Goldwyn (born Schumel Gelbfisz in the Warsaw ghetto) and sailed for America on the SS *Europa* with an army of models, assistants, and seamstresses, shaving six years off her official birthdate in the records of the ship's manifest.

Her Hollywood experience was short and mixed: she became tired of catering to infantile stars controlled by hypocritical tycoons. She got out as soon as she could but made sure she met with two of America's most important fashion editors, Carmel Snow of *Harper's Bazaar* and Margaret Case of *Vogue*, in her suite at New York's Hotel Pierre on Fifth Avenue before she left. Sailing back to Europe on the SS *Paris*, Chanel told Goldwyn future fittings for his movie stars would be conducted at rue Cambon.

Goldwyn's money, however, couldn't nullify her prickliness.

In 1931, she created dresses for the Gloria Swanson movie *Tonight or Never*. As expected, Swanson's luscious figure horrified her. The haughty couturière made a remark about Swanson being overweight during the initial fitting at rue Cambon and advised the movie star to lose a few kilograms before the last appointment in six weeks' time so she could slide into a show-stopping black bias-cut gown Chanel had designed. Swanson duly returned at the designated day a few kilograms heavier, much to Chanel's indignation. Even more horrific, Swanson declared she would try on the slinky gown over a rubberised girdle that Chanel could make for her. Chanel flatly refused. She was aghast. If you didn't fit the CHANEL silhouette, the silhouette would not conform to you. Fat was not in the CHANEL lexicon. She advised Swanson to do what she, Chanel, always did: stick to only champagne and caviar for the perfect figure.

The mythic Chanel diet was born.

Chanel was a fanatic when it came to body fat, employing a succession of intense Swedish masseurs she routinely ground to the point of exhaustion in her determination to remain waif-like and spare. And her relentless attention to body-shaming was not confined to herself or Hollywood stars. Anyone in her orbit, like the writer Colette who Chanel enjoyed a petulant relationship with, was fair game. Paul Morand in his loving recollections, *L'Allure de Chanel*, quoted her admiration of the writer and also her denunciation: 'I like Colette ... but she was wrong to let herself get fat ... Two sausages would have been enough for her, two dozen, that's just affectation.'[13]

The secret, as she told her friend Claude Delay, was, 'I think the reason I've never got fat is that I don't eat pork.'[14]

But she did enjoy ham.

If Boy Capel was the first golden goose Chanel managed to snare, her second was her diamond duke: Hugh Richard Arthur Grosvenor,

2nd Duke of Westminster, GCVO, DSO, British landowner, sportsman, and one of the wealthiest men in the world.

Though Chanel had swarms of lovers drawn from the rich milieu of artists, writers, and composers that habituated Paris in the 1920s and '30s (Picasso, Stravinsky, Dalí, and a string of notorious women like Misia Sert), no one approached 'Bendor' (the Duke's nickname) in terms of sheer opulence. The once-destitute orphan, talentless showgirl, and hot, young concubine was showered with jewels, especially large diamonds that would be shoved under her pillow or dropped inside bouquets of wildflowers or submerged in her soup, works of art, a racehorse, a sumptuous house in Mayfair, and 2 hectares of prime land near Roquebrune, an expensive area for real estate at Cap-Martin between Menton and Monte Carlo. Here, Bendor built her a magnificent mansion they christened La Pausa. He also gave her a Great Dane called Gigot ('leg of lamb' in French). Bendor had many dogs, one of which he called Jew.[15]

The attraction between the two was mutual. They were both imperious, promiscuous, cruel, charming, homophobic, prone to mood swings, virulently anti-Semitic, and visibly pro-German (Bendor was a member of The Link, a British right-wing, pro-German movement, and also reportedly kept a copy of *The Jews' Who's Who* within easy reach that claimed to list aristocrats that had Jewish blood coursing through their veins.)[16]

Of far more value to her when her life took a turn for the worse in the 1940s was the unrivalled access to British aristocracy and royalty that Bendor's position and status in British society provided her. She frequently dined with Edward, Prince of Wales, in London and Paris, and the Duchess of York (soon to be Queen following Edward's abdication) became a client. She partied with the best of them at their galas and soirées, then hunted and fished with them at Bendor's various hunting estates in France and Scotland. There's even a photograph of Chanel hunting wild boar at Bendor's lodge, Mimizan, south of Bordeaux with beagles and Chancellor of the Exchequer Winston Churchill and his son, Randolph.

These were the same Winston and Randolph who, in 1936, had dinner with Jean Cocteau and Chanel at the Ritz during the height of the abdication crisis. Cocteau remembered Winston got very drunk and sobbed in Chanel's arms about the fate of King Edward VIII.[17] Before that, Winston had immortalised Chanel in a 1928 watercolour portrait with her pet dachshund[18] and written glowingly to his wife, Clementine, of her calming influence on the truculent and lascivious Bendor:

> Coco is here in place of Violet [the Duke's wife]. She fishes from morn till night, & in 2 months has killed 50 salmon. She is vy agreeable – really a gt & strong being fit to rule a man or an Empire. Bennie vy well & I think extremely happy to be mated with an equal – her ability balancing his power. We are only 3 on the river & have all the plums.[19]

Bendor and Coco were violent with one another. There were monumental arguments and hysterical fights, when priceless jewels were flung overboard from Bendor's yacht, *Flying Cloud*, into the Mediterranean just to spite one another. Chanel's great friend and life-long apologist, Edmonde Charles-Roux, acidly described Bendor as 'a man who could brutalise women'.[20]

After five years of mauling and licking one another's wounds, they became best friends, recognising it was only a matter of time before someone really got hurt. But then, Chanel always recognised she harboured a violent, vicious temperament from a young age: 'I really was an awful girl, nasty and lying. I had destructive tendencies. Once I cut the window curtains in shreds to make dresses for my dolls. Another time I almost set the house on fire.'[21]

These destructive tendencies didn't improve with age. She observed later in life: 'I ... am an odious person.'[22]

Despite these well-documented distasteful qualities, Muggeridge had some sympathy with her current plight. He understood the terror that lurked behind the eyes of celebrities like Chanel, the vivid red scar of vulnerability masked by a seemingly impenetrable lacquered veil of French sangfroid. Paris, for all its surface glamour and formality, was in chaos without a credible measure of authority or law. The prisons, which Muggeridge visited, provided the most vivid example of this civic breakdown: '... there was total confusion; the judges having mostly disappeared or been arrested themselves, and the prisons being glutted with alleged collaborators, brought along by no one knew who, and charged with no one knew what.'[23]

But the deeper horror, the deeper fear was always lurking within easy reach:

> It was when darkness began to fall that one became aware of the breakdown; with no street-lighting, and the tall houses all silent and locked and boarded up, like sightless eyes. Inside them I imagined cowering figures, hopeful of surviving if they remained perfectly still and hidden. Then, as night came on, sounds of scurrying feet, sudden cries, shots, shrieks, but no one available, or caring, to investigate. It is unknown to this day how many were shot down, had their heads shaved, piteously disgorged their possessions in return for being released, but certainly many, many thousands.[24]

Muggeridge also had experience of the FFI and understood why people were wary of their debauched sense of omnipotence:

> I was never able to decide whether they were just a marauding gang, or whether patriotism or ideological fervour played some part in their activities and antics. They certainly took things from people – cigarette cases, jewels, money; anything like that ... Equally certainly, they were given assignments; to go to such a house, conduct a search, interrogate such a person, make an arrest, and even – as they boasted, but I never saw them do it – carry out an execution. If a door was not opened to them, they would batter it down; everyone cowered before them, and did what they were told.[25]

Paris was still a dangerous, unpredictable cauldron of repressed fears, envy, and malicious revenge. For many Parisians, however, the city was entering a new phase, a phase where the old Nazi terrors had simply been replaced by new French ones that were, in some cases, more insidious, sinister, and slyly performed than the former horrors. For someone as vulnerable and attractive to the mob as Chanel was, her rendezvous with the FFI was purely a matter of when and not if.

5

SAINT MUGG

Chanel had also been briefed by her network of contacts about the 41-year-old Cambridge-educated, anti-communist journalist, editor, novelist, playwright and satirist Major Malcolm Muggeridge.

The reality of their encounter was that it was she, not he, who had manoeuvred it towards reality. Muggeridge was perfect for what she had in mind.

She knew he was an MI6 officer assigned to the French Services Speciaux based in the Boulevard Suchet in an elegant mansion used by the Germans during the occupation as their naval headquarters. Aside from that, she probably recognised him from her occasional forays to Maxim's, where British and American officers were allowed to eat and drink for free (like Maison CHANEL, the restaurant was anxious to disassociate itself from the restaurant that was a favourite hangout of top-ranking Nazis during the occupation).

She had been told the Croydon-born son of H.T. Muggeridge, a lawyer's clerk who became the Labour MP for Romford, Essex, was well connected, a heavy drinker, and a sex addict (the BBC's official historian, Professor Jean Seaton, in her book *Pinkoes And Traitors*, covering the period 1974–1987, called him an 'incontinent groper').[1] He was also reputed to be difficult. His intelligence colleague, the historian Hugh Trevor-Roper, wrote in his wartime journals that he was nice but argumentative, prone to incandescent outbursts: 'Dining with Malcolm Muggeridge is like picknicking [sic] on a volcano. The climate, the elevation, the verdure, the scenery, the hock and the sandwiches are all perfect; but one can never be quite sure that there won't be an eruption.'[2]

He could be moody and capricious and was used to operating at the outer regions of the empire where he could generally do things his own way without interference from inferior superiors. He also had a reputation for hedging his bets which, when he later wrote up his account of meeting Chanel at rue Cambon for his memoirs, vividly illustrated this capacity of coming to a pompous verdict about something without actually disclosing which side of the argument you were on. The novelist Frederick Raphael exasperatedly described Muggeridge as an 'intellectual double-agent, his only decisive posture is of pretentious indecision: he knows where he doesn't stand.'[3]

Perhaps it had something to do with his profession and where he plied his trade and with whom. Working in Section V (counter-espionage branch) of MI6, Muggeridge's boss in the Iberian subsection was double-agent Kim Philby. Among his immediate colleagues were Graham Greene, whom he loathed as much for his thriller novels as his success with women, who looked down their noses at poor provincial Malcolm, grubby journalist and wannabe serious writer. Posted to Lourenço Marques in Mozambique by MI6, he had some sort of breakdown and became so unnerved by his job there that he once tried to drown himself in the Indian Ocean.[4]

Chanel couldn't believe her luck.

In Paris, things were less fraught for the well-heeled Major Muggeridge shuffling between the Rothschild mansion and its retinue of servants (where he argued with visiting Kim Philby on the necessity of withholding sensitive material from the Soviets) and Boulevard Suchet, the ultra-fashionable area where the Duke and Duchess of Windsor chose to reside after the war. He had an office overlooking the Bois de Boulogne, containing elegant, priceless furniture once belonging to the previous residents, which in the bitterly cold months of 1945 he cheerfully consigned to the flames of a fireplace.

He had no official 'boss' and spent his time doing secret odd jobs for various security services, which earned him a special *Croix de Guerre* and *Légion d'honneur* from the French government for undisclosed reasons. It was Muggeridge who pointed out to the French the incongruity of the Services Speciaux having the letters 'SS' painted on the number plates of their cars. With scorching memories of German SS troops during the recent occupation still fresh in the minds of ordinary citizens, the Services Speciaux was soon renamed DOER: Directorat-General des Etudes et Recherches.

She also knew one of Muggeridge's jobs was to visit prisons and interview the extraordinary collection of alleged collaborationists that had been banged up there. Invariably they were a motley bunch of former prominent politicians, prefects, various senior civil servants, military officers, sulking diplomats, writers, and soured journalists, all rubbing shoulders with an assortment of riff-raff accused of collaborating with the Nazis as paid henchmen, informers, agents provocateurs, and homosexual prostitutes. The cells, reeking of desperation and silent arrogance, were always overcrowded, loaded with five or six jostling, emotionally pent-up individuals, despite being originally designed for only one prisoner. Muggeridge thought he could use his legendary charm to prise open the secrets these wretched men possessed, but it was heavy going. Like the writer Albert Camus, he realised what charm really amounted to in such situations: 'You know what charm is: a way of getting the answer yes without having asked any clear question.'[5]

When not wading through the detritus of post-*Libération* French society, Muggeridge was also a kind of celebrity fixer, having been asked on his third day in Paris to keep an eye on P.G. Wodehouse (along with the new, uniformed *Observer* correspondent George Orwell) who was staying at the Bristol Hotel. The indefatigable comic writer was still reeling from the shabby treatment he had received from his contemporaries during his infamous broadcasts from Berlin, which had transformed him from a recognised national treasure into a figure of widespread official vilification. Chanel also knew Muggeridge had a secret that he was desperate to keep hidden from his superiors and his wife (in later years Muggeridge was nicknamed 'Saint Mugg' due to his moral diatribes against sex outside of marriage).[6]

Chanel's peasant cunning kicked in.

Muggeridge's secret provided her with the necessary leverage to secure his presence at her apartment, leverage that he later realised and sought to suppress in his published memoirs. Muggeridge thought he was clever. Chanel's genius was that she let him believe he was.

Chanel's leverage was Muggeridge's partner that night: a photographer friend of hers who she had known since the 1920s.

The dinner was arranged so Chanel could disclose to Muggeridge the wartime relationship between this friend of hers (possibly the American pupil of Max Ernst, Berenice Abbott) and an unnamed German officer. It was a tricky situation because her friend was also having an affair with Muggeridge despite being still in love with the German officer. She feared Major Muggeridge might think her relationship with him was only a ploy so she wouldn't suffer from *Résistance* and FFI reprisals after *Libération*. A British intelligence officer with the Services Speciaux had immense clout in spite of the casual manner Muggeridge sought to portray his activities in the aftermath of the occupation. The photographer begged Chanel to break the news to Muggeridge diplomatically over dinner.

Chanel saw this as a convenient chance to further her own contingency plans.

As it turned out, the ploy to placate Muggeridge was a disaster as the transcript of that taut, tension-filled encounter proved. The encounter was momentous not only in terms of the delicate truths at stake, but also significant (perhaps even crucial) in terms of its effect on Chanel's behaviour and activities in the following days.

We know Muggeridge considered it momentous, because he destroyed the photographer's initial transcript of the conversation that occurred that evening. This un-redacted version remained intact and virtually unknown until 1976 when Isée St John Knowles, founding president of The Baudelaire Society and Limouse Foundation Limited, stumbled upon it while researching a book on Muggeridge at the writer's own house. Muggeridge had deliberately tried to cover his tracks:

> While following the original document, it omitted all Chanel's references to the affair, which, in Muggeridge's words, were 'unseemly', 'insensitive' and even 'humiliating'. This transcript was typed by Muggeridge on yellow draft paper, and bears his corrections of typing errors handwritten in felt pen. Apart from the excised passages, of no relevance to Chanel's war, that document is an authentic record of the 1944 interview.[7]

Muggeridge clearly viewed the rue Cambon dinner as a 'humiliating' ambush by the two women, and it clearly influenced the tone he took in the 'interview' that followed. Another clue as to the devastating effect it had on his psyche was the ridiculous lengths he employed to camouflage and exorcise his pain in his published memoirs. Muggeridge had no qualms about lying, as he confessed: 'Diplomats and intelligence agents, in my experience, are even bigger liars than journalists.'[8]

Muggeridge's published account of his encounter with Chanel is breathtaking in its deceit:

> As it happens, I was to be taken to see her by an old friend of hers, F, who had appeared in Paris, covered in gold braid, as a member of one of the numerous liaison missions which by now were roosting there ... If Mme Chanel felt any uneasiness at my presence, she gave no indication of it; towards F she adopted an attitude of old familiarity, as though to say: 'Don't imagine, my dear F (she addressed him by his surname), that your being dressed up in all that gold braid impresses me at all. I know you!'[9]

While the elderly Germaine hovered around them, they enjoyed an intimate candle-lit dinner of filet mignon, red wine, real coffee, and silky cognac. Muggeridge marvelled at how she was able to source these delicacies when the rest of Paris was virtually starving. Chanel seemed 'immensely old and incorporeal'.[10] Perhaps reticent to admit achieving nothing of any value from the experience, but willing nonetheless to admit a kind of intellectual exasperation he later became famous for, he wrote:

> Afterwards, I tried to draft some sort of report on my evening with Mme Chanel, but really there was nothing to say except that I was sure the epuration mills, however small they might grind, would never grind her – as indeed, proved to be the case ... Alas, all ... I had done was to listen; fascinated, and even a little awed, at the masterly way she harpooned and skinned the braided F.[11]

In fact, Muggeridge, the aloof, dispassionate, satirical essayist was so enraged and ashamed of the contents of that cringing evening that he chose to shift the focus away from his joust with the formidable Chanel to her jokey jousts with the incredulous 'F'. Perhaps it was because the tenor and tone of the evening was permanently soured by the women's duplicity. As a consequence, the 41-year-old Muggeridge was less than impressed with the 60-year-old Chanel. He found her neither teasing nor endearing (although he used the encounter as a basis for his play *Liberation*) and certainly not alluring: 'My first impression of her was of someone tiny and frail, who, if one puffed at her too hard, might easily just disintegrate; her powdery frame collapsing into a minute heap of dust, as those frail houses had in the London Blitz.'[12]

In Muggeridge's withering opinion the interview had failed to reveal Chanel's wartime activities to any degree or in any depth. His anticipation of receiving an unbiased account from her was, as it transpired, inevitably limited by the traumatic conditions under which the interview took place and Chanel's possessive, intransigent personality. And yet, despite his dismissive evaluation of the exchange, the transcript does contain significant clues as to Chanel's state of mind and how these may have influenced what happened to her and how she reacted to the scent of perceived danger in the coming days. Gabrielle Palasse-Labrunie, Chanel's grand-niece, on seeing the interview for the first time in 2012, wrote: 'Movingly vivid to me, some forty years after Coco Chanel's death, is the sound of her voice transpiring from the words of that interview.'[13]

If that was the case, then Chanel's 'voice' was literally dripping with disdain. Although she patently needed to recruit this supercilious Englishman to her side, she couldn't resist the pent-up urge to indulge herself in a little outburst of not-so gentle mockery at his expense. Not to be outdone, Muggeridge returned her volleys with his trademark irony, fuelled and fortified no doubt by recent conversations with the *Services Speciaux*. Both tried to shine but the wit was strained, the feigned diffidence tired and jaded. It had been a long, hot, brandy and nicotine-draining night:

COCO CHANEL: I have heard so much about you, Mr. Muggeridge. I believe you have come to liberate us. How very solicitous of you.

MALCOLM MUGGERIDGE: Even so. Could I perhaps elicit some intelligence from you concerning your valiant deeds during these past years? By the way, please understand that I have liberated no-one and nothing.
C: Have you been acquainted with the FFI investigation?
M: If I wished, a copy of their report on you could reach me by tomorrow. But I would much prefer to hear your side of the story. Did the FFI demean themselves towards you with reasonable courtesy?[14]

Chanel was fishing. Although the FFI had not interrogated her yet, she knew it was only a matter of time before they went for her as they had gone for her friends. She tried to control her emotions, but she was bristling with indignation.

C: It is odd how my feelings have evolved. At first, their conduct incensed me. Now, I feel almost sorry for those ruffians. One should refrain from contempt for the baser specimens of humanity, for whom Libération amounts to shaving the heads of women who have slept with Germans.
M: Should I take it that you have a low regard for the Resistance?
C: A major shortcoming of the Resistance is the outnumbering, before long, of the genuine warriors by camera-carrying midgets intent on leaving a record of their purported heroism.
M: Surely General de Gaulle does not fit this description?
C: You're right. He is too tall to qualify as a midget.[15]

The future editor of the satiric magazine *Punch* failed to see the joke, or at least gallantly acknowledge it. He ploughed on:

M: Does he not inspire in you one spark of appreciation?
C: I wholeheartedly welcomed his eulogy of French valour, to which he attributed the Libération of Paris. Have you listened to him lately? He will soon be claiming that the Resistance has liberated the world. And why shouldn't he? A countless following of French half-wits will believe him.
M: Have politics ever riveted your attention?
C: No. Mediocrity doesn't appeal to me.[16]

Another zinger ricocheted around the room without acknowledgement. Chanel was having fun even if Muggeridge wasn't. Did their dinner companion snigger? Perhaps tired of the jousting, fed up with the catty insinuations, and obviously upset (no matter how hard he tried to disguise it) at how an evening of such promise had turned to shit, Muggeridge decided to get serious:

> M: If you were to write your memoirs, what wartime revelations would you make?
> C: This is such a difficult question, isn't it?
> M: Well, let me make it easier for you. Which side were you on?
> C: On neither side, of course. I stood up for myself as I always have done. Nobody has ever told Coco Chanel what to think.
> M: And what do you think about patriotism?
> C: What every Englishman thinks about patriotism, the last refuge of a scoundrel.[17]

Muggeridge threw her a bone he knew she would devour in her book-lined salon.

> M: Manifestly, Coco Chanel is well-read.
> C: That too, I owe to an Englishman.
> M: The Duke of Westminster? Surely, he wouldn't have wasted his time on books?
> C: I am referring to Arthur Capel. Does the name 'Boy' Capel mean anything to you?
> M: I'm afraid not.
> C: He was the man I loved.
> M: How nice.
> C: A true dandy.
> M: Does that make him any better than the rest of us?
> C: You are not a poet, Mr. Muggeridge. Otherwise, you wouldn't be working in espionage.[18]

Muggeridge was stung and Chanel knew it. He wasn't expecting the censor that, on the surface at least, seemed bordering on humiliation. Did he blush? Of course, a man like Muggeridge aspired to be a poet.

What person with literary ambitions working in intelligence at that time didn't? But this polite tête-à-tête was going nowhere.

The intoxicating, heady mix of rich food and rich drink, the closed, cluttered claustrophobia of the rich furnishings, and the abnormal Parisian heat contrived to produce a feeling of dopey entrapment in Muggeridge's mind. Add to that his sense of a shared secret sub-text between Chanel and his photographer lover during the interview and it was no wonder Muggeridge felt unnerved, even a little lost.

Provocatively, he decided it was time to turn things up a notch and he noticed, with faint amusement, that he could hear the blood throbbing in his head as he did so. Intuitively Chanel crossed her legs, sensing a turning point in the conversation. Muggeridge nodded:

> M: So I am not a poet. I venture to state, therefore, that during the years of conflict, you shared your life with a German. Indeed, you may still be doing so. Do you also assert that you are in love with him?
> C: What does it matter whether he be German or Chinese? Besides, what makes you think I am in love with him? I simply value his friendship. And even so, he knows very little about me.
> M: So, there were things you needed to keep secret from him?[19]

Chanel decided, for once, to use the unvarnished truth about herself to deliver her most cutting rebuke.

> C: Mr. Muggeridge, I have learnt to dissemble my true feelings. I have misled people, so many people, that I too could have worked in espionage.
> M: Who trained you?
> C: I trained myself. Long ago, 'Boy' Capel introduced me to 'Bludgeon the Poor!' (*Assommons les pauvres!*) which, rejecting resignation, informed my moral outlook for life. I was that pauper whom Baudelaire needed to shake out of passivity. I doubt whether you understand.
> M: Tell me about your German friend. Was he a Nazi?[20]

6

YOUR GERMAN FRIEND

Chanel took a long, deep drag from her cigarette, stared for a moment at the ridiculous Englishman slouched against her sofa, and wearily asked herself how to begin, where to begin, what to say about her notorious German friend?

Of course, all the talk, all the speculation about him was the result of her frantic efforts to save André; she knew that.

Everything she did, everything she agreed to do during those early days of the occupation was about André.

André Palasse was reputedly Chanel's nephew, born to her older sister, Julia-Berthe, in mysterious circumstances around the time they both left the Issoire orphanage. There is speculation the baby was actually Gabrielle's, not Julia's. Julia seems to have died a single mother around 1912 when André was 8 years old. At the time of his birth, a purported father was paid to supply the baby boy with the required surname (the baby was registered as André Palasse on his birth certificate), but when Julia died, the boy was orphaned.

Chanel rarely, if ever, spoke about her elder sister. Whenever she did, her comments were often oblique and contradictory. But then, Chanel always resisted the pull of family, as she once petulantly told Claude Delay: 'I don't like the family. You're born in it, not of it. I don't know anything more terrifying than the family.'[1]

But she also told Delay that Julia killed herself by slitting her wrists when she discovered her husband had a mistress.[2]

Whatever the circumstances of André's birth were, Chanel uncharacteristically cared for her nephew (André had been living with a local priest after the death of his mother) and brought him up as her own. By 1913, Boy Capel and Chanel were a domestic couple living in Paris when André came to live with them. However, André's manners and general deportment were so appalling during his stay that Chanel shipped him off to Beaumont College, the very same English boarding school that Capel had attended. The aim was to convert the unruly, provincial French schoolboy into something approaching Chanel's definition of a gentleman.

It seems to have worked. Before enlisting in the French army in 1940, André was running one of Chanel's fabric factories in Huddersfield, Yorkshire, where he and his family had moved to in the 1930s. He also oversaw Maison CHANEL's lace sourced from Nottingham and velvet from Manchester, plus wool and cotton from Carlisle.

By the time Chanel had left for the Pyrénées in June 1940, André, along with 1.8 million French troops following the collapse of the Maginot Line (an extension of concrete fortifications, military obstacles and weapon installations France constructed in the 1930s to discourage an invasion by Nazi Germany), had been taken prisoner, deported to Germany, and incarcerated in POW camps, *Stalags* or *Oflags*. Living conditions were primitive owing to overcrowding. Food was scarce, disease rampant. The number of French POWs represented 10 per cent of the adult male population. Over 100,000 French troops had already died.[3] Following the signing of an armistice on 22 June between Germany and Marshal Philippe Pétain's puppet French regime based in the resort town of Vichy, it was hoped the majority of these prisoners would be repatriated back to French government institutions. Progress was slow.

Meantime, Chanel had closed down Maison CHANEL. The effect was catastrophic. Around 4,000 seamstresses, artists, embroiderers, and shopgirls were out of work. Leaders in the fashion business accused her of heartless betrayal. Labour groups tried to get her to open again. Chanel was undeterred and unrepentant. She wrote to her estranged brothers, telling them to forget about counting on her for any future help: 'I've closed the business ... and I fear living in misery ... don't count on me anymore.'[4]

Chanel had no idea André was a POW or that he was suffering from tuberculosis until she arrived in the mountains and the small village of Corbères-Abères, near Pau, to stay with André's family at the château she had bought for him in 1926. An old lover of hers, Étienne Balsan, who had negotiated the sale of the property, lived nearby at Doumy.

It is curious Chanel did not head for La Pausa, her spacious villa in Roquebrune-Cap-Martin designed and built with Bendor in the early 1930s. Situated above the village of Roquebrune near Nice, the house had the regularly patrolled French border with Italy on one side and casual Monaco on the other. Its name derived from a local legend that Mary Magdalene 'paused' near the house's location on her retreat from Jerusalem following Christ's crucifixion. Perhaps it was her way of turning a blind eye to the activities of La Pausa's architect, Robert Streitz, who was an energetic supporter of the French *Résistance* during the occupation. Streitz used La Pausa's cellars as a base from which he relayed covert messages to agents and provocateurs. Jewish refugees also found La Pausa useful, employing its gardens as cover and a convenient bolthole prior to their escape across the Italian border.

Chanel was obviously covering herself against any accusations of collaborating with the *Résistance* by the Germans. Adopting a stance of 'plausible deniability' (a CIA term first used during the presidency of John F. Kennedy) – that she didn't know what went on at her vacant property while she was away – was perfectly reasonable. This is despite her and her German friend making several visits to La Pausa during the latter stages of the occupation, using it as a base for a couple of visits to Madrid on *Abwehr* business. She was obviously covering both bases: passively unknowing for the Germans and actively knowing for the French when the country was eventually liberated and her activities scrutinised.

Following the closure of her couture house and the dismissal of all employees, except those in the perfume boutique, Chanel ordered her director, Georges Madoux, to relocate all accounts and archives to a temporary office he was to establish in the Midi region of southern France. Madoux, however, was conscripted prior to the implementation of the plan and concluded his primary focus was to secure his family and personal belongings before addressing the administrative records of Maison CHANEL.[5]

In the confusion of those panic-stricken days of June 1940, it was every person for themself. Chanel's chauffeur refused to ferry her across the country in her Rolls-Royce, pleading with his employer they would be dangerously conspicuous, sitting ducks for all kinds of nefarious interventions. On these terms, the replacement vehicle cited by almost every biographer, a Cadillac, would have been equally conspicuous and targeted for attack. Consequently, Chanel recruited a replacement driver/bodyguard called Larcher (her regular chauffeur, like Madoux, was focused on his own family), using his own car, which had the benefit of requiring less precious petrol than the gas-guzzling Rolls-Royce now that rationing had come into effect.[6]

Chanel, Larcher, a secret stash of all the morphine she could buy, and a bag stuffed with cash were greeted by Katharina, André's wife, and his two daughters, Gabrielle and Hélène, at Corbères-Abères. A few days later other members of Chanel's retinue arrived. They included Manon, her chief seamstress, and some of her employees who had nowhere else to go – elderly women, lost and confused. Two other refugees were Angèle Aubert, who had been Chanel's right-hand woman for at least thirty years, and her pregnant daughter, Annick. A later blow-in was the socialite Marie-Louise Bousquet. The numbers swelled to fifteen after just a few days. It was a miracle they had made it through the dangerous terrain infested with people, German and French, alive to every kind of opportunity that might benefit them.

At least at Corbères-Abères they were reasonably safe, and there was enough food to eat, beautifully prepared by the Palasses' cook, Marie. They heard Pétain announce France's surrender over the radio on 17 June. Chanel allegedly wept. After a few more weeks of successfully hiding in the hills with still no concrete news of André apart from a perfunctory postcard from the Red Cross that he was alive, Chanel decided she had to connect with people of influence if she was to secure his release.

Another consideration was her dwindling drug supply. This meant Paris. It was the only solution. Plus, she had access to more cash there. But to get back to Paris, Chanel now required special passes (an identity card, an *Ausweis*, or a free-movement card, the *Passierschein*), which could only be issued at Vichy, the seat of the new collaborationist French administration of Pétain and Laval.

France had been cut in half by an arbitrary boundary or demarcation line (colloquially called 'the green line' because it was originally marked in green on the joint map produced at the Armistice convention in June 1940) that specified the area to be occupied and administered by Nazi Germany (known as the *Zone Occupée*) in the northern and western part of the country, and the *Zone Libre* (Free Zone) in the south.

This arbitrary line had its ridiculous anomalies, none more so than in the Touraine, where it ran along the course of the river Cher until suddenly amputating the beautiful renaissance Château de Chenonceau that was built across the bed of the river. In consequence, the main entrance to the château lay in the occupied zone, while the southern part of the château's long gallery was in the *Zone Libre*.

Only Vichy officials Pierre Laval and Fernand de Brinon had permanent free-movement cards through the *Zone Occupée*. Although many citizens ignored the requirement for papers to cross the line legally, Chanel could not take the risk of flaunting German laws and then getting caught if she were to plead André's case.

After a brief stay at Toulouse with Cocteau, Apelles Fenosa (a Spanish sculptor friend of Picasso's), and French actor Jean Marais to recharge the batteries and her drug supply, Larcher bought 45 litres of precious petrol on the black market to get them to Vichy. They set off in the unbearable July heat with Marie-Louise Bousquet and a female doctor as passengers. They managed to cover the 434km skirting the banks of the river Allier on country roads without being troubled by German tank battalions, renegade partisans, or marauding gangs of local criminals on the lookout for easy pickings.

The historian Julia Pascal describes Vichy, now three hours from Paris by train, as a louche town petrified in layers of the past:

> The town is a shock, a wild skyline of domes and minarets. Its elegant architecture is neogothic, neoclassic, neo-Alpine, neo-everything. At first sight, Vichy is a melancholy fragmentation of Bournemouth, Brighton, Bath, Baden Baden and Brigadoon ...

This town of mud baths and colonic irrigation grew rich as a cure centre for rheumatism and liver complaints. Its mineral-rich sulphurous waters, running warm from the surrounding Auvergne volcanic mass, promised soothing baths and massage and, to sweeten the nights, there were casinos, upmarket restaurants and brothels. From the 1880s to the 1940s, Vichy was a high-class Las Vegas (true to form, on 10 July the National Assembly met for the first time in the casino).[7]

Arriving in Vichy, Marie-Louise and Chanel (the doctor had mysteriously peeled away) ate at the Hôtel du Parc, where Pétain had an apartment and the War Office, Justice, Propaganda, Education and Sports Ministries were housed. The Hôtel du Portugal served as Vichy's Gestapo headquarters, and the Hôtel Algeria, where checklists for Jewish deportation were coolly finalised, was also nearby (renamed Hôtel Carnot, the Hôtel Algeria's name was cemented over by the town's council but the letters still bizarrely protruded, ghost-like, through the coating until it was later renovated). From the hotel, the Vichy regime drafted orders for 75,721 Jewish refugees and French citizens to be sent to death camps.[8]

The first thing that struck the hot and dusty couple was the number of people swarming around the town's cramped amenities (at least 130,000 displaced politicians, diplomats, bureaucrats, and hustlers) and the surprisingly festive atmosphere, everyone laughing and drinking champagne. They didn't realise it was the frenzied tip of a debauched, laissez-faire iceberg:

> Free sexuality was rife in Vichy. A contemporary account by the artist Henri Sjöberg, in his collection of drawings and writings, *Hors-Saison A Vichy* (Vichy Out Of Season), depicts the scene in the Ministry of Propaganda, room 243 in the Hôtel du Parc, where Pétain's government resided: a naked man and woman lie in postcoital exhaustion surrounded by champagne bottles. Pétain called for family values, forbade women to wear shorts or short skirts, abhorred divorce and demanded that women be mothers. Yet he married a divorcee, was a faithless husband and had no children.[9]

The second thing that struck them was how revered Pétain was. His picture was everywhere. The 84-year-old First World War hero was universally venerated in the zone as France's saviour and he enthusiastically portrayed himself as the country's grieving protector/father, declaring, 'France is a wounded child. I hold her in my arms.'[10] In Lyon, Cardinal Pierre-Marie Gerlier had exclaimed, 'Pétain is France. France is Pétain!'[11] School children in the Free Zone were required to ritually sing, '*Maréchal, nous voilà!*' (Marshall, here we are!). Everything smacked of a dictatorship, and everyone seemed to be wearing its Vichy symbol, the *Francisque* (the double-headed axe), as a lapel badge.

A more pressing concern for the two women was where to spend the night? Larcher was left to fend for himself. Fortunately, the vacant hotel room of Chanel's friend from Paris, André-Louis Dubois, a senior Vichy official, was made available to the women following his abrupt departure from the town (he was suspected of helping Jews with travel passes). The second issue of dwindling drugs was solved when the travelling doctor reappeared along with another old friend, Misia Sert. Misia had a compliant pharmacist who would sell them morphine for a ridiculous price. Chanel would pay whatever was required. All the doctor had to do was supply a script and they were in.

Things were looking up.

To round things off, Chanel sought out her friend Josée de Chambrun, an important figure in the Vichy regime. Josée, nicknamed 'Chérie-chérie', was the only daughter of Pierre Laval, deputy vice-president of the new government in Vichy and the spouse of Count René 'Bunny' de Chambrun, her lawyer, Laval's legal counsel and Pétain's godson! If anyone could advise her on what steps to take to free André, it would be René. Chambrun was to help Chanel in her later lawsuit against Pierre Wertheimer over her marketing rights to CHANEL No. 5 but at this time even he was powerless to effect André's release despite having unique access to the regime's two most prominent leaders. His advice was to return to Paris and seek out a sympathetic German powerbroker. He gave her a couple of names that might be useful, one of which she recognised immediately.

In 1942, René Chambrun was added to a list of French collaborators to be killed during the war or tried after it,[12] and was forever soiled, with Josée, for acquiring artworks confiscated from Jews between 1939 and 1945. Despite this stigma, he became the chairman of Baccarat, the manufacturer of exquisite crystal, from 1960 to 1992.

In the meantime, the only practical thing Chambrun could do was furnish Chanel (via the prefect of police) with the necessary *Ausweis* pass to return to Paris. It's worth reiterating how difficult these were to obtain and how other freedoms of movement past the demarcation line were also severely tightened up and rationed. People could only write letters to family members using cheap proforma cards and then checking off designated words (like 'in good health', 'wounded', 'dead', 'prisoner').[13] The occupied zone also reverted to German time, one hour ahead of the unoccupied zone. Movement between the two zones was not only actively barred; it was also dangerous. Chanel realised that, the way things were going, it would soon be impossible to return to Paris. It was now or never.

Larcher bought more petrol and Chanel, Marie-Louise, and the doctor began the long journey back. Reaching a roadblock that prevented everyone from passing through except Belgians returning home, Larcher had no other choice but to crawl through side roads jammed with cars trying to do the same thing. Finally reaching the spa town of Bourbon-Archeambault, the ancient seat of the House of Bourbon, they luckily found the one place where all the hotels had been booked out but no one had turned up because no one was allowed through from the north. They had only travelled 75km, but at least they were able to eat and sleep in three large rooms, each with its own bath.

When the frazzled travellers finally reached Paris, it was swamped with German soldiers. Swastikas flew above the Hôtel de Ville, the Eiffel Tower, the Arc de Triomphe, the Élysée Palace, and the Ritz. Posters on buildings and Métro stops either screamed, 'The English and the Jews have brought you to this sorry pass,' or barked, 'Abandoned peoples, put your trust in the German soldier.'[14] A banner hung from the French National Assembly announcing in thick black Gothic letters, '*Deutschland siege an Allen Fronten*' (Germany everywhere victorious).[15]

A curfew from 10 p.m. to 5 a.m. was in place, American films were banned, and displaying the French flag and singing the *Marseillaise* was vigorously suppressed by police. At night, citizens had to shutter their windows and turn off lights to prevent Allied aircraft using it for navigation. Paris was almost unrecognisable:

> Most conspicuous to the visitor were perhaps the thickets of black-and-white German direction signs on every street corner, pointing the way to this or that military post. Nor to be overlooked were huge banners, hanging from the façade of the National Assembly building and every other municipal building.[16]

Ronald C. Rosbottom writes in *When Paris Went Dark* about the unreal silence that had descended on the city, like dense smoke, for those left behind. There was also a new kind of danger that emerged from an unlikely source. People started disappearing from their homes, vanishing from work:

> ... there is no doubt, now that the archives are almost all freely open, that the French forces of order were active, not reluctant, collaborators with the Germans. Indeed, there is no way the Germans could have succeeded as well as they did in rounding up ... 'illegals' if it had not been for the help of the local police forces. The Germans quite simply did not have enough personnel to track and keep files on Jews or plan and carry out raids, arrests, and incarcerations.[17]

During the occupation, a mandatory labour policy called Service du Travail Obligatoire (STO; Obligatory Work Service) also contributed to the disappearances. The STO forced hundreds of thousands of French workers to live in Germany and contribute to the German war effort in slave-like conditions. From 1942, however, many French workers refused point blank to be forcibly conscripted into factories and farms in Germany, willingly going underground to circumvent imprisonment and eventual transportation to Nazi Germany. These réfractaires became the backbone of the *Résistance*.

For the occupiers, a soldiers' magazine, *Der Deutsche Wegleiter für Paris* (The German Guide to Paris), appeared, published by the Paris

Kommandantur. Further guides, such as the *Guide Aryien*, listed the Moulin Rouge and the Folies-Belleville as must-see attractions. These guides also helped soldiers locate other reliable places of entertainment such as Paris brothels that had been placed under German control at 43 rue de la Lune, 7 rue de la Grange Batalière, and 4 rue de Hanovre, as well as special clinics for the treatment of infections.

Paris had been turned into a Nazi holiday camp.

As a reward, an array of victorious German units were routinely rotated to France to rest and regain their strength under the motto *Jeder einmal in Paris* (Everyone once in Paris).[18] Beloved artists, such as Yves Montand and Les Compagnons de la chanson, entertained these recuperating soldiers, kicking off their careers during the horrors of the occupation. Even that icon of French culture, Edith Piaf, lived above L'Étoile de Kléber, an infamous bordello on the rue Lauriston that was often frequented by German troops and the Lafont-Bonny gang.

At 31 rue Cambon, CHANEL No. 5 was still being sold in the boutique, and there were often snaking lines of belligerent German soldiers queuing outside. But the main entrance to the Ritz was sandbagged and guarded by German sentries. Larcher and the doctor were handsomely rewarded and released by Chanel to make their own way across the slimy underbelly of unofficial Paris.

Marie-Louise unlocked her Avenue Foch residence. Chanel retreated to the fortress of Maison CHANEL and her untouched top-floor apartment. She dressed for dinner at Maxim's. It was time to bump into one of the names on Chambrun's list, the one she had recognised and felt most comfortable about soliciting help from.

Four years later, in the musty confines of her dimly lit apartment at rue Cambon, Major Muggeridge politely coughed, jolting Chanel back to the present:

M: Tell me about your German friend. Was he a Nazi?

Chanel rubbed out her cigarette in a bulky crystal ashtray already overflowing with butts stained bright red:

C: 'Spatz' cared for me with great affection. He still does. If anything had leaked to him about the stratagems I engineered during those harrowing years, his anxiety would have betrayed him to his colleagues. I could not afford to risk any of that knowledge in his hands.[19]

So Spatz knew nothing? Muggeridge should have asked but didn't.

7

SPATZ

Spatz (the German for sparrow) was 45-year-old Baron Hans Günther von Dincklage.

In August 1940, von Dincklage was a tall, blonde, and handsome attaché to the German embassy in Paris, aged 44. The easy-going ex-calvary officer was posted to Paris in 1928 and quickly established himself as a charming playboy with plenty of money. After divorcing his Jewish wife in 1935, he pursued multiple affairs with rich Parisians and mingled in the same social circles as Mademoiselle Chanel. Even the CHANEL organisation accepted she had known him for years before they began seeing each other seriously in 1940.[1]

To some sympathetic observers, Spatz was simply an aristocratic diplomat, a view reinforced by the absence of any hard evidence to the contrary. Even at the time of Chanel's death, this fantasy was vigorously upheld by her friends, as the biographer Hal Vaughan noted:

> Asked by *Women's Wear Daily*, the New York garment industry paper, in September 1972: '[W]as Chanel, Paris's greatest couturière, really an agent for the Gestapo?' (friend and biographer) Charles-Roux replied, '[Dincklage] was not in the Gestapo. He was attached to a commission here [in Paris] and he did give information. He had a dirty job. But we must remember, it was war and he had the misfortune to be a German.' Years later, Charles-Roux learned that she had been duped – manipulated by Chanel and her lawyer, René de Chambrun.[2]

For others in the know, von Dincklage was indeed an *Abwehr* spy, first recruited by German military intelligence in 1919 as agent F-8680.

Fluent in English and French, von Dincklage was perfect for Chanel. The difference in their ages (he was thirteen years younger) didn't seem to matter or warrant attention. He treated her with kindness and respect. As a member of the invading administration, he also provided access to the drugs she needed but couldn't get and, after some delicate negotiations (von Dincklage was not sufficiently senior to be accommodated at the prestigious Ritz), two small rooms were gratefully found for Mademoiselle on the top floor of the less luxurious rue Cambon wing of the hotel. The hotel built a small staircase into the attic from Chanel's suite, and she would live there until the end of the war. Chanel and von Dincklage would host dinner parties at rue Cambon, slipping back to the Ritz in the small hours. The baron also maintained a sumptuous, luxuriously furnished apartment on the Avenue Foch, complete with uniformed butler and well-stocked drinks cabinet.

Residency at the hotel was vital because residents were immune from food and wine rationing the Germans had imposed on the rest of the population. Only a few months into the occupation and many basic products had become scarce: trucks and cars utilised charcoal or wood pellets as alternatives to petrol; wooden soles for footwear replaced leather; hand soap was produced from suspiciously sourced fats and caustic soda; authentic coffee was simulated by toasting barley and combining it with chicory, while sugar was almost entirely non-existent unless you knew someone who knew someone who could get it for you in exchange for another something that was also entirely beyond your reach.

French citizens were being slowly ground into the dust of starvation, mainly due to the nation shouldering the hefty costs of financing the 300,000-strong occupying German army that took the form of a 20 million Reichsmark (RM) tax per day. Exchanging German currency against the French franc (FF) had been severely rorted to allow 1 RM to equal 20 FF. This arbitrary correction allowed for the organised plunder of French resources and led to persistent food shortages and malnutrition, especially among children and the elderly. The daily rations allocated to a French adult by the Nazis amounted to

350g of bread a day, 50g of cheese, and 300g of meat per week, plus a monthly allowance of 50g of rice, 250g of pasta, 200g of margarine, and 500g of saccharine. Jean Guéhenno in *Diary of the Dark Years* reported the resulting 1,300 calories a day was 'barely sufficient to keep people alive provided they remain lying down and don't work'.[3]

From August 1939 to July 1942, the cost of living in Paris increased by an estimated 65.5 per cent, while inflation ballooned by nearly 50 per cent. In the summer of 1942, French rations were slashed by a further 12 per cent, while increased food quotas for Germany were implemented. France produced over 2 million tonnes of grain, 350,000 tonnes of meat, 300,000 tonnes of potatoes, 150,000 tonnes of vegetables, 300,000 tonnes of fruit, and 600 million litres of wine for shipment to Germany.[4] Food speculation was rampant. Nazi authorities, soldiers, and traders bought everything on the cheap in France and relentlessly shipped it back to Germany on a continuous conveyor belt of greed that never stopped.

The sinister and fraudulent *bureaux d'achats* (central buying offices), used by unscrupulous elements of the German military and civilian government, represented the worst examples of this systematic economic abuse. They officially bought French goods for next to nothing with money the Vichy government gave them as reparations and then sold these goods on for a huge profit to the German military. The military, not to be outdone by Nazi bureaucrats, then charged the Vichy government again by presenting them with the bills for everything they had bought from the buying offices. It was a cruel farce, but it worked brilliantly for German and French speculators operating on either side of the occupation. The corruption was clearly visible and produced despairing anger among the citizens of Paris, who had a hard time getting food every day, while the people who ran the *bureaux d'achats* were living the good life on their backs.

To allay the growing threat of insurrection and pacify desperate Parisians, the German administration distributed food charts and tickets that could be exchanged for bread, meat, butter, and cooking oil. Everyone received a ration book from their local *mairie* (town hall) and Parisians were also required to collect coloured ration tickets for various foods from the *mairie* on nominated days. Tickets changed colour every month in an attempt to prevent forgeries. This couldn't, however, prevent lengthy five-hour queues when the shops opened, with seemingly endless lines snaking around the specified bakeries and butchers a feature of Parisian life during the occupation. People were frequently turned away with nothing to show for the time spent inching forward when things sold out. The situation did not improve with time. By 1941, everyone had ration tickets for items that often didn't exist in shops.

Hunger was a constant ache in the body. People rooted around in the garbage bins of major hotels, which soon had to be policed by soldiers to prevent rioting. Queues lengthened in front of shops. Scarce meat and meagre supplies of almost every other kind of food, including potatoes, forced people to eat what was once uneatable, as Parisians had once had to do during the German siege of Paris in 1870. Black market food was obtainable without tickets at exorbitant prices. Some farmers tapped into this lucrative source of easy money by distributing their meat to the black market at a huge profit. Counterfeit food tickets were also in circulation. Bartering overtook cash as the most popular means of procurement.

The Ritz's select clientele were shielded from all this disreputable stuff. It was a clean oasis in a sewer of human misery and, with a severe winter approaching, the hottest ticket in town.

Chanel also sought von Dincklage's help in the release of her nephew, André. For that, Spatz required a higher level of authority despite his ascendency through the ranks of the *Abwehr*. A mark of this progress was a visit to Berlin during the cruel winter of 1941 with a colleague, another impeccably dressed agent, the 39-year-old French traitor Baron Louis de Vaufreland, to personally meet with Adolf Hitler and his propaganda chief Joseph Goebbels.[5] The two of them had been sent by their boss, the shadowy Hermann Niebuhr (alias Dr Henri Neubauer), to be vetted by Berlin's top brass for higher duties and more sensitive clandestine operations. Soon after the visit, the homosexual Vaufreland was awarded the *Abwehr* code name Piscatory.[6]

Niebuhr, Vaufreland, and von Dincklage met Chanel in the spring of 1941 at rue Cambon, and a plan was hatched where Chanel could demonstrate how her impeccable English political contacts could be used as a back-door channel to influence relations between the two warring powers.⁷ As a sweetener for Chanel's cooperation (no doubt suggested by von Dincklage), Niebuhr mentioned that under German Aryan laws, there was a very good chance she could finally wrest legal control of Parfums CHANEL from her beloved adversaries, the Wertheimers. Chanel was sold. Not only was freeing André in the mix but a dearly held act of revenge was also within reach. Niebuhr promised to sponsor and expedite Chanel's Wertheimer claim through the appropriate channels.

Unfortunately for Chanel, things didn't quite work out the way she and Niebuhr envisaged, thanks to the Wertheimers' canny business manoeuvres prior to fleeing to the United States before the fall of France (more about that later). It was one more grudge for Chanel to bear, one more barb to store in her personal hurt-locker. Charles-Roux summed up the seemingly never-ending war of attrition between Chanel and the Wertheimers: 'They played the nastiest conceivable tricks on each other. Booby traps, ambushes, feints and double dealings, every form of machination – the list of hooks they baited for each other would be a long time completing.'⁸

The Nazis, of course, had other less palatable forms of leverage they could have used against her if all else failed, principally her exorbitant drug dependency. Count Joseph Ledebur-Wicheln, a colleague of Niebuhr, was well aware of her druggie reputation among the Ritz's favoured clientele because he was running some of them as his agents. They reported to the bemused count that von Dincklage was a daily visitor, often staying the night or escorting Mademoiselle to and from her apartment to evening soirées. She was often unsteady on her feet and hardly seen without von Dincklage on her arm. Von Dincklage's supply of morphine was the only thing keeping her in one piece, catty neighbours like Fern Bedaux reported.⁹

Once the Wertheimer scheme was out of reach, the second part of the deal was actioned. At 8 p.m. on 5 August 1941, Chanel and the Spanish-speaking Vaufreland travelled to neutral Spain by overnight train. From there it was envisaged Chanel could make a trip to England and gift her assorted important friends information vital to both sets of causes. Chanel knew this was a test of her credentials, her usefulness to the Reich, her commitment to undertake such missions, and her nerve. Fortunately, she had chosen the one skill she had in spades, which she knew might appeal to her German overlords: 'She was a facilitator. She knew everybody in Spain, she knew everybody in England, and she helped out the Nazis.'[10]

What occurred during that August through September 1941 visit to Madrid is still largely unknown. One thing we do know: Chanel never made it to England, but she did manage to work the diplomatic scene in Madrid and at least make contact with some English diplomats while holed up in a vast suite at the Ritz Madrid.

There is a record of a 13 August dinner party she and Vaufreland hosted for the British diplomat Brian Wallace and his wife, during which she nonchalantly recounted the banality of life in occupied Paris and tensions between France and Germany. Parts of the banter, as minuted by Wallace several days afterwards, are trifling amusements, an assortment of *amuse-bouches* (bite-sized amusements for the mouth) intended to titillate her guests. For example, there is the following breathtakingly hypocritical nonsense:

> There is a separate [*sic*] (German) commercial organisation and this is extremely active – Chanel gives a particularly grave warning about this: 'They are buying themselves into every business, covering it up in many ways so that when peace comes it is going to be extremely difficult to weed all the German interests.'[11]

Presumably here she is referring to those Aryan laws threatening Jewish commercial interests she herself tried to use to destroy the Wertheimers. But there are also fascinating glimpses amongst all the dross of Chanel's tactics in pitching to the British government the idea the Germans might be amenable to an armistice of some kind with a country they rather admire:

> The Germans are bitterly anti-French but generally rather pro-British (in that they have a great admiration for all that is British) ... The Germans hate and fear Churchill and divide England into Churchill and the rest. The latter they are convinced want peace; the former to exterminate Germany.[12]

The British didn't bite, and Chanel with Vaufreland returned to Paris. Back at *Abwehr* headquarters at the Hôtel Lutetia on Boulevard Raspail, Niebuhr must have been somewhat satisfied with Chanel's commitment because a few weeks later an emaciated and sick André somehow staggered up to his family's doorstep at Corbères-Abères without warning. Chanel was further rewarded with an official *Abwehr* agent number, F-7124, and the code name Westminster.[13]

By the time Malcolm Muggeridge came to write his memoirs in the 1970s, he wished he had 'found out all sorts of things – how she managed to get to and from Spain during the occupation, whether she also offered free scent to the German troops, who were her clients, associates and intimates in those years.'[14]

Incredibly, the 1941 Madrid moment was only obliquely canvassed at rue Cambon that hot evening in 1944:

M: What happened to your son?
C: He was eventually released. My joy was beyond words. It was as though the bells you heard chiming throughout Paris were all pealing together within me. If that boy had perished in a Nazi compound, I could never have gone on living. I would have killed myself.
M: What ransom did the Nazis exact from you for his release?
C: My not being more censorious towards them than I was.
M: Had you held out any promises to them?
C: I promised them that my close acquaintance with Churchill assured me of his steadfast trust. However, it took me quite a while to identify the right quarters in which to impart this intelligence. I liaised with generously-rewarded [sic] informers.
M: Did you make any further promises?
C: I didn't need to. I merely laid a trail for them to follow. By then, new opportunities were opening …[15]

Major Muggeridge rubbed the back of his neck and stubbed out his cigarette. It took all his earthly powers to stifle the gigantic yawn that was threatening to destroy the studious impassivity of his creased, tired face. It was time to wrap things up:

M: Where does Coco Chanel go from here? To London?
C: There's no point now. In these changed circumstances, the symbolic forcefulness of my endeavour is spent. As I now feel, I would wish to be borne off anywhere out of this world.
M: You may do so still, with your books to help you. What about that poet of 'Bludgeon the Poor!'? Can't he console you now?
C: Baudelaire, it is true, means more to me now than ever before.
M: Have you thought of writing your memoirs?[16]

It was the opening she had been patiently waiting for, the chance for corruption:

C: As a young girl, Mr. Muggeridge, I was very proud at overcoming a reading handicap whilst other girls of my age read abundantly. Don't ask me now to get the better of my plethoric spelling mistakes in order to write memoirs. Why don't you write them? I shall assent to your fee, regardless of its amount.
M: Give me one convincing reason, barring the financial incentive, why the memoirs of Coco Chanel should be worthy of my notice.
C: Because I am perhaps the only person you know who is brave enough to speak out against a *Libération* culminating in the shaving of women's heads; and because I do believe that I have been liberated, Mr. Muggeridge, not by those loathsome liberators of yours, but by my love for André.[17]

The superior Muggeridge didn't take the bait, brushed off the awkward bribe as polite banter and left with his former lover, Chanel's friend. It had been a long, bruising, painful evening, with both protagonists needlessly provoking and needling one another like a couple of truculent heavyweight boxing contenders talking up the box office during a media weigh-in.

But Chanel was not altogether unhappy at the way things had gone. In fact, she thought it had gone surprisingly well considering the context and the threat of disaster crackling in the unbearable heat of her apartment. Yes, she had momentarily lost her temper at one particularly irritating line of interrogation, but she had proved to herself that she was more than capable of matching wits with this

Major Muggeridge character, the smarmy, smug, supremely educated, opinionated Englishman, adroitly sparring with him like an old intelligence services pro. Not that she thought she wouldn't be up to it but, as with any athlete competing after a pause, there was an element of apprehension: those nagging voices in the head that questioned her capacity to compete at the highest level after a long layoff.

But these doubts were scotched during the first few seconds of their duel.

More importantly, her sublime plan of using Muggeridge as a well-placed courier to feed back her candid, perfectly plausible answers to his new colleagues at the *Services Speciaux* was in play. She had dealt calmly with all the old questions she knew would come up. Losing her temper just that once was not significant in the context of the range of subject matter that had been canvassed. She had not been fazed. Not in the slightest. If anything, she was a little bored having to repeat again and again what everyone already knew.

Her complacency at having survived what could have been a damming indictment of her wartime exploits should have alerted her to the dangers of appearing transparent with a man of Muggeridge's cunning, studied ambivalence. Everyone knew he couldn't be trusted, even intelligence colleagues like Hugh Trevor-Roper knew Muggeridge was mercurial with the truth when it suited him: 'I like poor old Malcolm Muggeridge. Of course, having no interest in the truth, he is obstinately wrong in most of his opinions.'[18]

Trevor-Roper penned these words in his diary a mere six months after Muggeridge's visit to rue Cambon.

Chanel was playing another dangerous game with someone she had never met. Luckily for her, there was nothing new in Muggeridge's probing interrogation, no killer punch, no dolorous stroke (this is despite what a later commentator described as its 'razor-edged'[19] approach). Chanel was mostly upfront about her special relationship with Spatz and another far more embarrassing and catastrophic association with a far more senior Nazi officer that would lead to another doomed, misconceived trip to Madrid. Perhaps the Major Muggeridge's reticence was due to the constraints imposed by the presence of Chanel's friend inside the stifling rue Cambon ménage. Who could say? At least it was over.

Chanel composed herself. Now it was just a matter of time. Things had to work their way through the system. She was stoic. She was confident. She had always believed she could ride out the controversy of her past dealings with her German friends with courage and guile. That was what she and von Dincklage believed was a natural, workable Plan A. There was also a Plan B. That too had been worked out. Its success would likewise depend on how her contacts responded to whatever pressures may be applied to them to abandon her or else give her up to the band of fanatics that wanted her to suffer.

There was nothing more to be done. She had done enough. It was well past midnight. While Léon and Germaine cleared up, Mademoiselle took off her make-up and glared defiantly at her dressing table mirror, a snippet of the evening's joust repeating itself in her mind on a never-ending sound-loop:

M: You confessed to me a moment ago that you had deceived many people. Do you now intend to deceive me?
C: If I intended to, would I forewarn you?[20]

8

AGENT F-7124

Les Fifis, when they did finally knock on Chanel's rue Cambon door in early September 1944, comprised two women dressed in dirty shorts and sandals, with American cigarettes hanging out of their mouths like punks from a Jacques Becker crime flick. Battered German semi-automatic machine guns were slung around their shoulders.

Dressed at that time in the morning (8 a.m.) in only a light dressing gown and slippers, Chanel was momentarily stunned by their gender and casual malevolence. Germaine was frightened but Chanel managed to use this as an excuse to take her back inside the apartment and whisper instructions. Although she was also permitted to wear something more suitable for her interview, a member of the detestable duo came inside to hurry Chanel up, and she left hatless with a bag clutched to her chest.

A dusty, dilapidated old Renault Primaquatre with a lugubrious modified wood gas generator clamped to its rear was waiting kerbside and she was bustled into it and driven off in the direction of the *Fifis*' headquarters on the Île de la Cité. And so began a process, repeated thousands of times that summer, which Major Malcolm Muggeridge himself described as, 'all things considered, one of the more squalid episodes in France's history, with, as it sometimes seemed, everyone informing on everyone else'.[1]

It was excruciating for the fragrant Chanel to be sitting in the same car as the two sweaty and unkempt female agents and their equally obnoxious driver, who kept on wiping his bulbous nose across his precious FFI armband.

Unlike his female counterparts, the man's armband featured the Cross of Lorraine, which signified he was part of an early group of French Scouts who had joined the *Résistance* in June 1940, carrying out intelligence missions and repatriating Allied airmen until they became part of the FFI proper in 1944. The cross signified an element of prestige for those veterans who wore it. The young female agents, on the other hand, obviously had to make do with homemade 20cm × 10cm stitched-together tricolour strips with the letters FFI scrawled in black on the white part of the strip. The rough quality of the band made no difference to the whiffs of official arrogance which spewed, uninhibited, out of their bodies along with their vile, rough smell.

Chanel hugged her bag tightly against her chest and undid the clasp so the scent of a handkerchief laced with pre-war No. 5 could caress and soothe her nostrils. Paris, in the sunshine, was glorious. People were smiling: men in shirtsleeves, women in faded summer dresses and sandals, children running around in search of Americans and free candy. Herds of black bicycles streamed along the rue de Rivoli, over bridges. In different circumstances she might have been basking in the sunshine flooding through the half-opened windows, but she was not. Her circumstances were altogether different. A semi-circular crowd shouting and yelling on a street corner reminded her of the reality of terror crouching benignly on every street, in every alley, waiting to pounce at the slightest provocation. It was a two-tone peace. She involuntarily shuddered.

At least they weren't headed towards the FFI's notorious subterranean headquarters under the great bronze Lion of Belfort (named after the colonel who had led the besieged French forces against the Prussianas in the siege of Belfort seventy-three years before) in the centre of Place Denfert-Rochereau. Originally conceived in 1935 as a shelter to protect Paris's administrative services and ensure their smooth operation in case of attack, it was never used for this purpose and instead became the nerve centre for the FFI during the *Libération* of Paris from 20 to 28 August. Chanel had heard so many dreadful stories about this damp and dirty command post located 20m underground, which could only be accessed by a slippery stone stairway of almost 100 steps, she could hardly swallow until she was sure she was being driven elsewhere.

Thank God she wasn't being interrogated there. She doubted how she would ever cope inside that grim reality and, again, was weirdly relieved when the Renault eventually spluttered and coughed in unison with its crusty driver, stopping outside the Préfecture de Police and its ancient sandstone façade freshly peppered with bullet holes.

The heat and light were blinding. She was determined to keep her footing. She was escorted into the building, along corridors littered with the refuse of a tense, bloody siege by the female *Fifis*, each holding one of her arms as if she were a violent, truculent criminal that had to be physically manhandled and coerced into a cell. Finally, she was dumped inside a vast room with broken windowpanes where three men in bad suits stood smoking in front of a desk and a single kitchen chair.

Chanel had been on an official FFI blacklist since 1942[2] and Spatz had prepared her for what probably would happen when she was taken in for questioning and the general approach that men of his type (intelligence operatives) usually took with prominent people in such situations. She must look concerned but not agitated; wary but not pitiful; solid, not defiant; controlled, not proud. This was her challenge, resurrecting a kind of deceptive fragility she had not projected for a while now. It was not exactly a new role, more a variation of others she had adopted at various times during her extraordinary ascendency from penniless orphan to millionaire couturière. She wasn't so sure, however, the persona she adopted, trialled with Major Muggeridge, would be suitable here. No, it had to be something less intimidating. Less ...

Of course (Spatz had counselled), after four long years of bitter occupation, the French would be different. How different was beyond anyone knowing as it depended on the people in the room at that particular time, what they had endured, how they had got there, the quality of their breakfast that morning, the severity of the razor nicks on their chins, her demeanour on entering, the sudden whiplash of emotion and energy she brought in with her, plus a thousand other little factors that coalesced into the prevailing reality that existed in that one, single defining moment. How successful the coaching was is unknown, but whatever transpired, Chanel would have to fight against her natural inclinations, as she told her friend Paul Morand:

'Arrogance is in everything I do. It is in my gestures, the harshness of my voice, in the glow of my gaze, in my sinewy, tormented face.'[3]

Although we have no exact record or transcript of what happened on that stiflingly hot day in September 1944, there are enough files of similar FFI interrogations contained within the 120 linear kilometres of archives at the Centre historique des archives du département de l'armée de terre at Château de Vincennes,[4] the vast Centre de Recherches des Archives Nationales,[5] and the miraculously preserved archives of the Préfecture de Police in Paris[6] to extrapolate and imagine what might have happened during the three hours Chanel was held for questioning at the Île de la Cité.

Chanel's three interrogators – let's call them fat, tall, and bald – formed the usual *épuration* committee of FFI intelligence officers enlisted for celebrity interviews. Let's imagine the fat one stubbed out his cigarette on the floor and opened a file on the desk while the bald one offered her a cigarette, which she accepted.

French authorities had been collecting information on Gabrielle Bonheur 'Coco' Chanel since the 1920s when she first became a person of interest. The contents were mostly gossip concerning her many relationships and burgeoning cocaine use. Things intensified in 1929 due to her close friendship with Vera Bate, a well-connected aristocratic Englishwoman suspiciously employed at Maison CHANEL since 1920 as Chanel's society facilitator. It was Vera who introduced Mademoiselle to the Duke of Westminster in 1923. Both Vera and her second husband, Colonel Alberto Lombardi, were being watched by the nascent French security services as suspected German spies (Chanel's association with Vera petered out when she left Maison CHANEL to work for couturier Edward Molyneux in 1930).

Ironically, Vera later denounced Chanel as a German spy near the end of the war.

On 26 January 1929, an intelligence report bluntly described Chanel as an *'ancienne demimondaine'*[7] who had been embraced by Parisian society and who had excellent contacts in the political and diplomatic world. On 20 January 1931, the incumbent Minister of the Interior, Georges Leygues, directed the head of the Préfecture de Police in Paris to initiate a discreet surveillance operation targeting the Lombardi–Chanel relationship, despite it having ended the previous year. Nonetheless, the investigation was to be conducted with due diligence given the severity of the case and 'the nationality of the suspects and the nature of their actions'.[8] There was also a passing reference in a 1934 file to Chanel's friendship with Winston Churchill.

From 1933 until 1935, Chanel's eager financial support of her cocaine-addicted lover Paul Iribe's far-right journal, *Le Témoin*, also brought her to the attention of the authorities. The journal's strident and aggressive patriotism, its ultra-nationalist derision of foreigners and Jews, often featured Chanel's likeness re-imagined as the iconic symbol of French liberty, 'Marianne', lying either prostrate at the feet of political gravediggers or being sentenced to death by unscrupulous world leaders. Chanel's connection was only severed when the emotionally volatile Iribe died of a heart attack while playing tennis at her villa, La Pausa.

Since 1940 the contents of her file had swelled dramatically, incorporating such FFI snippets as the unguarded comment she had made at an innocuous but lavish 1943 lunch party on the Côte d'Azur when she apparently declared that 'France has got what she deserves'.[9] It was certainly not a thin document that the fat one was leafing through. But perhaps the interrogation started off, as they usually did, with a completely unexpected opening gambit designed to knock the suspect off balance from the get-go. The bald interrogator asked innocently, 'When was the last time you visited Lévitan, Mademoiselle?'

Chanel blew a long, steady plume of smoke into that already smoky room. *So that's how things are going to go*, she must have mused.

When Paris was liberated from the Nazis, it was as if an immense rock had been lifted from the city, exposing the nefarious activities of a nest of vermin that had been hidden or absolved from official censure for the past four years.

One such discovery was an abandoned, damaged photo album in a nondescript building once used by German soldiers assigned to the 'Furniture Operation' (*Möbel Aktion*), the innocuous name designated for looting apartments owned by French Jews who had already been sent to the death camps. The snapshots displayed an array of furniture and household goods as if they were on show in a vast department store – which they were.[10]

The department store in the photos was called Lévitan. It was run by the Jewish businessman Wolf Levitan and was located at 85–87 rue Faubourg Saint Martin in the 10th arrondissement. After its confiscation, Lévitan became the place for Nazi officers to browse three floors of stolen Jewish household goods with their Parisian mistresses. The fourth floor of this wretched building became a dormitory for the 795 Jewish artisans working there, selected for their skills from the internment camp at Drancy in the north of Paris (the final stop for Jews before they were sent to extermination camps).

Today the album is kept in the German Federal Archives in Koblenz but it also appears in *Witnessing the Robbing of the Jews*, a 2015 book by sociologist Sarah Gensburger.[11] Photograph after photograph illustrates how the Nazis took everything, not just the expensive furniture or priceless artworks, but mounds of banal everyday objects such as warped kitchen saucepans, household equipment, even bedsheets. It is a cruel indictment of the unmitigated, malevolent greed of the occupiers. Of the almost 800 Jewish prisoners forced to work there, 164 were deported to death camps.

Chanel's three interrogators strolled around her like crows sizing up a carcass. It was put to her that her boyfriend, the German agent von Dincklage, as a senior Nazi official was entitled to take her to Lévitan and tell her to take whatever she wanted. Chanel denied this. She had never heard of the place. Where was von Dincklage anyway? Chanel said he'd fled the country after the failure of the 20 July assassination plot against Hitler. Where was he now? She shrugged. Most probably with friends in Germany (which was true).

The tall one then pounced: 'As an *Abwehr* agent ...'

The fat one interrupted him to remind her: 'F-7124.'

The tall one resumed: 'You naturally hated all Jews. Is that why you went after your business partners, the Wertheimers, using Nazi Aryanization laws?'

Chanel now realised her unguarded responses to Major Muggeridge's questions about her treatment of the Wertheimers had not gone unreported. She tried to play it back in her mind, the moment she briefly lost her temper with him and his sarcasm:

M: Turning to another fine hour – or was it? You are alleged to have availed yourself of Vichy regulations to break faith with your business partners. Would you disclaim that?
C: For heaven's sake! The situation has been presented to you in such a spurious light.
M: Please answer my question.[12]

Chanel resisted the urge to throw her drink at Muggeridge's face. She smiled. Whenever it got heated, she smiled. It was her way of signalling a devastating seriousness.

C: A fraud had been committed – one without precedent in my business. A fraud so blatant that it could have hit the headlines in the world's newspapers. Substantial bribes had been proffered. And snatched up by venal Nazis. Such was the plight others had wound me into.
M: Why were fraudsters resorted-to in the first place?
C: I will come to that in a minute. When I uncovered this shabby deceit, I was advised to invoke the full might of the Vichy regime to secure the arrest of every one of those wrongdoers. Naturally, I rejected this advice. No fraudster was prosecuted through any act of mine. Now I shall come to your question. What was the fraudsters' motivation in so ruthlessly double-crossing me? It was because, for personal reasons, I urgently needed to regain control of my business.[13]

Yes, she was provoked by Muggeridge's disdain but the way she recovered and brought the conversation back to her concern for André's welfare was masterful:

M: Why?
C: A close relative whom I treated like my own son, and who was in poor health, had been taken prisoner by the Nazis. Now, my business partners are Jews, influential Jews as it happens. I felt that before long, they would throw in their lot with the Allies. I could not imperil the captive André's life by my association with overt opponents of Nazism. My business partner was far from unaware of my predicament. He had also been made aware that I would not

disown our long-established ties, but that circumstances compelled me then to suspend our contract for a time.
M: Those business partners, did they actively support the Allied effort?
C: After a fashion, they did, mingling the sale of perfumes with anti-Nazi propaganda. In the event, my tirelessly publicised determination to wrest back control of the business neutralised most of the adverse repercussions on me from an unwilling association with their propaganda.[14]

At the Île de la Cité, Chanel again resorted to accusations of fraud and mismanagement. It was certainly the most visible aspect of her retaliation, but she was also incensed, cataclysmically incensed, by the way the Wertheimers had decisively outwitted her at the onset of the war when she should have been able to smash them to pieces. In hindsight, the genius of the Wertheimers' actions and their choice of confederates were to play a critical role when she needed to flee Paris and France in the next few hours. But during the time she was incarcerated at FFI headquarters, she certainly didn't know that.

She was also unaware, until she participated in von Dincklage and Hermann Niebuhr's wishy-washy Madrid plan in 1941, the full extent of the Wertheimers' manoeuvrings.

In June 1940, the Wertheimer perfume factory in Pantin, the suburb of Paris where No. 5 was manufactured, was destroyed by German bombing. In August, their other main perfume factory in Croydon, England, was also devastated around the time Chanel was taking refuge in the Pyrénées. Recognising the writing was on the wall for Jews and Jewish businesses in Europe, the Wertheimer brothers took action and fled to the United States. Before leaving, and without consulting Chanel, they 'sold' Société des Parfums CHANEL to an aircraft manufacturer from Bordeaux, Félix Amiot, whose business they had invested in since the early 1920s.

Fifty million French francs (which rapidly lost buying power when the franc was devalued against the Reichsmark) were transferred to

Amiot's account from the Wertheimers' Mannheim Mendelsohn bank. At their last meeting, the 43-year-old Amiot remembered, 'We said goodbye. Pierre asked me to help save what was possible and to look after his son Jacques who was in the military.'[15]

The deal was Amiot would hold the CHANEL business in trust for the Wertheimers. But incredibly, before fleeing the country, the Wertheimers made a catastrophic, uncharacteristic mistake that riled them and which they knew they would have to rectify the minute they reached safety. For some unknown, unfathomable reason, they failed to secure the formula for No. 5. How could they have missed it? Maybe they couldn't get to it because the Germans had locked down Paris, the city was in chaos, and they were on the run and couldn't get to their offices where it was buried in a safe? For whatever reason, they left without it.

Transiting through Spain and Brazil, Pierre and Paul Wertheimer and their families arrived in New York in early August 1940 and immediately set up a company to continue manufacturing Bourjois-branded perfumes and their cash cow No. 5 in America. In the meantime, from their huge brownstone houses on Central Park West and Park Avenue, they launched a new perfume, Courage, from the Bourjois brand and, once sales of Courage were on the rise, turned their attention to the burning issue on their minds: resurrecting No. 5.

The easy part was finding a suitable factory in Hoboken, New Jersey, near Manhattan to manufacture the perfumes. The hard part was replicating the necessary raw materials from a formula they didn't have. The other dire situation was that Jacques, Pierre's 29-year-old son, was still trapped in Bordeaux, France and in hiding from the Germans and their Vichy collaborators.

Thankfully, both the Wertheimers' business and family dilemmas were in the safe hands of a quiet, unassuming former official of the Toilet Goods Association of New York.

As part of the deal the American authorities struck with the family to set up the Bourjois company and manufacturing operations, the brothers were required to hire an American executive to navigate the spaghetti junction inventory of labour laws and regulations. Fortunately, they had one already on their books: Bourjois's vice-president since 1939 was 33-year-old Herbert Gregory Thomas of

Brooklyn. The Wertheimers could not have had a better go-to man than the erudite, imposing (he was almost 2m tall) Thomas. Born in Manhattan, he had been educated in Switzerland and attended the universities of Cambridge and Salamanca in Spain, as well as the Sorbonne in Paris before practising international law in Geneva and The Hague.

An ex-Guerlain executive, Thomas was the classic urbane businessman, fluent in several languages and wine connoisseurship. Inexplicably (at the time) joining CHANEL two months after Hitler invaded France, Thomas told *The New York Times*[16] that his new assignment was studying the industry's future needs, which included facilitating essential oils shipments from Europe. He was straight out of Central Casting, and the Wertheimers duly assigned their version of *Mission: Impossible* to him. He quickly set about delivering the required outcomes.

There was no time to lose.

In New York, Thomas was friendly with Manu de la Sota y Aburto, a delegate of the Basque government, whom he knew from Cambridge and Salamanca. When he was preparing to go to Europe to recover the formula of No. 5, Thomas looked for a name that would guarantee anonymity when he crossed the Spanish–French border through Hendaye, and he turned to Manu, who suggested Don Armando de Guevara y Sotomayor. And so, in the early autumn of 1940, Greg Thomas (as he liked to be called) left New York with false papers in the name of a fake Brazilian diplomat and, most critically of all, with a large suitcase full of Wertheimer-sourced Louis d'Or gold coins.

First stop Lisbon, Portugal, a neutral country but a country awash with spies. At the central train station, Don Armando boarded the Sud Express bound for Paris, with two days and nights of travel through occupied France. Arriving at the Gare d'Austerlitz, he made his way to Galeries Lafayette, plastered with posters announcing the department store was about to come under Aryan administration. The perfume department, he reported to the Wertheimers, was crammed with Germans buying up as much No. 5 as they could carry. Business was booming, which meant Chanel was also cashing in. The Wertheimers were selling 60,000 bottles a year despite an ongoing world war. While in Paris, Don Armando also managed to retrieve the precious No. 5 formula from Félix Amiot (probably Amiot realised he didn't have the capacity or resources to manufacture it on his own, so it was a relatively easy release).[17]

Securing the formula was obviously crucial for two symbiotic reasons: without it, it couldn't be manufactured and the precise raw ingredients integral to its production could not be identified.

Heading towards the epicentre of French perfumery at Grasse with his fake papers and gold coins, Don Armando crossed the zonal demarcation line and arrived on the Côte d'Azur in the Free Zone. From Grasse it was 30km to the valley of the Siagne, near Pégomas, and the source of the No. 5 ingredients that could never be substituted by replicas: Grasse jasmine blossoms and roses. Don Armando was in the market for supplies of their concentrates, and he had the currency to pay for it. CHANEL's supply came from the fields of the Mul family, exclusive suppliers to the company since the perfume's creation in 1921. Félix Amiot, the new president of Société des Perfumes Chanel had already alerted them to Don Armando's intended visit once the formula had revealed its secret raw ingredients.

Back in Paris, Chanel was completely oblivious of what was about to be transacted. Unlike the recipe to make the perfume, the maths of its composition was relatively simple: each 30ml bottle of CHANEL No. 5 uses the floral essence of more than 1,000 jasmine flowers and a dozen roses. To make 1 litre of jasmine concentrate requires 660kg of flowers: Don Armando required 300kg of this concentrate, produced from 350 million jasmine flowers, to produce the half a million bottles of No. 5 the Wertheimers stipulated were needed. There was no way around these numbers. The Mul family set to work, transfixed by the gold now in their possession.

While this operation was underway, and with the No. 5 formula safely tucked away on his person, Don Armando focused his attentions on finding Pierre Wertheimer's son, Jacques, who had been initially captured and held in a POW camp, but now, in the chaos after the fall of Paris and with Félix Amiot's help, had gone to ground in Bordeaux.

Félix Amiot was far from being a puppet of the Wertheimers. In retrospect he was their saviour, the saviour of the CHANEL business (the canny Amiot probably used some of the 50 million francs the Wertheimers gave him before they left France to bribe his business associate, Luftwaffe Reich Marshal Hermann Göring, to quarantine the business from other marauding Reich officials) and, as we shall see, the saviour of his illustrious bête noire, Coco Chanel herself. It was Amiot who also pointed Don Armando in the direction of an unscrupulous French Foreign Legion deserter and his rich-girl American lover who might be able to smuggle Jacques out of France.

Mary Jayne Gold's monied background allowed her to fly her own plane around Europe, visiting luxury hotels, skiing at top destinations in the Alps, and associating with other wealthy individuals. In 1940, Gold was enjoying life in a Paris apartment when Germany invaded France. Her plan, like many exposed expatriates, was to head 800km south to the lawless port of Marseille and catch a ship back home. But on the way down, Gold encountered a person who changed her mind and her life, recording it for posterity in her memoir, Crossroads Marseilles, 1940.[18] In Toulouse, a collecting point for hordes of European refugees, Gold met an American student, Miriam Davenport, a native of Boston. Davenport also recorded their encounter, recalling that Gold told her:

> That she was a rich woman and that should I run short of cash, she would love to help out. She was planning to go fetch her little dog from where she had left him on the flight south, then go on to Marseille where she would cable home for money and return to the States.[19]

Neither Gold nor Davenport left France.

In Marseilles, the two women threw in their resources with Varian Fry, an American journalist and intellectual, who had created the Emergency Rescue Committee to assist Jewish and anti-Nazi artists and intellectuals to leave France. The committee also provided refuge for individuals fleeing persecution and expedited their transit through France's mountainous border regions to Spain and neutral Portugal, or clandestinely transported them on freighters bound for North Africa and various ports in North and South America.

They were helped by Raymond Couraud, the former French Foreign Legionnaire turned local gangster who became Gold's lover. 'Killer' (as Gold affectionately called him from the way he murdered the English language) had fought the Germans in Norway and was a decorated war hero.

After the fall of France, Couraud became a legionnaire but deserted when his outfit was posted to the main Legion base in Vichy-run Algeria. Despite his combat experience, Couraud certainly didn't resemble a physical killer. Wearing spectacles, he looked like a gaunt, beleaguered bureaucrat. Bored with hiding from the Vichy authorities, Killer convinced his girlfriend, Gold, to buy him a small fishing trawler under the pretext that he and twelve other legionnaires could sail to Gibraltar and continue the fight against the Nazis from England. Gold bought the idea. What she didn't know was that Couraud was really using the boat to make money, smuggling people and contraband in and out of France via North Africa and Spain.

Which is when he encountered the gigantic Don Armando and his emaciated French companion who the don wanted conveyed on Couraud's boat to Morocco. The third part of Greg Thomas's mission was completed when Jacques Wertheimer finally made it out of France aboard the American Export Lines 7,000-ton transatlantic steamer Excalibur, arriving in New York from Lisbon on 21 November 1940.

Flush with money, Couraud was unfortunately arrested by the Legion for desertion soon after the Morocco trip and was locked up in Marseille's military prison, Fort St Nicolas, near the harbour. Released in December 1940, he deserted again, joining a Corsican gang in Marseille renowned for their cruelty (Don Armando made use of this gang to ship bulk quantities of No. 5 raw materials out of the country). Making even more enemies than when he was operating on his own, Killer stole Gold's diamonds and fled to Britain where he somehow managed to hook up with the Special Air Service (SAS). He was decorated for gallantry by the British, but even the completely mad and unmanageable SAS eventually dismissed him for disobeying orders.

While all this was going on, Don Armando had melted away into the background, and the urbane Greg Thomas returned unobtrusively to New York with his precious cargo of 50kg of absolue de jasmine in early 1941. The other 270kg of jasmine concentrate, plus other raw materials, required an intervention from Thomas's contacts at the American Perfume Association to allow their entry into the United States.[20]

Following US entry into the war on 7 December 1941, Thomas took leave from the Wertheimers and officially joined the Office of Strategic Services (OSS), precursor to the post-war Central Intelligence Agency (CIA), and became one of its most effective operatives. He was Chief of Station at Madrid and Lisbon and was responsible for running OSS agents into France. In 1945 he was made president and later chairman of CHANEL, Inc., a job he held until retiring in 1972.

OSS records were sealed for sixty years after the war, and Thomas features a few times in the 35,000 files, including a note on the alias he assumed in 1940 to transact his mission for the Wertheimers.[21] The only interview he gave where he spoke obliquely about his exploits was in 1989 with Phyllis Berman and Zina Sewaya for *Forbes* magazine.[22] Founder and *grand maître* of the Commanderie de Bordeaux in the United States, French *Légion d'honneur* recipient, Thomas died after unsuccessful brain surgery in 1990.

In Paris, Chanel was informed of these Wertheimer manoeuvres (i.e. the Amiot Société des Parfums CHANEL deal and the Hoboken factory) by her *Abwehr* boss, Hermann Niebuhr. She became 'drunk with rage'.[23] According to her friend and early biographer Edmonde Charles-Roux, 'the Wertheimer clan would see what she was made of. She was Aryan and they weren't. She was in France and they were in the United States. Emigrants ... Jews. In the eyes of the occupying power, in short, she alone existed.'[24]

9

THE PROPERTY OF JEWS

The heat was becoming unbearable inside that vast, gloomy smoke-filled interrogation room on the Île de la Cité.

The bald man took off his jacket and hung it on a hook at the back of the door. Chanel reached for her handkerchief, dabbed her face, and asked for a glass of water. The fat man went to fetch it. The glass was smeared with grease, but she drank it, wincing before resting it on her lap. The questions continued.

She had been betrayed, she said. Again. Like she had been when the love of her life, Boy Capel, told her before he died that her couturière business was wholly owned by investors and all the money she was making was not hers to keep.

Yes, her interrogators agreed, and her first impulse was to spitefully mobilise her German friends and collaborators for revenge, like Baron von Dinklage, the Vichy commissioner for Jewish Affairs Xavier Vallat, René Bousquet (future secretary general of the Vichy police), the *Abwehr*, and even Otto Abetz, Hitler's ambassador in Paris. Was that not the case?

Chanel asked for a cigarette. The tall one rolled up his sleeves as if he was just getting started. There was another name, the slimy French traitor Baron Louis de Vaufreland, her interrogators had omitted, but they were mostly correct.

The bald interrogator produced a yellowy press clipping from the Nazi-controlled *Le Soir* newspaper and dangled it in front of her face. 'You were so confident of getting hold of the Wertheimers' business you couldn't wait to boast about it, could you?' he asked. Chanel squinted at the paper's interview with the famous Coco Chanel in which she discussed plans to reopen the fashion house she'd closed in 1939 on the eve of war. Published early in the Nazi occupation of Paris, it featured a pen-and-ink drawing of Chanel looking fierce and determined in a black turtleneck.[1] Above it was a story about de Gaulle being sentenced to death *in absentia* by the Vichy regime.

Chanel shrugged, as if to say, 'What does it matter?' That was the least of her caprices. Her virulent reaction to being outplayed by the Wertheimers manifested itself on several other fronts, including the little-known introduction of rogue fragrances under the brand name Mademoiselle Chanel. These rogue CHANEL products included a No. 1, a No. 2, a No. 3, and a No. 31. It's unclear if each bottle had a unique aroma or they were all the same. Pierre Wertheimer and Ernest Beaux (the creator of No. 5) were acutely aware of these provocative fragrances and Wertheimer/Amiot, through CHANEL lawyers in France, moved to block their distribution.

Chanel knew she was in breach of her contract with Parfums CHANEL but had no idea who this Félix Amiot was. When she was informed he was the new Aryan owner of the perfume group, she went into overdrive. In New York Parfums, Chanel's new perfumes were seized by customs agents, which catapulted her relationship with that bastard Pierre and this new bastard Amiot to a whole new level.

Though Beaux distanced himself from the red-and-gold bottled Mademoiselle CHANEL No. 1, recent chemical analysis directed by Dr Philip Kraft of Givaudan (the Swiss-based manufacturer of flavours, fragrances, and active cosmetic ingredients) in 2007 proved it bore Beaux's chemical 'signature'. The Kraft research team sent a sample to Christine Ledard, who analysed it using GC-chromatography and GC-olfactometry. The findings were published in the October 2007 issue of *Perfumer & Flavorist*, entitled 'From Rallet No.1 to Chanel No.5 versus Mademoiselle Chanel No.1'.[2]

The tests revealed Mademoiselle Chanel No.1 was similar in concept to Beaux's construction of Rallet No. 1. The absence of the aldehyde cocktail which Beaux effectively employed in Rallet No. 1 and CHANEL No. 5, was notably absent in Mademoiselle CHANEL No. 1. In contrast, 25 per cent of the Mademoiselle formula comprised a novel ingredient that was only recently introduced in the

1940s (Beaux was known to be a constant and meticulous experimenter of new materials).

Although the exact origins of Mademoiselle Chanel No. 1 and the other Mademoiselle Chanel fragrances remain uncertain, we do know that when Pierre Wertheimer finally returned in 1946 (strangely as a Mexican citizen) he reluctantly agreed to give Coco Chanel another 2 per cent of the profits of Parfums CHANEL. Mademoiselle Chanel No. 1 duly vanished from the shelves of Maison CHANEL. The spurious Chanel-fuelled publicity campaign claiming bottles of American-made No. 5 perfume were fake also subsided.

As part of the deal Chanel struck with the Germans, proceedings against Jewish ownership of Société des Parfums CHANEL were indeed inaugurated. Letters of denunciation began to arrive at the Vichy government's Jewish Affairs Department demanding the Aryanization of CHANEL perfumes. Claiming Amiot's purchase of the company was a sham and that Jews were still in charge, on 8 February 1941, the government appointed Georges Madoux as provisional administrator of CHANEL perfumes. To speed things up, Chanel personally wrote to Madou on 5 May 1941, a toxic letter that somehow made its way into the file on the desk in that oppressive office on the Île de la Cité: 'Parfums Chanel is still the property of Jews ... and has been legally 'abandoned' by the owners. I have an indisputable right of priority. The profits that I have received from my creations since the foundation of this business ... are disproportionate.'[3]

Chanel's campaign coincided with increasingly horrific German reprisals against Jews in occupied countries. In France, approximately forty-nine concentration camps were constructed at breakneck speed for use during the occupation, the largest of these hideous structures installed at Drancy. These heinous arrangements escalated rapidly. In early 1942 they were merely punitive: Jews over the age of 6 were forced to wear the yellow star with *Juive* or *Juif* scrawled in black across it; and adult Jews were restricted to the last carriage of trains on the Paris Métro. But by July, things had drastically changed. Over several days over 13,000 Parisienne Jews were arrested by pro-Nazi French authorities in an operation known as the Vel' d'Hiv Roundup.[4] They were sent to Auschwitz and gassed.

Out of a Jewish population in France estimated at around 350,000 in 1940, by war's end about 75,000 had been exterminated by the Nazi and Vichy regimes for simply being born at the wrong time, in the wrong place.[5]

Louis de Vaufreland tried his best to break the impasse between Chanel and the Jewish Affairs Department. Through a friend of his, Prince Ernst Ratibor-Corvey, he arranged a meeting between Chanel and the lawyer Dr Kurt Blanke, a repellent man who practically lived in his Gestapo office at the Hôtel Majestic and was responsible for using Nazi laws to confiscate Jewish property. In fact, the 40-year-old Blanke also ran the activities of the odious Entjudung (the elimination of Jewish influence) for the Nazis in Paris.

But not even Blanke could break the impasse.

By June 1941, Göring's influence had kicked in, scuppering Chanel's Aryanization plans, and Blanke was forced to close the file: 'I can conclude in good faith that the Bourjois perfumery has passed into the hands of the Aryans in a legal and correct manner and that no grievance can be made against Mr. Amiot.'[6]

But Chanel was unrepentant and undaunted. She kept up her private war against the Wertheimer/Amiot hegemony. The bitterness never ever completely left her. Paul Morand in his 2017 book, *The Allure of Chanel*, wrote she had a 'kind of solid appetite for vengeance that revolutions are made of'.[7] Even so, she was also extremely pragmatic when it came to where the bulk of her money originated.

Major Malcolm Muggeridge had asked the key question a few days before her internment at the Île de la Cité:

M: Will you ever consider working with them again?
C: I will. In the past, even when our partnership better resembled a slanging match, our relationship somehow survived.
M: Naturally, I cannot comment on the fraud you allege, since I am not in possession of the facts. Even so, can you reasonably expect influential Jews to remain silent in the face of an ideology which vows to oppress their people and many others? Would you concede that the resolute gearing of their business to promoting the Allies should override personal factors, however pressing?

Chanel surprisingly conceded the point but, tellingly, rammed home her unique sense of entitlement:

> C: I go along with that. I could not expect them to take any different line, and therefore took matters with the fraudsters no further. But I can never forgive their withholding their trust when I needed it at a critical point in my life.[8]

Amazingly, there are historians who think the perfidious scheming of Chanel and de Vaufreland to wrest control of Société des Parfums CHANEL using Nazi Aryanization laws was undertaken at the behest of the Wertheimers themselves. They believe it was a bizarre double-cross ploy by the Wertheimers to protect their perfume business and keep Amiot on his best behaviour.[9]

Such historians cite other dubious arrangements between high-ranking Nazis and eminent Jews where the threat of extermination was a mere ruse to camouflage mutually advantageous financial benefits. Applying that logic to the case of Société des Parfums CHANEL, presumably Göring was aware of the Wertheimers' conspiracy against the Reich and was actually bribed by Amiot to indulge Chanel's scheming before stepping in and squashing it. What a fantastic, serpentine plan!

The catch is these cosy, devious arrangements were often invented in hindsight to sanitise deals that Jews had no choice but to acquiesce to.

This was not the case with the sale of Société des Parfums CHANEL to Félix Amiot: he was doing the Wertheimers a huge favour in precarious times. There was no need to enter into a pact with malicious, avaricious Nazis. Such partnerships were extremely dangerous, terrifying, and prone to sifting allegiances. One small slip, one small offence, one small bad impression and you could wind up dead. Even if such deals were commonplace, that doesn't mean it was a game for everyone, especially for a refined Jewish family like the Wertheimers, scared out of their wits enough to flee to America and leave one of their own (Jacques) behind in their desperation to survive. This particular conspiracy theory just doesn't add up.

The tall man asked Chanel if she wanted a break. She cringed at the thought of what she might find in the filthy bathrooms of this once beautiful building. 'How long is this going to take?' she asked. The tall man shrugged.

If Chanel felt she was being unduly singled out by the newly victorious French post-*Libération* regime for heavy-handed treatment, while her beauty and fashion competitors were getting off comparatively lightly, she was probably right. Chanel certainly wasn't alone among the fashion world's elites when it came to dangerous entanglements with Nazis.

Today L'Oréal has a portfolio of thirty-six international brands such as Yves Saint Laurent Beauté, Lancôme, Cacharel, Giorgio Armani Beauty, Kiehl's, Aesop, Diesel, and Viktor&Rolf, with a net income of over four billion euros a year and roughly 88,000 employees in 2020. Not generally known are the billions of litres of paint manufactured by a L'Oréal-managed company that was supplied to camouflage Nazi Germany's battleships, U-boats and other war machines. Rewarded with vast wartime profits, the L'Oréal family's ascendancy towards untrammelled wealth features in Tom Sancton's book *The Bettencourt Affair*, published in 2014.

Eugène Schueller, a chemist, created L'Oréal (formerly L'Auréale) in 1919 after discovering a new method for manufacturing hair dye. He later immersed himself in Nazi politics and economic theory throughout the 1930s, funding the French anti-communist and anti-semitic outfit La Cagoule (or 'Hood'), which aimed to overthrow governments and firebomb synagogues to advance their right-wing goals. Scheuller even chaired meetings at L'Oréal's HQ for members of the La Cagoule organisation.[10]

After the Nazi invasion of 1940, Schueller used his right-wing connections to tap into lucrative Nazi war procurement contracts. Between 1941 and 1944, L'Oréal's profits soared along with Schueller's personal wealth. After the war ended, Schueller was charged with collaboration and tried in the French courts, but definitive proof of any impropriety couldn't be found. His cause was also helped when eminent witnesses testified to his character and nationalism including a very young François Mitterrand, future French president. He was naturally acquitted, and his company continued to prosper.

Schueller's tentacles reached into every corner of post-war French society. Former colleagues of La Cagoule like Jacques Corrèze, serving a ten-year sentence for war crimes, were often taken care of when they were released and given positions in L'Oréal companies around the world.

Schueller's family were also heavily involved in extreme right-wing politics. His son-in-law and successor as Head of L'Oréal, André Bettencourt, served as a Nazi propagandist for Joseph Goebbels, Hitler's Reich Minister of Propaganda from 1933 to 1945. After the war, Bettencourt and his father were repeatedly sheltered from prosecution by the ascendant Mitterrand. After his background was revealed in 1994, André quickly transferred his shares in L'Oréal to his wife, Liliane. The avalanche of money continued to roll in. Liliane Bettencourt, who died in 2017, became the world's richest woman and fourteenth richest individual with a net worth of US$44.3 billion. In 2023, her daughter, L'Oréal heiress Françoise Bettencourt Meyers, became the first woman to achieve a personal fortune of US$100 billion.[11]

The L'Oréal story is not unique. The 'whitewashing' of European businesses after the war included minnows and titans such as BMW, infamous for its use of Nazi slave labour throughout the war; IKEA, whose founder, Ingvar Kamprad, was an unashamed and virulent Nazi party member; Hugo Boss; and BASF (shorthand for its original name, Badische Anilin- und Sodafabrik), the German chemical and electronics company that made mustard gas for Nazi extermination camps. Like people, companies did what they did in order to survive. It was easier to say yes than say no and suffer the consequences. Turning a blind eye to atrocities, iniquity, cruelty, and humiliation while counting the money will always exist and will always find willing collaborators and apologists. It is a fundamental feature of the human condition. Indeed, choosing whether to join in or not is fundamental to being human.

Before she could express her contempt at the unfair way she was being treated to her interrogators at the Île de la Cité, Chanel's session was abruptly terminated in the most extraordinary way.

A door was suddenly opened into the room, obscuring whoever was behind it. The fat man was summoned. Then the bald man was summoned, leaving only the tall man alone with Chanel. After a short time both men came back into the room, and the fat one gestured irritably at the open door. 'You may leave now, Mademoiselle,' he told Chanel. She didn't wait to be told a second time and marched out, escorted by the tall man.

Squinting from the glare of the harsh afternoon sun, she offered an American cigarette to the tall man while they waited for a taxi. A pretty girl rode past them on a rickety bicycle. Chanel looked at her black, alligator-strapped, 18-carat-gold Patek Philippe wristwatch. It was just over three hours since she'd left rue Cambon.

'What happens now?' Chanel asked him.

The tall man shrugged again. Chanel understood and nodded.

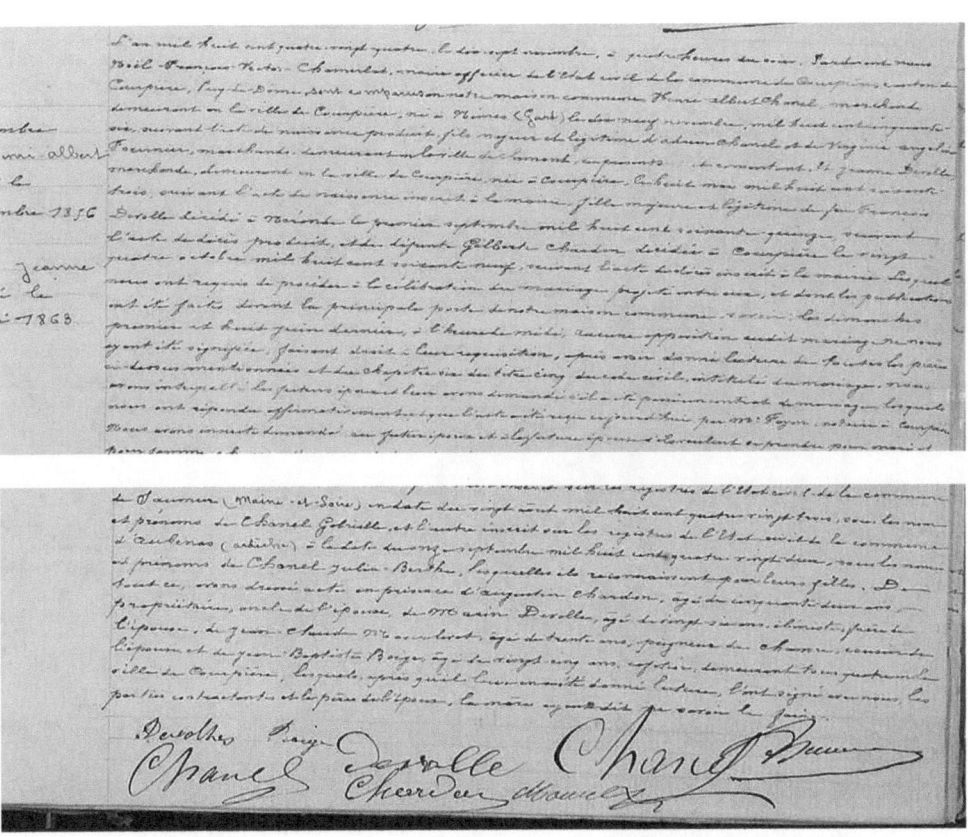

Birth certificate of Gabrielle (Coco) Chanel in Saumur (Maine-et-Loire) in 1883 with misspelt surname. (Archives du Maine-et-Loire, public domain)

Marriage certificate of Henri Albert Chanel and Jeanne Devolle in Courpière (Puy de Dôme) in 1884. (Public domain)

Coco Chanel in 1920 with her famous bob cut. (Pictorial Press Ltd/Alamy Stock Photo)

Pierre Wertheimer in 1924 when the Wertheimers and Chanel made an agreement to create Parfums CHANEL. (Public domain)

Chanel on the balcony of her suite at the Hôtel Ritz before the war. (© Photo Roger Schall/Schall Collection)

Chanel and Winston Churchill hunting in France, 1921. (Public domain)

From left to right: Chanel, Misia Sert and Madame Philippe Berthelot at the beach on Venice's Lido, 1920s. (Tallandier/Bridgeman Images)

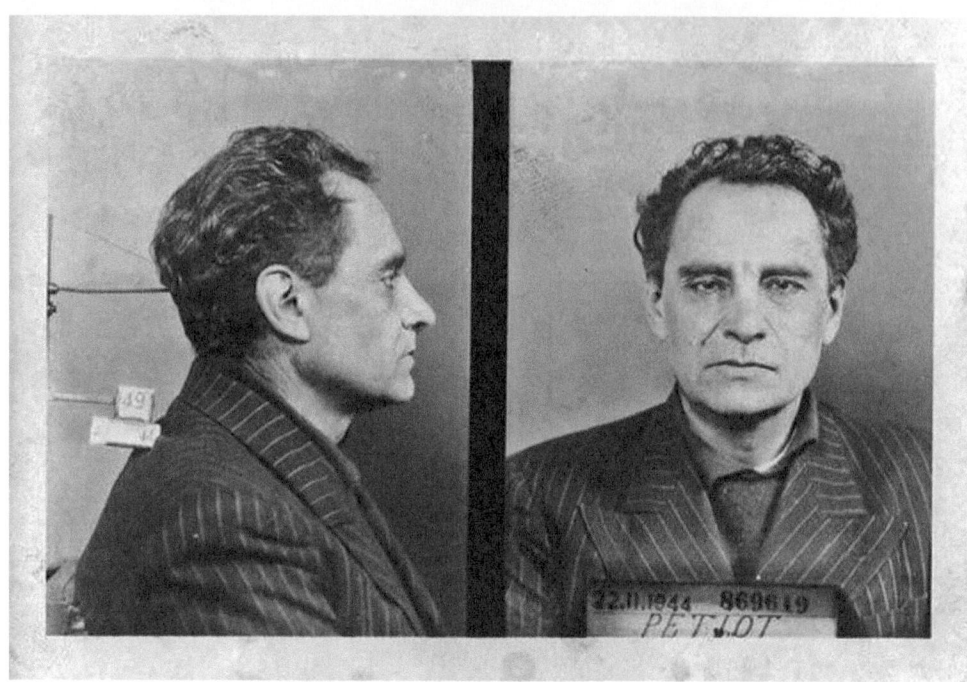

Marcel Petiot photographed on 22 November 1944. (Public domain)

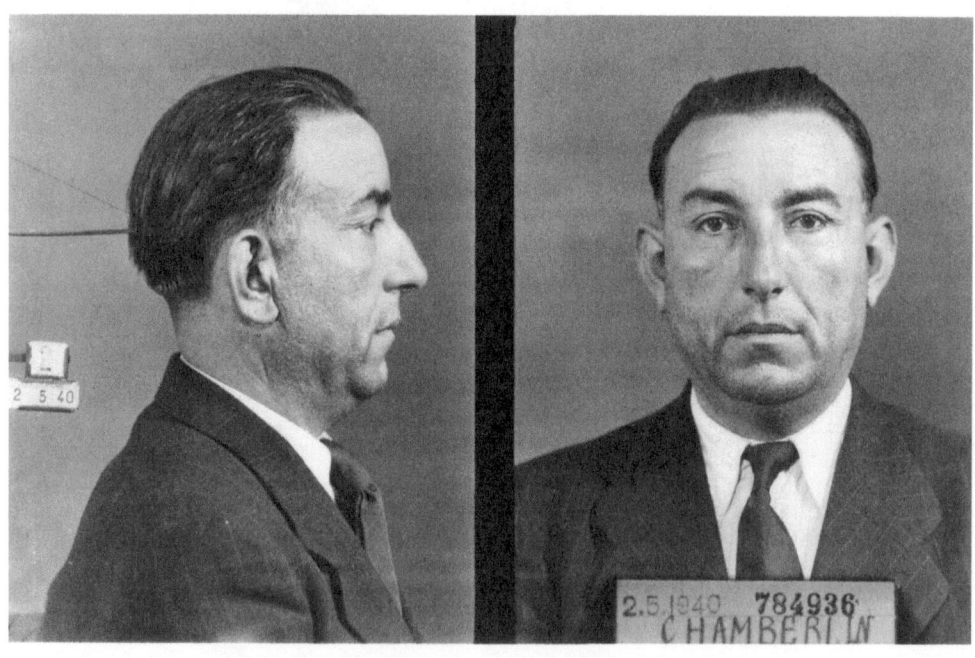

Legal identity photograph of Henri Chamberlin (Henri Lafont) taken on 2 May 1940. (Public domain)

A newspaper photograph showing, in the foreground, Henri Lafont (left) and Pierre Bonny (right) as their verdict is read out by the Court of Justice on 11 December 1944, sentencing them both to death. (History and Art Collection/Alamy Stock Photo)

Von Dincklage's photograph accompanying his application to enter Switzerland in December 1944. (Swiss Federal Archives, CH-BAR E4301#1992/36#1493*, Az 200766, VON DINCKLAGE, HANS, 1896.12.15, D, 1939–1951)

Von Dincklage in 1938. (Public domain)

Félix Amiot (second from left) photographed in 1969. (Photo by Nir Maor, public domain)

Walter Schellenberg as an SS *Oberführer* in 1943. (Photographed by Kurt Alber, Bundesarchiv)

Spring 1945: civilians queuing outside a patisserie on a street in Paris. (piemags/archive/military/Alamy Stock Photo)

The National Assembly in Paris decorated with the slogan 'Germany is winning on all fronts'. (Bundesarchiv)

Jewish women wearing the yellow star in Paris, June 1942. (Bundesarchiv)

French *Résistance* fighters engaging with the enemy during the battle for Paris, August 1944. (Public domain)

French collaborators, with swastikas painted on their faces, are marched through the streets of Paris on 27 August 1944. (US Signals Corps, public domain)

Portrait of Malcolm Muggeridge in 1935 by Amrita Sher-Gil. (Public domain)

A Paris street in 1945 showing two cars which have been converted to run on wood fuel. (piemags/archive/military/Alamy Stock Photo)

The legendary *Gang des Tractions Avant*'s preferred getaway vehicle, the front-drive Citroën 11CV Traction, on the road in France. (Public domain)

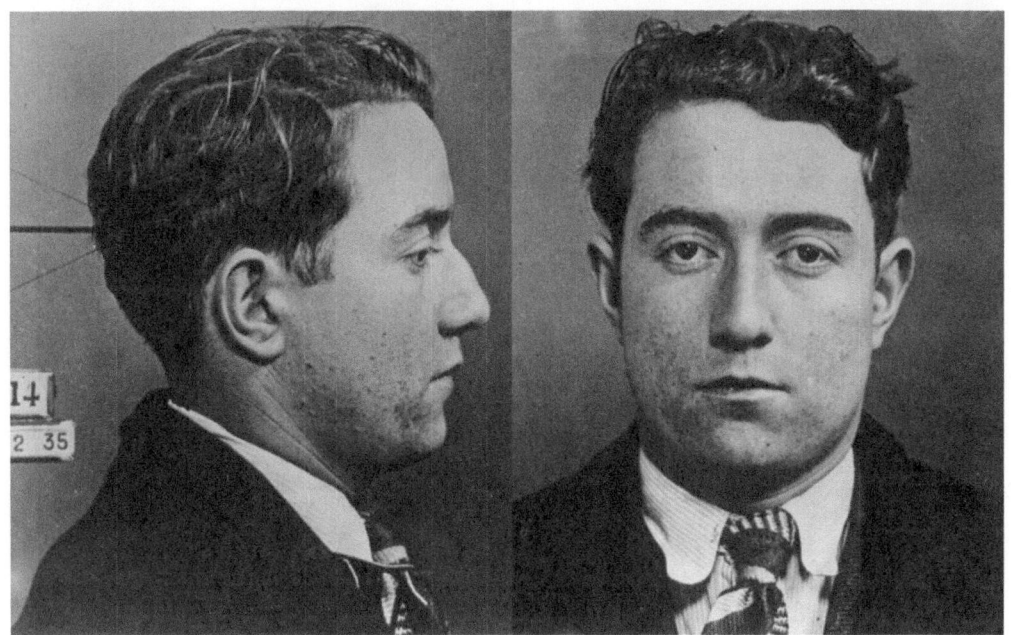

Pierre Loutrel, aka Pierrot *le fou*, aka Crazy Pete. (Public domain)

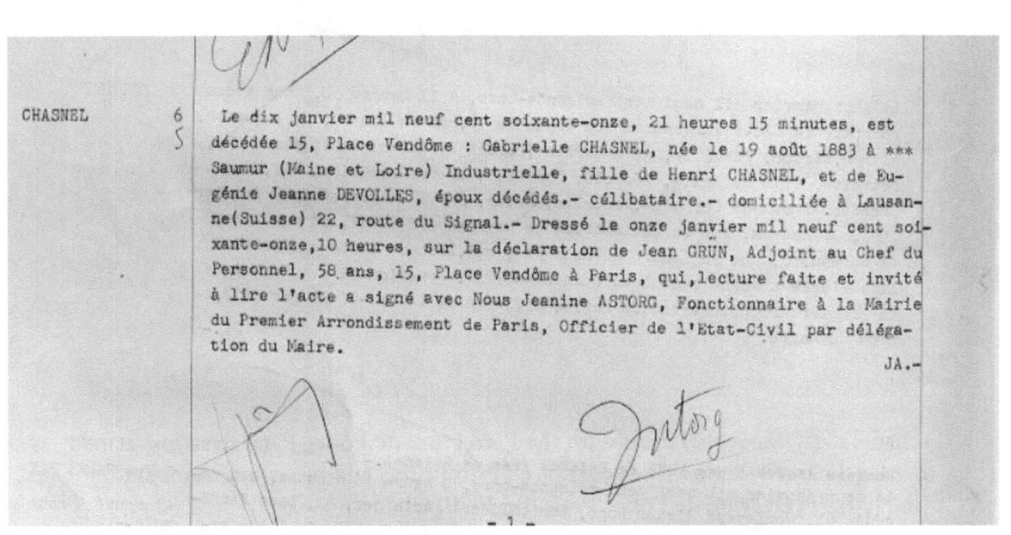

Chanel's death record with misspelt surname intact. (Public domain)

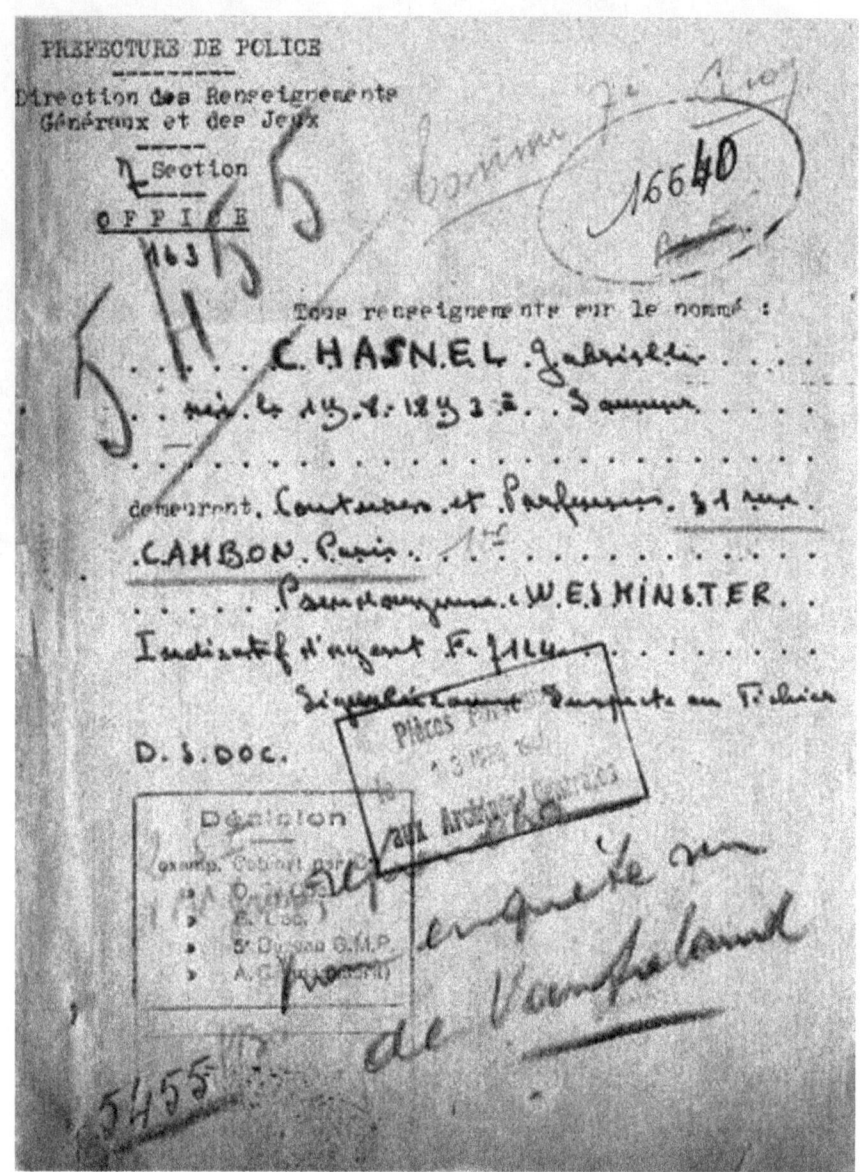

Chanel's *Abwehr* registration with the Préfecture de Police Paris showing her legal name (Chasnel), code name (Westminster) and her agent number (F-7124). (Préfecture de Police Paris, BA1990, Chanel)

10

DEAR WINSTON

Germaine burst into tears when she opened the door to the apartment at rue Cambon and found Chanel waiting outside, cool as a frozen daiquiri. The two hugged on the threshold and Chanel wafted in, shuddering theatrically from the experience she had just been through, kicking off her sandals and lighting a cigarette.

It was at this moment that she reputedly, allegedly, supposedly, reportedly said that her old friend, Prime Minister Winston Churchill, had intervened on her behalf with the FFI (through his ambassador, Duff Cooper) to have her released.

It is a myth that has persisted for over eighty years:

Her grand-niece, Gabrielle Palasse Labrunie, recalls that when Chanel returned home, she told her maid, Germaine: 'Churchill had me freed.'[1]

… Chanel had managed to have Winston Churchill save her.[2]

Chanel was released within a few hours, saved by the intervention of Winston Churchill operating through Duff Cooper, the British ambassador to de Gaulle's French provisional government.[3]

Speculation abounds about how Chanel managed to avoid being indicted and tried as a spy, but she most likely owed her gentle treatment to intervention from her British connections, especially Churchill.[4]

After the Libération of France, Coco was arrested by the French resistance forces for her wartime activities. But Churchill, a close friend of one of Chanel's former lovers, the Duke of Westminster, is said to have intervened on Coco's behalf; she was released after 24 hours. Immediately on her release, Coco Chanel left France for Switzerland.[5]

A few days later she was arrested, but Winston Churchill made a phone call, and she was soon released.[6]

As cited by most, if not all, Chanel biographers, the implication is that Churchill was personally informed of her detention at the Île de la Cité inside the three hours she was there. It was the genesis of four prevailing mysteries that occurred and converged within the next twenty-four hours of Chanel's life that have never been fully explained or proven but have been perpetuated nonetheless by every notable Chanel biographer.

Mystery one: what and who precipitated Chanel's unexpected and abrupt release from her ad hoc interrogation by the FFI in September 1944? The blanket response in all Chanel biographies is that Churchill, operating through the personal intervention of his friend and ambassador to France, Duff Cooper, obtained her release.

This was a time before the internet, emails, mobile phones, and text messaging. For Chanel's maid, Germaine, or her butler, Léon, to send an international long-distance message from a war-torn country to reach the personal office of a wartime leader in the middle of conducting an ongoing war, even by telephone, would have been an incredible feat (it is doubtful Chanel had one at rue Cambon or, in its absence, access to a radio transmitter).

Not only was it logistically incredible but also physically incredible as there weren't that many private telephones in France to begin with in 1944. Many people simply didn't have a phone at all, and when they did, service unreliability was as high in France as it was in more saturated, sophisticated telephonic areas like America and Britain. And, of course, most telephone lines in and out of Paris were disabled during the fighting to liberate Paris. Telephones in Parisian households were also a threat and a source of terror. In the early years of the occupation, the Gestapo had developed a means of using them as microphones, so many of them were unplugged by their owners and never connected again, or thrown away. If Chanel did have a working telephone, it was almost certainly bugged, a fact von Dincklage would have known. Whether he let his mistress in on the surveillance is unknown.

Putting aside the likelihood of the Chanel household having access to a reliable telephone (or the availability of a working public telephone *cabinet* at a local café, *bureau de poste*, or the nearby Hôtel Ritz) and then somehow directly reaching Churchill's office, there is the added unlikelihood of Churchill immediately putting aside more pressing things and reaching back out to his French counterpart, the imperious de Gaulle, to negotiate her release.

And not just anyone's release but a notorious French citizen and collaborator! He would, in effect, be responsible for an even greater diplomatic feat: successfully navigating through the length and breadth of French bureaucracy in a city still trying to sort out and administer basic living conditions for 2 million people and its liberating army. Plus, he or one of his officials in faraway Britain, even an official at the British Embassy in Paris using his imprimatur, would then have to do all this in the generally accepted three hours that Chanel was away being interrogated.

Maybe by some fluke or sensational alignment of luck and technology it did actually happen, but on the surface it appears it would have been a considerable stretch, like the 'magic bullet' cited by the Warren Commission's investigation into the Kennedy assassination.

An additional complication is that Churchill had left London on 5 September by train for a meeting with US President Franklin Roosevelt in Quebec, Canada. The journey, via the ocean liner *Queen Mary* and a Canadian National Railways train, took six days. Churchill was unwell throughout the trip, gloomy, bad-tempered, and moody. His staff found him flat and uncommunicative most of the time. Even General Sir Alan Brooke, Chief of the Imperial General Staff, Britain's highest-ranking army officer and Churchill's closest military adviser, wrote in his diary the prime minister 'looked old, unwell and depressed. Evidently found it hard to concentrate and kept holding his head between his hands.'[7]

He was consequently left alone with his 'Black Dog' (the name he gave his depressive condition), which is what he wanted. How Chanel's staff might have reached him, and whether or not he was in a fit state to respond to any urgent requests for help, is problematic (he eventually returned to London on 26 September).

Then again, this wasn't the first time Chanel claimed she had the Prime Minister of Great Britain's ear whatever the situation or prevailing diplomatic circumstances. Unfortunately for her, this exaggerated claim she and von Dincklage bandied about occupied Paris (possibly to deflect the enormous amount of Nazi money funding Chanel's burgeoning drug intake) brought her to the attention of SS General Walter Schellenberg, Reichsführer Heinrich Himmler's intelligence chief. It not only precipitated a catastrophic relationship with Schellenberg she went to great financial and political lengths to cover up after the war; it also put her in great personal danger.

Sometime in November 1943, Chanel and von Dincklage travelled to Berlin as guests of Schellenberg. Eschewing the daily '*Alte Tante Ju*' air service from Le Bourget airport to Berlin's Templehof airport, which used a Junkers 52 aeroplane, the couple instead plumped for the sedate sleeper train service that left Gare du Nord at 11.17 p.m. and arrived the next day at Berlin's Zoologischer Garten station at 9.34 p.m. Met by SS officers and orderlies who carried their bags, the couple were driven in a limousine through the blacked-out, bombed streets of Berlin to their SS guesthouse at Wannsee, a salubrious lake resort to the west of Berlin ... the same guesthouse where SS General Reinhard Heydrich held his infamous Wannsee Conference to workshop the extermination of Europe's Jews.

The next day the two met with Schellenberg, SS Brigadeführer Walter Schieber, and Major Theodor Momm at the Reich Security Main Office at Berkaer Strasse, once a nursing home for Jews until the SS seized it in 1941. No doubt the discussions were bugged. Schellenberg fancied himself as quite the secret agent, as his loving description of a former office at the Foreign Intelligence Ministry and its hidden accoutrements testifies:

Microphones were everywhere, hidden in the walls, under the desk, even in one of the lamps ... My desk was like a small fortress. Two automatic guns were built into it, which could spray the whole room with bullets. All I had to do in an emergency was to press a button and both guns would fire simultaneously ... Whenever I was on a mission abroad I was under standing orders to have an artificial tooth inserted which contained enough poison to kill me within thirty seconds if I were captured. To make doubly sure, I wore a signet ring in which, under a large blue stone, a gold capsule was hidden containing cyanide.[8]

Although no verbatim transcript of the meeting can be found, a summary was later given by Schellenberg to British MI6 interrogators after his capture in 1945. Parts of it were deliberately omitted from the file the British eventually shared with their OSS buddies for unknown reasons.[9,10]

As part of the financial deal Schellenberg struck with Chanel before he was released from Allied captivity in 1951, having served time for war crimes, he never mentioned her Berlin visits or the plan to contact Churchill in his autobiography *The Labyrinth*. But Chanel *did* tell Major Muggeridge about her Schellenberg/Churchill plan when she was interviewed by him at rue Cambon in August 1944. In fact, she was quite candid with the MI6 officer about how she 'targeted the man whose vulnerability I could turn to my advantage'.[11]

According to the OSS file, Schellenberg's reason for meeting Chanel was purely because she 'knew Churchill sufficiently to undertake political negotiations with him. [She was] an enemy of Russia and desirous of helping France and Germany, whose destinies she believed to be closely linked.'[12]

Chanel was correct about Schellenberg's vulnerability. He admitted he was ill and stressed out by his workload: 'I was finished after eight weeks in a lightless cell.'[13]

Which perhaps explains the green light he gave to the cockamamie plan the group came up with that snowy morning in November 1943:

> ... it was agreed: a certain Frau Lombardi ... should be released from an internment camp in Italy and sent to Madrid as an intermediary. Frau Lombardi was an old friend of Frau Chanel ... Lombardi's task would be to hand over a letter written by Chanel

to the British Embassy officials in Madrid for onward transmission to Churchill. Dincklage was to act as a link between Lombardi in Madrid, Chanel in Paris, and Schellenberg in Berlin.[14]

Frau Lombardi was Vera Bate née Arkwright, the well-connected Englishwoman now married to Colonel Alberto Lombardi who had introduced Chanel to the Duke of Westminster in 1923. Vera was suspected by the Italians of being a British informer and her 'Dear Winston' letters to her childhood friend Winston Churchill were routinely intercepted by the Italian secret police.[15] She had been interned at Rome's women's prison since 12 November 1943 but was removed to Bagno a Ripoli concentration camp near Florence on 22 November soon after the Schellenberg meeting broke up. From there she was escorted to Paris, where Chanel and von Dincklage were waiting, a detail at variance with Schellenberg's testimony that a week after she was freed, she was flown to Madrid.[16]

Travel documents for the trio were received on 17 December 1943 and they left by train for Hendaye on the Spanish border, where SS Captain Walter Kutschmann delivered a large cache of money to Chanel for the operation codenamed *Modellhut* (Model Hat).[17] But after they arrived in Madrid and checked into the Hôtel Ritz, their bizarre plan quickly unravelled and descended into farce.

Both Vera and Coco were working to entirely separate agendas, known only to themselves and certainly not to von Dincklage or Schellenberg. The latter were caught completely unawares when, according to Schellenberg's OSS file:

> On her arrival at that city (Madrid) ... instead of carrying out the part that had been assigned to her (Vera) denounced all and sundry as a German agent to the British authorities. The result of this, however, was not only was Chanel denounced as a German agent but also Spitzy (an *Abwehr* agent). In view of this obvious failure, contact was immediately dropped with Chanel and Lombardi ... Schellenberg does not know wether [sic] any communication was subsequently handed to Churchill through this woman (Vera).[18]

The letter to Churchill has not been discovered.

Vera went along with the Madrid plan as a means of escaping to Britain once she was safely in the embrace of the British authorities. Chanel also saw it as a means of escaping to Britain (presumably with Dincklage in tow?) as she disingenuously told an astonished Muggeridge:

MUGGERIDGE: ... What were you hoping to achieve?
CHANEL: My freedom.
M: I don't understand.
C: England still lay beyond my reach. I couldn't travel there without German authorisation.
M: Why England?
C: To settle in London and make it my home. My heart has always leaned towards England, and with the close friendship of Winston, the hero who brought hope to the world, I could not imagine a happier life for myself.
M: We have focused up to now on your Nazi connections. Nevertheless, if your strategy was to succeed, it would also have called for British contacts.
C: It did: Hoare.
M: Our man in Madrid?[19]

Chanel's capacity for deviousness and disinformation is clearly illustrated during the following ludicrous exchange:

C: He did his best, considering how impeded he was.
M: Did you divulge your true goal to him?
C: I acquainted him first with a plan which was a pretext, masking my true goal. This smoke-screen was a secret peace plan I was required to convey to Churchill. That was why I had approached Schellenberg in the first place. That plan, Winston would have used it to light his cigar with. Nevertheless it supplied me with the opportunity to travel to Madrid. Even the very cautious Hoare at first agreed that, under cover of the smoke-screen plan I should implement my own.
M: You say that he agreed at first. Am I to infer that he later changed his mind?

C: He mistrusted a professed friend of mine who was journeying with me, and whom I had saved from execution by the Italian Fascists. She was English, on friendly terms with Winston and Westminster. Hoare's suspicions proved to be justified: she betrayed me.[20]

Muggeridge put it to her that one of the reasons the plan was doomed from the start was that no one could fathom why Vera was rescued from an Italian prison and included in the operation in the first place. Chanel did not enlighten him, other than to say Vera was out of her mind and had turned to herself and Churchill for help.

M: How in the end did she betray you?
C: She falsely reported me to Hoare as being Schellenberg's mistress.
M: Was there any substance in that?
C: Mr. Muggeridge, disregarding the fact that I am old enough to be Schellenberg's mother, I would feel nauseated to be coupled with a man whose ideology has debased our hearts.[21]

Despite Chanel's protestations the rumours of her debasement persisted in certain circles throughout her life and beyond. Only the passage of time and fading memory conspired to retrieve her reputation in England.

M: Did your friend's treachery jeopardise your own plan to reach England?
C: It wrecked it. The Nazis helped Vera's rescue in return for her involvement in Schellenberg's peace plan. Clearly, I had no intention of implicating her, but that plan was my only means for getting her safely to Madrid.
M: How did Schellenberg react?
C: I assured him that the Vera shambles had left his initial design undamaged; that in no time, Churchill would be in better health and that a meeting would be convened in London thereupon. All the while, I feared that he would find my explanation implausible. He summoned me to Berlin.

M: Did you go?
C: I had no choice. At our interview, he told me unequivocally that he had lost confidence in me; that I was a mere amateur, playing in a world of professionals.
M: Close to the mark, wouldn't you say?
C: I'll let you be judge of that, Mr. Muggeridge.[22]

11

NOT YOUR FINEST HOUR?

What Chanel didn't divulge to Major Muggeridge was that the real reason Vera was involved in Modellhut was because it was Vera, and not Chanel, who had the closer relationship with Churchill, and a letter coming from her would stand more of a chance of reaching Britain's prime minster. Chanel also withheld the fact that before she and von Dincklage left for Paris, she asked Henry Hankey, a senior British diplomat attached to the British Embassy in Madrid, to forward a six-page letter[1] handwritten on Hôtel Ritz notepaper to Churchill. That letter asked for his assistance in transporting Vera, now trapped and detained in Madrid, back to Italy and her husband.

Between denouncing Chanel and being placed under house arrest in Madrid, Vera had somehow changed her mind about escaping to Britain.

The letter, and Hankey's covering note (describing Chanel as someone 'who claims to be a personal friend'[2] of the PM) duly arrived at 10 Downing Street, but Churchill wasn't there to see it. He was in Tunisia recovering from a severe bout of pneumonia and didn't return to Britain until 19 January 1944. By that time, Chanel and von Dincklage had returned to Paris in disgrace, leaving Vera to fend for herself.

Yes, it was not 'her finest hour',[3] Muggeridge teased.

But Vera Lombardi was determined to reunite with her husband. She followed up Chanel's letter with a scribbled one of her own in March 1944. This time the intermediary was the daughter of Chanel's old lover, the Duke of Westminster. And this time Churchill did get it and did take action, though it took a while. Reunited with her husband, she sent a thank you letter to Churchill dated 9 May.⁴ Vera Lombardi died in Rome six months after her reunion with Alberto.

Operation *Modellhut* was to haunt and incriminate Chanel for the rest of her life. Not only was it a threat to her reputation, and indeed her life, it wrecked her relationship with the British authorities, especially in relation to her claims of being close to Churchill and indeed his ambassador to France, Duff Cooper. Chanel tried it on again with Muggeridge during that steamy, stifling night at rue Cambon: 'The fate of the world hinged on one man – a friend of mine, Winston Churchill. He, and he alone stood up to Hitler.'⁵

Writing later of that interview in his memoirs, Muggeridge conceded there was some truth in her assertion:

> [I] asked her if she often saw Churchill in those days [before the war]. Oh, yes, she said, she knew dear Winston well, and used to play piquet with him, making a point, of course, of always losing, as otherwise he'd be in a bad temper (*mau vaise humeur*). She felt sure, she said, that he'd never come to Paris without seeing her. I didn't say so, but I felt equally sure that he would; in fact, had.⁶

Muggeridge's sensational hint that Churchill had secretly visited France in the immediate aftermath of *Libération* and, during the course of his visit, had seen Chanel, might just be another one of Saint Mugg's enigmatic throwaways designed to titillate his acolytes. But then again, it might not. We may never know the truth of it, but what we can say from the available facts is that Chanel's close Churchill relationship was an immense exaggeration, one of many exaggerations spilling out of a catalogue bulging with deceits that Mademoiselle garnished and repeated and promoted throughout her entire life in her unyielding quest to Win and not Die.

Another manifestation of the 'Churchill got me out of the FFI interrogation room through the intervention of his ambassador Duff-Cooper' scenario was that Chanel had documents with her from Churchill that somehow could be used to secure her release:

> In fact, Chanel had been questioned in Paris soon after the *Libération* in August 1944 by the *Forces françaises de l'intérieur* (FFI). There was

speculation that she had produced letters from Winston Churchill, assuring her of his support, in order to counter any potential accusations of collaboration.[7]

This suggestion raises questions that a trawl through the relevant archives have not answered thus far: what were these 'letters'? When did Chanel obtain them? What did they contain? Where are they now? And, of course, why would a French authority take any notice of this foreign intervention, especially a British intervention on behalf of a celebrity French citizen known to have been a collaborator, with a French police file filled with the testimonies of corroborating French witnesses?

It also doesn't matter that Churchill might have had compelling reputational and legal issues[8] to intercede on Chanel's behalf. The fact is that time, distance, and technology separated him *from* acting on her behalf. It consequently makes any intercession by Churchill suspiciously implausible. And then there is the small matter of proof, despite biographer Axel Madsen's assertion that he witnessed British Foreign Office files that were 'inadvertently declassified'[9] in 1972, which showed Chanel possessed secret information that might have embarrassed Churchill. It just doesn't stack up.

What of Duff Cooper and his alleged Churchillian instruction to 'protect Chanel'[10] as reported by her friend and biographer Paul Morand, an extraordinary directive that was confirmed by another of her besotted friends, Edmonde Charles-Roux? In practice, Cooper was only in a position to carry out Churchill's alleged request after 13 September 1944, the date he left London with his wife, Diana, to take up his post as Ambassador of France.[11] For the next two weeks he was consumed by embassy appointments and the minutia of setting himself up. (For the first few weeks they were living at the Hôtel Bristol, on the same floor as the alleged Nazi collaborator P.G. Wodehouse and his wife; Cooper had them evicted when he found out.) This included a tour of German torture chambers on 23 September conducted by Paris's new Prefect of Police, Charles Luizet.[12] The interaction with Luizet would have been the perfect occasion to bring up the Chanel issue except, by this time, she had already fled Paris and France for Switzerland.

So really, Cooper would only have been able to help Chanel after 13 September. The timing would have been extremely tight as the only indication we have of the date of Chanel's FFI interrogation is approximately two weeks after de Gaulle's victory march down the Champs-Élysées on 26 August.[13] That would put it around 10 September ... three days before the Coopers touched down in Paris in a comfortable Dakota escorted by a swarm of forty-eight Spitfires.[14]

Let's say, for arguments sake, Chanel *was* arrested by the FFI after 13 September. For the distraught Germaine and Léon, getting a message to Ambassador Cooper would have been easier than contacting Churchill. Perhaps they used Major Muggeridge as an intermediary, with Léon tracking him down at either Victor Rothschild's mansion on the Avenue Marigny or his own elegant office on Boulevard Suchet overlooking the Bois de Boulogne? Would Muggeridge have bothered doing anything, given his documented antipathy towards her? Probably just enough to ensure if things went belly-up, there'd be no recriminations heading his way during the course of any investigation. Cooper and Muggeridge knew one another by reputation before the war and professionally during it. Cooper had been impressed by Muggeridge's intelligence[15] though Muggeridge, typically, was more ambivalent about Cooper's street-smarts and intellectual capacity for being an ambassador:

> Duff Cooper had a useful propensity, which now afflicted him, of seeming to fall asleep, or perhaps actually falling asleep, when a conversation went on too long, or failed to hold his attention. One became aware that his eyes had closed, his chin fallen onto his chest, his breathing become audibly regular. Then, suddenly, he would come to.[16]

Not a very appealing attribute for an ambassador posted to a crucial post in wartime. If Muggeridge had tipped Cooper off about Chanel's arrest, could Cooper have interceded on behalf of a renowned French citizen? He was, after all, the new dozy ambassador finding his feet among new, ravenous French bureaucrats eager to show the world they were firmly in control of things. Not only is the timing off; the likelihood of Cooper ever succeeding in this area is also suspect.

Cooper's wartime diaries, such as we have, record no mention of Churchill's instruction or Cooper working to free Chanel. The caveat here, as noted by his son and editor, John, is that:

> There is a distinct possibility, on the other hand, that my father may have during the later years of the Second World War and after wielded the blue pencil himself. The handwritten volumes are untouched, but for the years 1944 and 1945 and the first five months of 1947 we possess only typescripts.[17]

So, to be fair, we will probably never know for sure. There is, however, another theory: Chanel was released by the FFI because she had documents on her person, or was able to point to the existence of documents, that proved she was really a member of the *Résistance*, playing a double role in addition to serving as an informant for the Nazis.

The basis for this claim rests on photographs of documents, previously unseen, that surfaced in mid-September 2023 at a London exhibition dedicated to Chanel presented by the V&A Museum. After passing through an assortment of over 200 outfits, which included a 1956 black lace strapless evening gown owned by 1950s supermodel Anne Gunning, a *marinière* blouse from Chanel's 1916 spring-summer collection, the actor Lauren Bacall's pink tweed two-piece suit, and a minimalist black silk trouser suit worn by Diana Vreeland, visitors to the 'Gabrielle Chanel: Fashion Manifesto' retrospective exhibition were presented with a potpourri of artefacts dealing with Mademoiselle's wartime past.

The first blockbuster document on show was a photograph of a certificate allegedly showing Chanel's membership in the *Résistance* between 1 January 1943 and 7 April 1944, which adroitly describes her as an '*Agent Occasionnel*'.[18] Another show-stopper highlighted her spectacular affiliation with the 'Eric' *Résistance* network and listed her code name as Coco.[19] The exhibition's curator, Oriole Cullen, interviewed by *The Guardian* newspaper, said at the time:

> We have verification from the French government, including a document from 1957, which confirms her active participation in

the resistance ... The new evidence doesn't exonerate her. It only makes the picture more complicated. All we can say is that she was involved with both sides.'[20]

Tragically, *The Guardian* article didn't divulge how the curators found the documents. This oversight was rectified by French historian Dr Guillaume Pollack, the author of a book on the history and administrative mechanics of *Résistance* networks in 2022.[21] After learning of the V&A documents, Dr Pollack spent weeks tracking their origin, finally finding the source file squirrelled away in the French military archives at Vincennes. But there was a problem, he later told France 24, the French state-owned international news television network: 'When I opened up the file, something struck me right away: It was basically empty. Aside from two official documents, there was nothing there. I've rarely come across such a dry file.'[22]

Normally such files are bulging with all kinds of information describing the *Résistance* activities of a person, activities which are then backed up by the inclusion of several third-party testimonies. The files, carefully assembled by the French government shortly after the Second World War, were required to adhere to specific legislation that outlined in detail the conditions under which a citizen could be officially classified as a bona fide member of the French *Résistance*: 'If one thing is clear, it is that in order to be called a *Résistant* (member of the *Résistance*), you need to have been active as such and recognised (by others) as such. In this case, there is none of that – not a single trace.'[23]

In Pollack's view (reiterated to the author), the V&A certificate with Chanel's name on it is not convincing proof of her membership of a movement that was frequently cited by collaborators and enemy agents to cover up their activities. The other V&A document, flagging Chanel's role in the epic Eric network, also puzzled Pollack.

Eric was a French *Résistance* network that mostly operated in the Balkans. In Pollack's opinion, although René Simonin (Eric's leader) returned to Paris in 1943 and the network operated from the French capital for an additional year, there is no reference whatsoever to Chanel in network documentation, aside from the V&A affiliation certificate located in the military archives and displayed at the exhibition. The other 'strange'[24] thing about it was that the word 'Eric' had clearly been written over a whited-out section of the document.

Dr Pollack also said, in the France 24 interview in November 2023, there are questions about the actual date Chanel's *Résistance* membership certificate was purportedly issued. Chanel was 74 years old in 1957, when the card was allegedly stamped – well after the *Résistance* had been disbanded. The question is, if Chanel really was a member of the *Résistance*, why did she keep it secret? The fact it was hidden for so many years doesn't make sense. Unless, of course, keeping it under wraps was designed to keep at bay the plethora of questions from former *Résistance* fighters who would have demanded she provide details on what she did, where, when, and with whom. In summary, Dr Pollack suggests Chanel may have manufactured the documents to rehabilitate her tarnished reputation after the war when several different *Résistance* veteran organisations emerged and started probing claims made by various celebrities. Needless to say, he has 'doubts, huge doubts'[25] about the documentation incorporated in the V&A's 'Gabrielle Chanel: Fashion Manifesto' retrospective exhibition. The anomalies are too apparent to ignore: 'The certificate proves nothing.'[26]

On balance, the whole 'Churchill rescued Chanel via his ambassador Duff-Cooper' scenario, and even the more recent 'Chanel released herself because she was actually a member of the *Résistance*' thread, appear to be clever smokescreens devised and circulated by Chanel and her friends to camouflage the real source of her release from the mercurial grip of the FFI that sultry morning in September 1944.

If that was the case, the question is then, who might have had the prestige, clout, fast access to the right people, enough traction with unhinged elements of the FFI to secure an agreement to let her go, and sufficient motive to effect Chanel's release during the three hours she was incarcerated at the Île de la Cité? It was certainly not Major Malcolm Muggeridge, who Chanel originally thought might be a decisive influence with the French authorities if anything went wrong. That was before their testy and mutually disdainful encounter over dinner with Muggeridge's embarrassed and nervous lover. She had miscalculated there.

But a *Résistance* commander would probably fit the bill. As her friend Edmonde Charles-Roux so adroitly put it, way back in her 1974 biography:

Only protection from very high places could restore to Gabrielle the freedom which others less guilty than she had lost. So she must have been saved by an order that could not be disobeyed. Whose order? No trace of it, nothing remains that will enable us to answer this question with the slightest degree of certainty.[27]

Whose order?

Perhaps someone with a proud history of undermining the German occupation and war effort on a daily basis, who fought in the streets for the *Libération* of Paris with General Philippe François Marie Leclerc de Hauteclocque, and who now had the tacit approval of de Gaulle's provisional government in bringing to justice collaborators hiding like vermin in the cracks and crevices of the damaged city. Someone who embodied the brooding Catholicism of the Parisian mind, an artist, a poet (and occasional ghostwriter of Chanel aphorisms that were sprinkled like fairy dust across fashion magazines throughout the 1950s). Maybe the man who captured the lonely soul of the people in his veins and was a mirror of their tremulous fears, desires, and weaknesses.

Perhaps a former lover who had a devastating love for Chanel, who knew about her transgressions and bad decisions and who had forgiven her, could never forget her, and could never leave her to the vicious caprices of marauding thugs roaming Paris like a pack of tormented wolves. A man who would die in 1960 at the age of 70 endeavouring to find 'the sublime simplicity of true reality'[28] with his estranged wife via the ancient Benedictine monastery Abbaye Saint-Pierre at Solesmes:

I live in retreat. I work the land, I grow vegetables, I raise Siberian rabbits that are as beautiful as Christmas toys. I harvest miraculous melons. I try, finally, to live in the healthiest way possible, the simplest way, and the most logical too, in accordance with the doctrine to which I have converted.[29]

It was here, that this man, Pierre Reverdy, great leader of the *Résistance* and lauded poet of France, wrote the very last poem of his life for his beloved Chanel.

If such a man was the source of Chanel's freedom in September 1944, why would she or he seek to hide their illustrious collaboration? Perhaps because they had struck a deal in the immediate aftermath of *Libération*. For his part, he would do whatever he could to keep her safe in the days to come when he knew, more than anyone else, what was likely to happen to an easy FFI target like her. For Chanel, there were some friends and ex-collaborators like Serge Lifar (the Ukrainian dancer and choreographer from the Ballets Russes and Paris Opéra Ballet who she had hidden in her rue Cambon apartment when the FFI came knocking)[30] that she would never give up.

But there were others, such as the expendable Baron Louis de Vaufreland, who worked the Nazi hierarchy with her in their ill-fated attempt to wrest control of Société des Parfums CHANEL from the Wertheimers' proxy, Félix Amiot, that she could and did. It was an easy sacrifice to make. Her acolyte Carmel Snow, legendary editor-in-chief of *Harper's Bazaar*, got it back to front when she wrote in a letter to her family: 'Apparently her German was the most beautiful of the Germans, spoke English perfectly, and was the tops of a Spy [sic], for years before the War started. Evidently Coco never denounced anyone, or I presume she would be in jail.'[31]

It was precisely because she denounced the well-known traitor de Vaufreland, or more accurately betrayed his whereabouts, that she escaped jail.

12

DON'T LOSE A MINUTE

At the time of Chanel's arrest in early September 1944, the threat to her life was real and imminent.

De Gaulle's provisional government was on the cusp of establishing special courts to deal with collaborators. Citizens guilty of major acts faced death by execution. Others, found guilty of the newly invented crime of *indignité nationale*, lost their right to vote, run for office, and practise certain professions. A noose was tightening around the throats of suspected traitors, like France's most famous couturière.

Mystery one: Who had the leverage to arrange Chanel's release from FFI interrogation?

Her former lover, now revered *Résistance* commander Pierre Reverdy, knew she was in danger, serious danger, and was the most likely person of authority who could have arranged her release from FFI interrogation. Remember, Reverdy was the one friend who told her at the start of the war that 'war was a time to hide, lie low and keep quiet'.[1] It makes sense then that Reverdy (reputedly a serious, taciturn, and sombre man) was the most likely person who Chanel instructed her maid, Germaine, to contact after the two FFI female agents knocked on her apartment door and she momentarily went inside to change. Such a move on Chanel's part is also plausible in terms of the relative ease of contacting Reverdy (as opposed to the impossibility of trying to get a hold of either Churchill, Muggeridge, or Cooper), his clout with the FFI, timing (he was active in the city), and motive (their ongoing affection despite her collaborationist notoriety), plus of course the deal they had struck.

In the days following *Libération*, the *Résistance*, FFI, and groups of communist fighters had banded together to form the FTP. Together with civilian police officers and Leclerc's army, they gradually wrested control of Paris away from the Germans. In the ensuing confusion and brittle peace, the detested traitor Baron Louis de Vaufreland had gone to ground. The *Résistance*, in particular, were desperate to detain de Vaufreland. Not only was he a Nazi agent (tagged as a '*V-Mann*' on German *Abwehr* documents which, in the nomenclature of the Gestapo and *Abwehr*, meant he was a trusted agent); he was also a Nazi recruiter and uninhibited thief who had conspired to send many *Résistance* fighters to their death.

Tipped off by Chanel (though not wholly for the reason Hal Vaughan states in *Sleeping with the Enemy*),[2] Reverdy's band of *Résistance* fighters found the baron hiding in the Paris flat of Count Jean-René de Gaigneron and hauled him off to the Île de la Cité and then to the former Jewish concentration camp at Drancy. The baron would reappear at a later date as a witness in a future judicial investigation into Chanel's wartime activities. For now, he was left wondering how Reverdy had tracked him down and why he was treated so violently. It was almost personal, he later recalled.

At the rue Cambon a few days later, with the FFI at her door, Chanel called in her part of the deal with Reverdy.

Reverdy was also probably involved in the second mystery that occurred during Chanel's last twenty-four hours in Paris before her Swiss exit. It is alleged that as soon as she returned to her rue Cambon apartment after being released by the FFI, 'Chanel's maid Germaine told Labrunie (Chanel's grand-niece) that soon after Chanel "left her rue Cambon apartment abruptly ... she had received an urgent message from (the Duke of) Westminster" through some unknown person telling her: "Don't lose a minute ... get out of France."'[3]

Mystery two: Who warned Chanel she had to leave France immediately when she returned to her apartment at rue Cambon?

Her grand-niece, Gabrielle Palasse-Labrunie, later confirmed to the biographer Hal Vaughan in a telephone interview on 12 February 2012 that the unknown person conveying Westminster's message was in fact ... Ambassador Duff Cooper (who hadn't yet arrived in France!).[4] The problem with assigning this crucial intervention to an eminent Englishman across the English Channel mirrors the impracticalities associated with the answers perennially given to explain the first mystery. In this case, however, the questions are, how was this warning conveyed – by telephone, messenger or other? And how did the messenger know Chanel had been interrogated? The telephone context has already been covered, so the most likely origin of the communication to rue Cambon involved a messenger. Given that assumption, there is no record of Bendor reaching out to Chanel either in his family's Eaton Hall archives or in the diaries of his contemporaries.

The most likely source confirming this initiative would have been Duff Cooper, and there is nothing in the official release of his diary entries for late 1944 that even hints at his acting as a go-between (noting of course his son's admission that these 1944 entries showed signs of later editing). And then, of course, how would Bendor have received such intelligence when he was not securely plugged into the intelligence services or any other covert organs of the British government? Add the timing factor and the Westminster/Cooper theory appears unconvincing, another case of misdirection by Chanel's adoring household, the well-meaning and naïve Palasse-Labrunie, and of course her manipulative, conniving grand-aunt.

Again, Pierre Reverdy and his band of *Résistance* fighters would have been the most well-placed, expedient, and well-informed source of this particular piece of advice to Chanel. That is, of course, if it ever truly happened. But then again, something like a well-placed nudge in the ribs must have occurred to have triggered her decision to flee the capital without a moment's hesitation:

Within hours, Chanel left Paris in her chauffeured Cadillac limousine headed for the safety of Lausanne, Switzerland.[5]

A few days later, she fled to Lausanne, Switzerland, where she would later be joined by Dincklage.[6]

Immediately on her release, Coco Chanel left France for Switzerland.[7]

In September 1944, Coco piled her luggage into her Mercedes and had her chauffeur drive her to Lausanne, Switzerland.[8]

If anything, the warning confirmed what she had intuitively realised after the FFI interrogation: her days in Paris were numbered.

Mystery three: Why did Chanel attribute her release to Winston Churchill and her warning to leave the capital immediately to the Duke of Westminster?

Probably to protect the reputation and honour of Reverdy. It was a noble thing to do, which some cynics might say is completely at odds with what we know about her. And yet, imagine if it was leaked or revealed to the citizens of Paris that one of the nation's most revered *Résistance* commanders had aided and abetted a detested collaborator such as the infamous Coco Chanel to escape a justice that most Parisians expected her to face. Such information probably would have led to a seismic backlash against Reverdy that even his friend Charles de Gaulle would have been hard-pressed to ignore. If anything, Chanel's deceit in naming Churchill and Westminster as her heroes, two foreigners who could neither confirm nor deny such an accolade because of its Anglo-French sensitivity, is a subtle and oblique corroboration of the Reverdy link to her FFI release and subsequent warning.

Mystery four: How did Chanel leave Paris in her own car?

The generally accepted means of her escape is perplexing. After the Germans occupied France in 1940, they methodically and indiscriminatingly took all the fancy cars and motorbikes away from their owners, either requisitioning them or carting them back to Germany. Many owners, such as the writer Georges Simenon, took to hiding their treasured automobiles in country barns, burying bikes in tarpaulin-lined ditches, or completely dismantling them and stowing them in basements.

When Chanel returned to Paris in 1940 after travelling to the Pyrénées and Vichy to secure the release of her nephew, André, either the Rolls-Royce or Cadillac she had left behind would almost certainly have been confiscated, and she would have been left without a personal car for the duration of the occupation. Despite losing her personal car, she would, as the companion of a highly placed German intelligence officer like von Dincklage, have travelled around Paris in von Dincklage's assigned Grosser Mercedes staff car. Travelling the Métro would have been unthinkable and unnecessary for Mademoiselle.

Aside from the unlikelihood that Chanel had access to a Mercedes or a Cadillac after *Libération*, the other and perhaps more devastating factor that limited her escape from Paris by automobile was the chronic lack of available civilian petrol (indigenous oil production was non-existent in France and all imports were halted at the onset of the war). Unlike the massed horse-fuelled assaults of the First World War, the Second World War was run on petrol. Without it planes, long-distance bombers, tanks, battleships, submarines, and supply trucks would have ground to a halt. These new machines required tonnes of oil. Erwin Rommel commiserated in his diary that 'neither guns nor ammunition are of much use in modern warfare unless there is sufficient petrol to haul them around … a shortage of petrol is enough to make one weep.'[9]

Another tank commander, American General George Patton, was of a similar view on the primacy of oil, telling his beleaguered commander General Dwight D. Eisenhower, '… my men can eat their belts, but my tanks have gotta have gas.'[10]

Romania's Ploiesti fields supplied the oil for Germany's war machine, as did the oilfields of the Caucasus at Maikop, Grozny, and Baku after the Soviet Union was invaded in June 1941. The nation's remaining oil reserves were produced in Germany, as synfuel. Germany had little oil but mountains of coal, relying on substantial deposits of bituminous and brown coals (lignite) for 90 per cent of its energy in the 1930s.

By the time the Germans were on the run in 1944, they were so starved for fuel that hundreds of tanks and cars literally sat abandoned unscathed in French fields and roads. Oil was more expensive than diamonds or gold. Even the other side were having problems. The Supreme Headquarters Allied Expeditionary Force's (SHAEF) Chief of Supply wrote to the US Under Secretary of State for War on 16 September 1944, forced to admit:

> The greatest difficulty to be overcome in the distribution of relief supplies at the present moment is lack of adequate road transport ... The lack of transport has the effect of increasing the requirements of imported supplies as collection and distribution of indigenous production is rendered difficult or impossible.[11]

The only fuel that could be had (due to continuing French domestic production) was coal and wood. Hence the majority of cars not requisitioned by the Nazis in France used modified wood-fired gas generators precariously mounted on trucks and automobiles to burn charcoal or wood pellets when gasoline became almost non-existent for non-military use.

The wood or charcoal when heated in an enclosed container like a tank gives off methane, which is piped to the engine. Though it could power the vehicle, the methane could only produce a maximum speed of about 30kmph and the power ratio was exceptionally low. The boilers themselves were often towed behind the car or bolted to the trunk/boot and looked ugly and cumbersome. They were also chronically unreliable. The engine performance was routinely abysmal, and it took a lot of charcoal or wooden scraps to even travel a short distance. A full 'tank' could possibly keep you moving for 50km. Another drawback was the risk of gas poisoning from the carbon monoxide content of these often-homemade generators leaking into the cab.

In my view, it is highly unlikely Chanel and her bags of cash and drugs made an immediate and unplanned getaway from Paris in a modified coal/wood-fired car that could barely do more than 30kmph, a vehicle that would have been an easy target for misadventure as it visibly wheezed through the meandering suburbs towards sanctuary on a whim and a prayer. It was also unlikely this was the Plan B her lover von Dincklage, with input from her well-connected and conniving lawyer, René de Chambrun, had arranged if things quickly worsened for her after *Libération* (which they did) and she felt threatened and intimidated (which she did) by French officials.

I suggest the most likely way Chanel escaped Paris in September 1944, given the prevailing shortages, breakdown in civil authority, and violent instability in the city, was by utilising the one outfit she had links to that was more powerful than either the Nazis or the French authorities or even the Allies in the French capital to help her — an organisation that had the know-how, network, and bravado to execute a quick getaway, and which had unfettered access to all kinds of identity papers, plus a reliably fast vehicle with unlimited litres of precious fuel: organised crime.

13

GANG DES TRACTIONS AVANT

Criminal gangs in Paris operated with the full knowledge and willing collusion of the German occupying authorities, developing symbiotic relationships with the various arms and agencies of Nazi Germany's military and intelligence institutions.

It would have been impossible for the Nazis to occupy Paris so wholly and completely without the aid and complicity of the gangs. Just to feed and billet troops required an enormous and consistent amount of daily coercion to repatriate goods and divert food production to German forces. The gangs proved willing accomplices, and they became, as the occupation progressed and things seemed to be working the way the Nazis envisaged them working, unsupervised and powerful, a law unto themselves with commensurate levels of influence and wealth.

Of all the criminal gangs operating at the time in France's *le milieu criminel* (criminal environment) or *le milieu interlope* (illegal environment), no gang was more formidable, organised, feared, resourceful, and reckless than the legendary *Gang des Tractions Avant* (GTA).

Not only were they feared, the GTA were so well connected, politically and judicially, they comprised the most infamous set of untouchable criminal figures operating in French metropolitan areas since the Terror of the 1790s. Unlike other criminal syndicates, however, they dispensed with secrecy, and their principal exponents were well known by the public for being involved in high levels of organised crime without apparent public censure. They were only hated by the Paris police, who were envious of their power and wealth and determined to wrest control of these monopolies from them without mercy.

And of course *Le Milieu* (the umbrella term for French criminal society) controlled the only two things, apart from transportation and money, that Chanel needed to survive in the aftermath of *Libération*: drugs and fake papers.

The three main drugs trafficked and used in France during the wars were (in order of consumption) cannabis, cocaine, and heroin. Heroin, mostly produced in Afghanistan, was transported via Belgium or the Netherlands, with the city of Lille being the major hub for trafficking. The safer route through the Alps region was left to the control of guerrilla Albanian gangs, who even the roaming paramilitary Nazi death squads, known as the *Einsatzgruppen*, avoided if they could.

The cocaine market was then and now the second-largest drug market in France. It evolved in the 1930s when Corsican gangsters Paul Carbone and François Spirito shipped morphine from the opium fields of Turkey and Lebanon to Marseille, hired French chemists to process it at pop-up labs in the suburbs, and then trafficked it throughout the world. During the war, most of it arrived through two primary entry routes. The first through the port of Le Havre, transiting from Ecuador or Brazil. The second route was via French Guiana, where it was transported by road from Suriname and then trafficked by Algerian, Armenian, and Corsican mafia-style groups operating from Marseille. Cannabis mainly came from Morocco, transiting through Spain.

Chanel, of course, was well aware of *Le Milieu*'s drug operations and could testify first-hand to their reach and prolificacy within both the Nazi administration and obsequious French haute society during the occupation. *Le Milieu*'s expertise in fake *Résistance* documents was a recent commercial offshoot that blossomed significantly in the months prior to and after *Libération* when collaborators such as Chanel sought to whitewash and legitimise their past activities from avenging authorities with valuable *Résistance* bona fides.

Chanel, von Dincklage, de Chambrun, and their social set had well-established links with *Le Milieu*. It was a social connection that reached its apogee with notorious Parisian underworld gangster

Henri Lafont (aka Henri Chamberlin) and the infamous cocaine and sex-fuelled parties he hosted at his sinister establishment at 93 rue Lauriston in the 16th arrondissement.

Lafont's gang was called various names: the Carlingue, the French Gestapo, and the Rue Lauriston Gang. The Germans called them *Active Grupp Hess* after their German contact at the rue Saussaies headquarters. Invitations from Lafont and his sick sidekick Pierre Bonny (the most celebrated police officer in France before he was jailed for corruption) were never ignored. Everyone turned up. Lafont was the exterminating angel of Paris with a capriciousness for cruelty that could turn on a centime. It was easier for the Nazis and the haughty French demi-monde to accept and subject themselves to compromising situations under duress than remain unsullied and exposed to all kinds of unnecessary and unforeseen dangers forced upon them by a whimsical gangster like Lafont. Besides, the champagne, food, and girls were the best in Paris. Former French football captain and close Lafont confederate Alex Villaplane (the first player of North African origin to represent France) always made sure of that: 'While ordinary Parisians starved, Lafont prospered, with sumptuous dinners and orgies, affairs with high-society women and the finest food, clothes and jewellery.'[1]

The late Le Point journalist Philippe Aziz,[2] and more recently the English writer Christopher Othen,[3] have written extensively on the Lafont and Bonny gang, detailing their lurid escapades and crimes.

Lafont, the illiterate street-rat orphan from the slums of Paris, liked to model himself on the genial Signor Ferrari from the 1942 Warner Bros. film *Casablanca* portrayed by Sydney Greenstreet. He was even known to parrot Ferrari's most famous line in the film: 'As leader of all illegal activities in Casablanca, I am an influential and respected man.' Unlike Ferrari, Lafont had a penchant for cultivating orchids, an incongruous hobby that defied his hard-man reputation. Or maybe it enriched it?

His rise to the top echelon of terror began in 1940 when the Nazis arrived in Paris under-prepared to subdue and occupy a nation of 41 million people. They needed help from the right kind of people, people like themselves. A big, triple-chinned, black brilliantined thug like Lafont, eager to make money and unfazed by how he did it, was what they were looking for.

A chance encounter in a French prison was all it took to set Lafont on the road to immense wealth and treachery: 'For four years, I had all the most beautiful women, orchids, champagne and caviar by the bucketful. I lived the equivalent of ten lives.'[4]

He was lucky and he knew it:

I had a bare arse and empty pockets ... Fucking hell, at thirty-eight years old I was in total shit and here comes Fritz to offer me money, honours, respectability, the good life. They shake my hand, feed me, treat me with respect, not like the French who want to send me off to Guiana (site of a French penal colony). I'd have to be the king of idiots to refuse and I'm not the king of idiots.[5]

He became *Abwehr* agent 10.474.R. With the authority and willing connivance of his recruiter, the overwhelmed *Abwehr* officer Hermann Brandl known as 'Otto', Lafont secured the release of thirty handpicked career criminals from Fresnes prison in Paris to create his gang of Nazi enforcers. They soon evolved from trading in black market goods and protection racketeering to mercilessly hunting down Jews and *Résistance* members. In 1942, ditching the blonde and affable Otto, Lafont (by this time partnered by Bonny) moved from the *Abwehr* to the Gestapo and became even more powerful and dangerous.

While Chanel and her cronies – like Jean Cocteau; Maurice Chevalier; Vichy official Paul Morand and his eclectic wife, Hélène; the Francophile German ambassador Otto Abetz and his stunning French wife, Suzanne; the former lawyer and journalist Ferdinand de Brinon, now Vichy ambassador to the Nazi government in Paris; and of course her lawyer, René de Chambrun, and his wife, Josée (daughter of Vichy leader Pierre Laval) – sipped black market Krug champagne, helped themselves to delicacies from Maxim's and wandered in their dinner suits and their finery from room to room while masked nudes performed sex acts on Lafont's guests, in the cellars below rue Lauriston, gang members dressed in SS uniforms were torturing Jews, *Résistance* fighters, black market competitors, and other mutual enemies of the Reich.

There were even auctions where *Résistance* officers suspected of possessing premium-grade Allied information were sold off to the highest bidders from competing branches of the SS, Gestapo, the *Abwehr*, and other elements of the German administration. After these entertainments, Lafont would speed off with a party of his guests in one of his white Bentleys, headlights blaring, German sentries saluting, to a restricted nightclub for more champagne, more cocaine, more of everything.

Mostly everything was anything to make a buck. The gang was only interested in making money and whatever it took to keep it. Aziz tells one of many such stories in his book *Tu trahiras sans vergogne*:

> Following a tip-off from a source in the Périgueux Gestapo, Alex (Villaplane) and three of his men burst into the home of Geneviève Léonard, accused of harbouring a Jew. They ransack the house ... Alex seizes the 59-year-old mother of six by the hair. 'Where is your Jew?' he shouts. The lady refuses to answer ... Alex picks her up brutally, pushes her into a neighbouring farm, hitting her with his rifle butt on the way, and there he forces her to watch an appalling scene: men from the BNA (Brigade Nord Africain, a squadron of fighters drawn from destitute immigrants created by Lafont in 1944 to cleanse the Périgord region for the SS) torture two peasants in front of her.[6]

After being beaten senseless, the two peasants were doused in petrol and set on fire, then machine-gunned from close range. By this time, Villaplane was an honorary SS sub-lieutenant.

After the Allies landed on French soil in June 1944, the Lafont gang mined new avenues of cruelty and bestiality. Capturing eleven *Résistance* fighters at Mussidan, a small village in the Dordogne on 11 June 1944, they shunted them into a freshly dug ditch and machine-gunned them to death. The prosecutor at Lafont, Bonny, and Villaplane's trial after Paris had been liberated detailed their catalogue of infamy with disgust:

> They pillaged, raped, robbed, killed and teamed up with the Germans for even worse outrages, the most awful executions. They

left fire and ruin in their wake. A witness told us how he saw with his own eyes these mercenaries take jewels from the still-twitching and bloodstained bodies of their victims. Villaplane was in the midst of all this, calm and smiling. Cheerful, almost invigorated.[7]

As the Allies got closer to Paris, the gang realised the Nazis were doomed, and they focused their energies on inventing measures to save their necks from the guillotine when France was liberated and de Gaulle's officers took over. One new business opportunity that emerged in the final days of the occupation, which was not only lucrative but could also be used as a convenient and plausible excuse for clemency, was the facilitation of celebrity getaways to relatively safe countries like Spain or Switzerland.[8] For a hefty price, in cash or kind, criminal crews like the *Gang des Tractions Avant* (named after its preferred getaway vehicle, the superb front-drive, low profile, six-cylinder Citroën Traction Avant 7 saloon) would more or less guarantee safe passage through Allied and German lines in a vehicle driven and guarded by experienced thugs unafraid of anyone or anything, all this with the added bonus of 'genuine' identity papers. For some prominent Parisians with dirty reputations and a cache of dirty money at their disposal, this criminal service was a last resort and as much of a sure thing as they could buy when all other avenues of escape or civil rehabilitation appeared doomed.

Another calculated gang ruse was orchestrating public displays of mercy, allowing many of the people they were supposed to be hunting to escape, thereby cultivating the pretence of working with the Nazis while helping to save *Résistance* compatriots. In the opinion of the same prosecutor, Lafont's gang, and Villaplane in particular, excelled themselves in this new enterprise:

> [A witness described Villaplane] arriving in a village in a German car and wailing the following: 'Oh, in what times we live! Oh, ours is a terrible era! To what harsh extremes I am reduced, me, a Frenchman compelled to wear a German uniform! ... Have you seen, my brave people, what terrible atrocities these savages have committed? I cannot be held responsible for them, I am not their master. They are going to kill you. But I will try to save you at the

risk of my own life. I've already saved many people. Fifty-four, to be precise. You will be the 55th. If you give me 400,000 francs."[9]

However, by September 1944 when the time came to execute her escape plan, Lafont's gang was of no use to Chanel. Lafont, Bonny, Villaplane, and other gang members had been rounded up and imprisoned, awaiting trial (they were later executed by firing squad on 26 December). The plan, probably worked out by von Dincklage and René de Chambrun and paid for by Chanel well in advance, seemed to be in tatters. Once again she found herself abandoned. Luckily for Chanel, another Le Milieu group operating in the Pigalle quarter of Paris comprising members of the Carlingue, corrupt police officers, and rogue criminals expelled from the *Résistance* was still intact and thriving. The GTA would have represented, in a rapidly diminishing array of choices, her only viable alternative in the circumstances and it would explain how, like other prominent collaborators in the same desperate situation,[10] she was able to escape Paris after she was released by *Les Fifis* and warned to leave the country immediately.

Chanel's best contact would have been a figure well known to her from the Lafont parties: Pierre Loutrel, widely known by his nickname of Pierrot le Fou (Crazy Pete), who was France's first public enemy number one and a leader of the GTA.

It would have been a dangerous relationship for Chanel to reactivate but she was out of options. Loutrel wasn't called Crazy Pete for nothing. Mercurial, cruel, violent, he was a member of Lafont's Carlingue from 1941 to 1944, with a reputation as a cold-blooded murderer in the same vein as Villaplane. He was also a trusted Gestapo executioner. Like the rest of Lafont's gang, he tried to gain the confidence of the *Résistance*. In his case, by mowing down an inconsequential German officer drinking beer on the terrace of a quiet café in Toulouse with a machine gun. Not buying his sudden transformation from French criminal to French war hero, the French authorities came after him with a vengeance. Seared by the experience, he retreated back into Le Milieu and quickly formed his own outfit, the GTA.

Other likely candidates Chanel might have tapped for transportation out of Paris include the tall, bespectacled 24-year-old René *la Canne*, or René Girier, also nicknamed *The King of Évasion* on account of his many impossible escapes. He got the name René *la Canne* (René the Lame) from a bullet he received in the leg on a heist that went wrong, which gave him a limp for the rest of his life. René's speciality was armed attacks and having a way with elderly rich women, who he often beguiled with his good looks and rough charm. If he did chaperone Chanel into exile, it was probably because he was chosen for this reason. Despite her legendary sangfroid, Chanel could be jumpy under stress, and this was easily the most stressful moment of her life. Add a dose of desperation and she probably had to self-medicate herself to get through the ordeal of hurtling through the night in a fast car driven by wanted killers.

Like most gang members, René lived life on a knife's edge. Throughout the 1940s and 1950s when he was active, he escaped seventeen times in eight years from prisons and was released in 1956 thanks to one of his glamorous visitors, Princess Charlotte of Monaco.[11] She housed him after his release near her château in Marchais. He then became her driver (René never had a licence) and drove her to the wedding of her son, Prince Rainier III of Monaco, to Grace Kelly. Although René *la Canne* published his autobiography several times under different titles,[12] he never mentioned driving Chanel to Switzerland in 1944. Maybe he wasn't aware who his 'mark' (client/victim) was that night? No names. No questions.

Another candidate (though less likely) was Émile Buisson, Loutrel's accomplice and successor as public enemy number one after Loutrel died by accident from a freak gunshot wound on a botched armed heist in 1946. Buisson was a killer with over thirty murders to his name and hundreds of grievous robberies. He cut his *Milieu* teeth working for Lafont before joining up with the GTA. Jailed at 16 for malicious pickpocketing, menacing the elderly for money, and possessing an arsenal of offensive weapons, he was exiled to Shanghai with his brother for five years. Returning to France, he picked up where he left off and became even more of a menace. Even *Le Milieu* were wary of rubbing the mercurial Buisson up the wrong way. He was universally regarded by police and colleagues alike as criminally insane and was eventually guillotined in 1956.

It is highly likely (though we have no hard evidence except for some clues in previously cited private correspondence between organised crime figures at the time) that with ash in her mouth and whatever remaining cash, clothes, jewellery, and drugs she could stuff into a couple of battered Goyard valises, Coco Chanel slid into the back seat of a criminal gang's fast getaway car to escape the imminent threat of public vilification and death. She had to disappear. Germaine, her maid, and Léon, her butler, could follow later with her other things after securing the rue Cambon apartment. Was she scared? No doubt. But let's imagine this was her only way out and she took it because how else *could* she have escaped so quickly?

Such a journey, whether facilitated by the services of a bunch of crooks or less plausibly by her own means, was still either going to lead to her survival, extortion for more money, kidnapping, bodily harm, release at her destination, or possibly all of them. Using organised crime meant that at least she had three of the four requirements necessary for her evacuation from Paris: access to a fast, reliable vehicle (the French affectionately referred to the Citroën Traction Avant as the *Reine de la Route*, 'Queen of the Road') with unlimited litres of priceless fuel, an escort armed with a proven mix of bravado and arrogance to pull it off, and tailored German/*Résistance* identity papers that could be used in any eventuality. The only thing that remained to be verified was the network, the safe route the getaway car would use to arrive at Chanel's final destination: Lausanne, Switzerland.

Why not England?

There were a few reasons: after the *Modellhut* fiasco in Madrid, the less-than-enthusiastic attitude exhibited by MI6's Major Muggeridge during their meeting at her rue Cambon apartment when she first floated the idea, and the silly name-dropping and spurious claims about high-level British support Chanel bandied around Paris after *Libération*, she rightly felt time and distance were the best course of action to heal the fractured relationship with Britain's establishment. Besides, it had to be Lausanne because, after her mid-1920s No. 5 deal with the Wertheimers, that's where she secretly banked all her money. Buckets and buckets and buckets of money safely secured in the vaults of her inviolate Swiss bank, the Union de Banques Suisse. And, of course, the Swiss were very, very discreet. As James Bond author Ian Fleming wrote: 'In Switzerland you can cover up all your sins.'[13]

For the route south to Lausanne, her transporters would have likely used one of the old, tried-and-tested *Résistance* escape lines that helped stranded Allied soldiers and airmen evade capture by the Nazis. The 'Pat Line' as it was called (also known as the 'O'Leary Line' and the 'PAO Line') provided desperate men and women with food, clothing, bogus identification papers, and escorts to Marseille. From there, these people were guided to neutral Spain and then home via British-controlled Gibraltar. Albeit with a significant variation at Dijon, this was the likely line south Chanel took towards exile in Switzerland.

The 550km route would have taken about seven or eight hours without any breaks and barring any setbacks or breakdowns. Ten hours would be closer to the mark. Depending on the lateness of her departure, Chanel may have used a safe house in the suburbs before heading off in the early hours of the following morning to avoid suspicious *Résistance* eyes that were on high alert for anything that may have been, well, considered suspicious.

Let's not forget there was still a war on, with vicious battles, demented Nazi rear-guard actions, and deadly assaults continuing to play out for another eight months or so.

If no safe house was involved, the getaway car would have followed the river Seine east along the right bank, past the fossilised Notre-Dame cathedral across on the right and the Gare de Lyon on the left, then swung left at Bercy, shadowing the river Marne from Charenton-le-Pont before leaving it forever after skirting the Parc du Tremblay. Plunging due south beyond the town of Lognes, the car would have headed eastwards towards the ornate Château de Vaux-le-Vicomte. There was no stopping there or at the medieval city of Troyes. At some stage, after circumventing Dijon, they must have changed their Parisian license plates to plates prefixed with the letters 'WH' (*Wehrmacht Heer*/Army Command) denoting a German staff car, and scrubbed out the 'FFI' sign that would have been attached to the doors as a precaution in Paris.

Troyes had been liberated from the Germans on 26 August, Dijon on 11 September, which meant the no man's land beyond Dijon was still viciously contested by British SAS operatives armed with Vickers K machine guns mounted on jeeps seeking to disrupt German lines of communication. There was also the danger posed by ad hoc, uncoordinated *Résistance* forces and the dreaded 2nd SS Panzer Division Das Reich, which had left its base at Toulouse to reinforce Paris and the Normandy beachheads.

The Burgundian countryside was consequently an extremely risky area to be travelling through. Adding to the above mayhem, between Dijon and the closest official Swiss border crossing at Vallorbe, the French terrain was occupied by rogue military groups, liberated prisoners and roving criminals from French internment camps, remnants of the Vichy state, fanatical SS forces determined to defend their demented Ordensstaat Burgund (a proposed SS-controlled Burgundian state that would act as a buffer against France), and starving refugees who sought to ambush unprotected supply trucks, fleeing families, anything that was moving, disabled, or easy prey for attack.

Unlike Chanel, most of the people heading south were on foot, travelling for weeks dressed in rags, surviving for days without food, and then scrambling for food that had fallen off carts along the road.

It must have been a harrowing experience for anyone working their way through this violent maelstrom of desperation to Swiss safety. Not least because along with the deserving, there were also deserting soldiers and numerous political and industrial refugees with despicable backgrounds like the 'Italian Goebbels' Dino Alfieri, Gestapo chief Rudolf Diels, SS officers like Franz Sommer, and pockets of ex-Vichy regime ministers, intellectuals, scientists, and collaborators mixed in with the innocent, such as Fernand, Marquis de Brinon, described as one of the architects of French collaboration with the Nazis during the 1930s. As a high Vichy official, de Brinon and other remnants of the Vichy leadership (such as Pétain and ex-prime minister Pierre Laval) were evacuated by the Nazis to Sigmaringen Castle in southwestern Germany, an enclave created to thwart their capture by advancing Allied forces. Here, de Brinon was selected as president of the rump government in exile. It proved to be only a temporary respite as he was eventually arrested by the Allies and held with his Jewish wife in Fresnes prison. After the war he was tried for war crimes, found guilty, sentenced to death, and executed by firing squad at age 61, on 15 April 1947 at the Montrouge military fort in Paris.

Chanel was never in the same category as these unrepentant atrocities but nor was she completely innocent of opportunist Nazi collaboration. Even so, her escape from imminent harm, possibly death, was a personal triumph. Navigating through the horrors and melee of a disintegrating Nazi-dominated Europe required special skills, diamond nerves, trust, and determination. How could anything after this upset or deter her from achieving whatever she wanted? Practically nothing.

Reaching her pre-paid destination, an exhausted but no doubt exhilarated Chanel was deposited unscathed at the chic Hôtel Beau-Rivage on the northern shores of Lac Leman. She probably got out of her dusty, growling getaway car completely unfazed, as if the entire journey was the most normal thing in the world to do. Escorted to Junior Suite 460 with her precious valises by an astonished manager, the most famous fashion couturière in the world could finally flop on a well-made bed, inhale the cool scent of freshly laundered Swiss linen, and fall asleep.

14

WHO HAS SEEN COCO?

By the end of the Second World War, 580,000 French men and women had died.¹ Overall military deaths totalled about 150,000. Estimated civilian casualties amounted to 150,000, comprising 60,000 deaths from aerial bombing, 60,000 from the *Résistance*-related activities, and 30,000 executions by occupying Nazi troops. The overall number of POWs and deportees was around 1.9 million. Approximately 240,000 perished in captivity, while 40,000 were victims of forced labour atrocities in Nazi death camps.²

The toll on the national psyche was also immense. But the horrors of the past and the almost pathological desire to bury certain distasteful memories and facts deep underground quickly turned to practical frustrations with the present, especially with unwanted visitors who had seemingly overstayed their welcome and were taking their own sweet time in leaving: the Americans.

Hilary Footitt's study *War and Libération in France: Living with the Liberators*³ explores the complications arising from the relationship between the liberated and the liberators. The French were conflicted by gratitude for their liberation and resentment as the Allies, especially the Americans, seized control of their country. The relationship consequently deteriorated to such an extent that it became mired in tension and mistrust: the French struggled to reassert their national identity and rebuild their national dignity, while the Americans tried their best to ignore the defeated nation that had capitulated to Nazism, maintaining the right to continue their own operations without interference.

When the Americans first arrived, they were greeted with enthusiasm and a sense of profound relief bordering on adulation, but the sheer size of their forces and the relentless needs of their vast war machine soon stretched the population's goodwill to breaking point. Friction between American troops and the local population became common. By mid-1945, the hostility felt by both sides was palpable.

Initially, the French found themselves in the embarrassing position of hosting people whom they were compelled to accept into their homes out of sheer need rather than pleasure. However, the dynamics did not conform to the typical host–guest relationship in which the guest relies on the host and the host exerts a kind of paternal dominance over such a relationship. Despite requiring American assistance and financial aid, the French were bitterly offended by their continuing dependence on such hand-outs. They were naturally eager to quickly reconstruct and rejuvenate their lives by reclaiming the territory they had lost to the Germans, territory which many French believed was now occupied by another occupying force, the Americans. They were also exasperated by the Americans' total lack of interest in the cultural and social revitalisation of France, concluding the occupiers were focused solely on what reconstruction efforts were useful in supporting their remaining war endeavours.

As a result, the French adopted a position of prickly disillusionment as the Americans slid into a bunker of baffled frustration and impatience with simmering French ingratitude. They each dismissed the other as arrogant and haughty foreigners who did not appreciate what the other had to offer or their unique qualities.

Added to this national, angst-soaked psychological sandpit was the growing feeling the German occupation was no worse than the current occupation. Despite overwhelming evidence to the contrary, the haunted, bitter faces of the French as the terrifying winter of 1944–45 approached betrayed the extent of their simmering feelings. The more things changed, the more they didn't:

The inconveniences and discomforts of daily life seemed endless. Telephones were not the only service out of order. Candles were constantly needed, since the electricity failed at least twice a night.

For many, the winter cold was a more terrible memory than the shortages of food. Susan Mary Patten, staying with friends at a château on the Loire, was asked by their little daughter if it was true that in America people could sit in a drawing room without an overcoat on. In the Louvre, a British officer, seeing a crowd packed close to a picture, marvelled at the French appetite for culture. But when he came closer he saw that they were all trying to stand close to a grille dispensing hot air … In cafes, there was only fake coffee or gaze, a sickly carbonated drink …[4]

Things were getting worse, not better. Two days after Christmas 1945, the French franc was devalued, some say gutted. France was now eighty-four times poorer than in 1914.[5] Everybody was looking ill and old. It was a new kind of torture: there was no bottom to the abyss; it just kept on going. Only the young, feverishly embracing the new freedoms and ignoring the new poverties, were annoyingly optimistic.

Some of the more resilient survivors realised something had to be done to dispel the gloom and despair pervading everything everywhere, to remind people what France had and will always have, no matter what … or else the death spiral was likely to suck down those very things that could not be lost or destroyed under any circumstances.

The French fashion industry had been one of the first cultural pillars of French society to react to this sense of national rescue, though the scarcity of suitable fabric impeded the relaunch of full pre-war fashion shows. To vault this hurdle, it was decided that representative haute couture collections would be presented on static miniature mannequins, or dolls, in a show called *Théâtre de la Mode*.

Two hundred and twenty-eight dolls measuring 70cm in height were worked upon by couturières, jewellers, milliners, hairdressers, and theatre designers to be presented at the Museum of Decorative Arts (adjacent to the Louvre) on 28 March 1945. Over 100,000 people visited the show in the first weeks. After the exhibition ended, the dolls were exhibited elsewhere in Europe (Barcelona, London, Copenhagen, Stockholm, and Vienna), moving in 1946 to New York and San Francisco. Returning to Paris, they were packed up and forgotten in a basement until 1952 when they were acquired by the small

Maryhill Museum of Art in Goldendale, Washington, which restored them and their sets.

British Pathé filmed the show featuring embroidered evening gowns, meticulously tailored suits, beachwear, shoes, gloves, handbags, hats, even silk underwear created by Balenciaga, Lucien Lelong, Schiaparelli, Nina Ricci, Pierre Balmain, and Christian Dior (who had not launched his Dior label yet). Cartier and Van Cleef & Arpels provided jewellery. *The New York Times* called it the 'back-in-business show'.[6]

Back in business, yes, but it was not a complete resurrection from the decimation that some industry figures were fond of publicising, despite the unpalatable facts:

> Fashion historian Dominique Veillon estimated that couturières saw their turnover in 1943 increase to 463 million francs from 67 million in 1941. Jacques Fath, who started trading as a couturier only in 1939, was able to increase the number of his skilled staff from 176 in 1942 (many of them drawn from other houses that had been forced to close) to 193 in 1943 and 244 in 1944.[7]

To survive, it made sense for Paris's working designers to maintain business connections with the German purchasing offices. Visibly supporting the *Cercle Européen*, a rabid ideological clan who promoted Nazi ideas, was also crucial and 'significant career insurance'.[8] Marcel Rochas and Maggy Rouff became the most visible collaborators in this respect after they presented a private show for *Cercle* dignitaries in November 1940.

But they weren't the only ones. Fashion magazines could publish photographs of what Parisian women were wearing until February 1943. At that point, the Germans, sensing they were unwittingly popularising clothes their own women in Germany could not own, banned their distribution. Haute couture after this could only be bought with a special ration card given to 200 German women and 19,015 French women.[9] After that, couturières like Jeanne Lanvin and Maggy Rouff branched out into designing theatre and cinema costumes. In 1943, another correction was implemented, and only actresses – or the 'actress' girlfriends of German officers – were allowed to buy long gowns.

The *Théâtre de la Mode* did its job, paving the way for French domination of the couture industry for the next twenty years.

But, of course, the name on everyone's lips, the *monstre sacré* in the room, was not there. Where was Coco?:

I have lost my poor Coco,
Coco my dog who I adore,
Close to Trocadéro,
He is far if he still runs.
I must confess, my greatest regret,
In my lost cruelly known,
Is it over my man cheating on me,
Coco was more faithful to me.[10]

Coco was away having a good time, doing what she enjoyed most: making money, living well, taking drugs, and indulging her voracious passion for revenge. Her induced exile in Switzerland demonstrated the core traits she carried through life: cunning and resilience, determination, and control of her narrative. Despite the multitude of friends and lovers, she was essentially a loner, a comet that set her own trajectory: 'Chanel cannot get along with the pack; she can adjust herself only to the particular.'[11]

She had money when she first arrived in Lausanne and spent it staying at the Hôtel Beau-Rivage for an extended period. But she soon tired of its clientele, the desiccated dowagers in black lace and the gnarled old men hobbling on walking sticks, everyone playing cards silently like old film stars after dinner on the terrace. It was all so dreary and dull.

The hotel's inhabitants were prisoners sleepwalking in warped time, a time of stupendous comfort and entitlement savagely expunged by the ravages of war.

Like emaciated zombies, these well-heeled aristocratic émigrés emerged from their Beau-Rivage suites, the men corseted in ancient winter tweed suits (raw silk in summer) with white spats and gloves, a beige bowler or a Panama hat, a carnation or rose in their buttonholes, walking stick in hand, sporting the impressive, well-trimmed moustache of an outdated English calvary officer.

The women appeared uniformly in something loose and flowery, vaguely Parisienne, superbly tailored though a little dowdy. Trotting behind them were their dogs, dogs of all breeds, temperaments, and degrees of training, but all inclined to instinctively lift their legs on the immaculate flower beds of the hotel's gardens whenever they had the chance of fresh air.

Most of them, their stomachs and palates irrevocably ruined by decades of high living, mountains of cigars, and reservoirs of brandy accompanied by a kaleidoscope of syrups and elixirs, would take luncheon at the same hour every day on the terrace, where they were invariably served the same dish (consommé de la soupe in winter, poached seafood in the summer), the same watered-down Rauzan-Ségla *deuxieme cru Bordeaux* served from a crystal decanter, and the same *eau de vie* with their coffee. This ritual avoided unnecessary staff interactions while they, undisturbed and gently sloshed, intermittently drifted off into reveries of past times when they only had to lift a finger for an old family servant to attend them in loving anticipation of their unconscious needs.

Chanel picked up the habit. In Switzerland lunch, wherever she lived, never varied from *soupe aux légumes, filet mignon, riz sans beurre,* and *compote de fruits.*

At 5 p.m. the émigrés returned to take tea and cake at the same table, maybe even a peeled cognac-soaked pear, this time dressed in a change of clothes, something grey and supple perhaps. Something English and comfortable. In the evenings, they sat alone or played cards in shrunken, shiny dinner jackets or perhaps a revived, distant CHANEL relic that still wore well and which they had managed to save from the debacle of the past five years and the demands of a merciless, ravenous austerity. Or else, like the titled Poles sprinkled among the hotel's indoor plants like gigantic totems with unpronounceable names and provenances going back centuries, they were served a tray of cakes for their hors d'oeuvre, a second tray instead of the roast main course, and yet more cakes for dessert while a steady stream of pre-First World War vodka was poured down their throats to accompany this stupendous performance.

Or perhaps they were spirited in from leafy villas secreted here and there in the Swiss countryside by chauffeur-driven vintage cars that had escaped the grasp of uncouth Germans on the hunt for war booty. In the open cab might have been a kid-gloved chauffeur and a liveried footman. In the passenger compartment, behind smoked-glass windows, might have been an old man with a short white beard trimmed to a point or an old lady with long white hair coiled like a fat, sleeping cobra on her crown. The hotel's porters would then compete amongst themselves, hoping for a sumptuous tip for the care they took in helping the old man, a skeletal frail creature in a thick sealskin-collared coat, muffler, and grey felt hat, into a wheelchair bound for the dining room. Lunch or dinner, it did not matter. The ritual was the same.

If they were resident at the hotel, at the conclusion of their outing, a footman would turn their wheelchair fully around before the lift doors closed so the old boy could raise his felt hat with a trembling hand in a benediction to fellow guests who happened to recognise him. If not, it was a watery, pop-eyed stare into nothingness before the lift bore him or her back to their delicately lit room on the second floor facing the lake.

Every one of these people knew who Chanel was and either tried to hide their recognition or furtively catch her eye whenever Mademoiselle felt like leaving her balcony with views of the mountains to make an appearance. Most of them had been her client at one time or another. She never acknowledged them. In the lobby of the hotel, they stepped respectfully aside, the men raising their hats, the women dropping their eyes in a kind of curtsey of acknowledgement. A silence would then fall as everyone followed Chanel's stiff back with their eyes as she strode purposely in a fog of morphine towards the terrace, or lobby, or dining room and disappeared. Then the talk would begin. Hadn't she aged? What was she wearing? Did you hear about so and so? Where's her German friend? I hear she is broke. What is she doing here?

It was too genteel to last. Chanel tried to alleviate the boredom by switching to the Lausanne Palace hotel for periods, but it never worked. Then, in 1946 her sophomoric existence at the Beau-Rivage and the Palace was shattered by a series of incidents that would have sunk a lesser mortal.

15

ZOMBIE

Early in 1946 Chanel received news of an irritating business setback care of her old nemeses, the Wertheimers.

Pierre and Jacques had recovered Parfums CHANEL from the wartime custodianship of Félix Amiot (albeit after some unappetising legal arm-wrestling when the collaborator Amiot was told acquiescing to the Wertheimers' request would save 'his little neck' from revenge-seeking French authorities)[1] and once again were cranking up production of their most lucrative asset. But there was bad news for Chanel. Pierre travelled to Switzerland to personally tell her that the wartime profits from sales of No. 5 amounted to only a ridiculous and paltry US$15,000.[2]

Chanel, naturally, was livid. She responded by instructing her lawyer, René de Chambrun, to countersue the Wertheimers for back royalties and selling fake products, i.e. the American No. 5, that she always maintained were demonstrably inferior and detrimental to the brand CHANEL. She also insisted that ownership and all pre-war rights be returned to her. If this was refused, she threatened to revive her red-labelled Mademoiselle Chanel and bring out a new and 'original' Mademoiselle CHANEL No. 5.

It was a sensational and cunning ploy, and it had the desired effect. The urbane and charming Pierre was horrified. He knew she knew she would do it, and he knew she knew he would countersue and so on and so on. It had the legs of a Greek saga and a mischievous, almost Jacobean thirst for treachery and revenge. Where was the end to all of this? There was no end. It would drag on and on, playing out over the years across one bad development after another. Chanel would always find ways of funding successive actions. She would never stop. It was just too horrible and debilitating to contemplate. Another Chanel war was in no one's best interests (except possibly Chanel's), especially where the future prosperity of the brand CHANEL was concerned.

The prospect of such a Promethean struggle (for stealing fire from Olympus and giving it to humans, Prometheus was bound to a rock and had his liver repeatedly eaten by an eagle in an infinite cycle of pain and torture) was anathema for Pierre. He duly trooped back to Lausanne and settled out of court with Chanel. According to de Chambrun, in 1947 the Wertheimers agreed to pay her US$400,000 in cash[3] (Professor Garelick called it US$326,000 in back royalties)[4] and 2 per cent of world sales (the equivalent of US$25 million a year in modern currency)[5] of No. 5 plus the rights to produce her own scents (but without the numeral 5) from Switzerland. Chanel had won but she couldn't be bothered with all the rigmarole connected with manufacturing perfume. So she went after an even better deal more suited to her present needs, which she got. In exchange for relinquishing all her perfume rights, she received a monthly payment from the Wertheimers, who also covered all her living expenses, taxes, and food bills. Not a bad outcome.

Chanel was once again stupendously rich. She used the money to eventually buy a stucco, three-storey hillside villa in Lausanne, which she decorated with her customary panache in Louis XV antiques and gilt-framed portraits. She also bought three homes for André Palasse and his family: a house in the wine-growing region of Lavaux, an apartment in Chexbres, and a villa embedded in woods near the village of Lutry within the canton of Vaud.

Meanwhile, her German friend, Baron Hans Günther von Dincklage, had been conniving to join her in Switzerland, even applying for Liechtenstein citizenship (which would allow him automatic entry) but was denied on every appeal. In October 1945 he was holed up with his mother at his aunt's estate, the crumbling Rosencrantz Manor, near Schinkel in northern Germany, when he was caught with a large amount of foreign currency by the occupying British. Under questioning, his companion, an American GI called Hans Schillinger, admitted the money was freely obtained from Mademoiselle Chanel for von Dinklage's personal use. Schillinger (an associate of Chanel's photographer friend, Horst) pleaded he was just a courier. The British confiscated the money and released the men. When they later tried to return it to Chanel, she declined to accept it, citing her reluctance to notify the French government she was in possession of a substantial amount of undeclared foreign currency. She suggested the British donate it to a charity of their choosing. What happened next is unknown. By early 1946 von Dincklage had finally been granted Swiss entry, and he and Chanel resumed the stylish and well-upholstered lifestyle they had enjoyed during the war.

Another financial outlay was prompted by another nasty turn of events in April 1946, just a few months after her reunion with von Dincklage. Out of nowhere, a French court issued an 'urgent'[6] warrant to bring Chanel to France for questioning. On 16 April a presiding member of the court, Judge Roger Serre, ordered French police and border officers to escort the wanted Chanel back to Paris. In May, Serre widened his investigation using powers under French penal code article 75 concerned with dealing with 'the enemy'.[7] Serre's order was in line with the de Gaulle government's avowed post-war mission to identify and cleanse French society of collaborators and other vermin who had profited during the German occupation without exception (although, in practice, there were a lot of high-profile exemptions): 'French military and civilian courts tried or examined 160,287 cases in all. While 7,037 people were condemned to death, only about 1,500 were actually executed. The rest of the death sentences were commuted to prison sentences.'[8]

News of this warrant must have sent a tremor of terror through Chanel's nervous system. Apart from the stigma associated with being wanted by the French state for questioning on such a damaging subject, there was also the very real threat in Chanel's feverish imagination of being kidnapped by a covert French police team and bundled out of Switzerland against her will. There was always talk at the Beau-Rivage and Lausanne Palace of people, friends, former associates who had suddenly disappeared and then popped up weeks, months later behind bars, awaiting trial in places like Nuremberg or (much, much worse) the Soviet Union. Was she tempted to hire protection? Perhaps the thought crossed her and von Dincklage's mind?

It would not have been an unreasonable response in the circumstances. This time the threat to her freedom was an official French court as opposed to an ad hoc, rag-tag, semi-sanctioned FFI outfit that had picked her up and brought her in a dilapidated Renault to their headquarters on the Île de la Cité in September 1944. This time her presence was sanctioned and enforced with the full legal might of the French state allied to a police force more than capable of employing nefarious measures to ensure the people's need for revenge was satisfied. This time it was more than serious. This time she had no one in authority to turn to and intercede on her behalf. She was an expatriate who had fled the country when her neck was on the line, a graphic expression of guilt in most people's eyes.

There must be something she could do? She couldn't, wouldn't, just sit on her hands like some calcified geriatric zombie and meekly comply with this detestable court order. It was not, and never had been, in her nature to do such a thing. To simply roll over like one of Bendor's spaniels. What would everyone say? They had finally got her; her luck had run out; Chanel was weak; Chanel was finished.

The counselling she received from the wily and sly de Chambrun (who was also fending off collaborationist accusations and consequently had legal problems of his own) was firstly to point out to his client that she was not, crucially, under arrest. The French warrant was solely focused on bringing her in for questioning or, to be more exact, seeking her cooperation to be questioned. There was also no deadline or time limit on her cooperation, which meant the process of her attendance in Paris could be extended, stalled indefinitely. De Chambrun advised her to cooperate, it would only make things worse if she didn't, but first she must take steps and the time she had at her disposal to nullify the potential for damage. She would be silly not to. Chanel was anything but silly. To pay for this nullification she shrewdly created, with de Chambrun's help, a trust fund, COGA ('Coco' and 'Gabrielle'), which was used to discreetly funnel money towards her various causes, namely those people who had information, knowledge, or solid evidence of Chanel's wartime activities that could be detrimental to her survival.[9]

Like the former Chanel collaborator, SS Brigadeführer and Generalmajor der Polizei, Walter Schellenberg.

Schellenberg had been captured by the British in June 1945 while trying to orchestrate his surrender on favourable terms and was undergoing trial for war crimes at Nuremberg. He was ill with a chronic liver condition and clinically depressed. To avoid prolonging his agony, he proposed a tantalising deal with the authorities. In exchange for a shorter sentence, he would rat out his fellow SS and SD (*Sicherheitsdienst*, Security Service) colleagues in prison. When told in the summer of 1946 he would be held over for a further trial (the so-called Ministries Trial) he let it be known he was writing his memoirs. The news was not well received by anyone remotely connected to the detestable former chief of the Combined German Secret Services.

According to Edmonde Charles-Roux,[10] de Chambrun informed Chanel of Schellenberg's proposed memoir and a message was passed to him in Nuremberg that Chanel was willing to finance a home for him and his wife in Switzerland while he was incarcerated. It was enough to seal the deal. On 4 November 1949, Schellenberg was sentenced to a paltry six years in prison but released after two years for ill health. On his release, COGA paid for Schellenberg's cancer treatments and subsequent funeral when he died penniless in Turin, Italy in 1952. *The Labyrinth: Memoirs of Walter Schellenberg, Hitler's Chief of Counterintelligence* was published posthumously in 1956 without any reference to Chanel.

This left one other substantial threat for COGA to deal with: Baron Louis de Vaufreland. But things were not so easy here. Chanel was in for a rude shock. The baron, who she betrayed to Pierre Reverdy to save her skin in September 1945, was Judge Roger Serre's star witness in the case he was compiling against France's most famous couturière. The 48-year-old Serre had been grilling the crushed, bewildered, and distraught baron for months.

If Sere was expecting a quick resolution to Chanel's case, he was gravely mistaken. Chanel's stalling and unavailability, either due to sickness or unavoidably pressing family matters, finally ran out on 4 June 1948 when she appeared before the Court of Justice in Paris to answer questions first requested of her a full two years earlier. In the intervening time, two things had happened: Judge Serre had been replaced by Judge Fernand Leclercq, and her nephew, André Palasse, had been interrogated by Judge Serre on 20 November 1947 before he handed over Chanel's case (over fifty pages of detailed analysis) to Judge Leclercq.

Chanel's and André's testimonies, recorded by court stenographers, are both a matter of record.[11] All the following excerpts are obtained from that record. Obviously, she had been coached by de Chambrun. Even so, she was not prepared to concede a millimetre, not one. It was her word against theirs and, as she knew, it was all about the performance. Besides, what were these people? Only traitors, deviants, and war criminals themselves. Sadly the transcript, dry as it is, does not convey Mademoiselle's haughty and scathing delivery.

In summary:

Chanel denied she was a friend of de Vaufreland adding (just for good measure) that 'he was visibly of abnormal morals and everything in his manner of dressing and of perfuming himself revealed what he was. I didn't trust him. If he was in relations with certain Germans, they could only be of a sexual nature ...'

Chanel had met de Vaufreland in 1941 at the Hôtel Ritz. De Vaufreland knew all about André's imprisonment: 'Vaufreland claimed he could bring him back. I accepted the offer Vaufreland spontaneously made ...'

Chanel denied she was in contact with German officials when meeting de Vaufreland:

> He never introduced me to any German, and the only German I knew during the occupation was the Baron Dinchlage [sic], established in France before the war and married to an Israelite ... I never knew any Germans by the names of Neubauer or Niebuhr ... de Vaufreland did not present me to the Germans with whom he had relations.

When confronted with sworn testimony from von Dincklage's former *Abwehr* boss, Hermann Niebuhr (now working for US Army counter-intelligence), that was also confirmed by the incarcerated de Vaufreland about her explicit, consensual relations with the *Abwehr*, Chanel replied: 'I protest against his declarations which are clearly implausible. I have no memory of a German that Vaufreland introduced me to.'

Chanel denied she was a registered *Abwehr* agent F-7124: 'I never was aware of my registration in a German service and I protest with indignation against such an absurdity …'

Chanel denied she had travelled with de Vaufreland to Madrid to facilitate André's release:

> It was completely by accident that we met on the train … After my nephew's return, I asked de Vaufreland to put some distance between his visits … after a year of captivity he (André) couldn't bear that sort of person (homosexuals) … I maintain I never asked anything from Vaufreland, neither for my nephew, nor for the trip I wanted to make to Spain.

Chanel denied she had sought de Vaufreland's help in using Nazi laws to Aryanize her business: 'I never asked de Vaufreland to be involved with the reopening of my perfume business … I didn't ask anything of him.'

To round things off, Chanel used her well-worn ploy of arranging 'for a declaration to come from Mr. Duff Cooper, former British Ambassador, who would be able to attest to the respect I enjoy in English society.'

The only potential glitch was André's testimony:

> [de Vaufreland] … declared that thanks to his relations with the Germans, I had been liberated. Mademoiselle Chanel also told me that she had asked Vaufreland to use all his influence to get me freed … I cannot be sure that Vaufreland had me freed; I have no proof of it. I repeat – I only knew what Vaufreland and Mademoiselle Chanel told me.[12]

Inexplicably, there is nothing in the record that indicates whether Judge Leclercq brought this apparent anomaly to her attention. Neither is there any reference to the statement the former *Abwehr* agent Count Joseph von Ledebur-Wicheln gave to MI6 in 1944 (probably because national agencies never share intelligence) that described von Dincklage's and Chanel's visit to Berlin in 1943 to meet with Himmler and Schellenberg.[13] The disastrous Modellhut mission was also never brought up.

Chanel must have been relieved things had gone so smoothly. Her testimony was never really challenged in any detail, probably because the court had a mountain of other cases to process. It didn't matter anyway. It was all a pack of lies. One can almost hear the exasperated intake of breath from Judge Leclercq as he turned the page of questions he had prepared for her, which she batted away without hesitation. Maybe he too was tired, even relieved, when he had nothing more to ask?

Chanel's answers had barely taken up a morning of the court's time. Not only was she now free to return to her sedate life and the companionship of von Dincklage in Switzerland (after first stocking up with a cache of hard drugs difficult to obtain in that country), she and her lawyer also considered the collaboration case against her now closed. It was time to move on and enjoy things: life, freedom, the future, her money. And yet ...

Except she couldn't, which is perhaps why she periodically entertained the idea of re-editing her past history to alleviate the vast tracts of boredom she was powerless to eradicate in dreary exile in dreary Switzerland. Drugs could only obliterate the present, but a well-written, forthright biography could distort a millennium. She knew what she was doing, as she once let slip to the American journalist Janet Flanner in 1931: 'Chanel ... refuses to read any book that tells what really happened, as she hates history: it is so dead.'[14]

The former Vichy official Paul Morand and his wife, the Romanian princess Hélène Soutzo, were penniless and stranded in a Swiss pension de famille when they were befriended by Chanel and supported with gifts of cash and accommodation. In the winter of 1946, during the time she was resisting the French Court of Justice, the Morands were her guests at the luxury Badrutt's Palace Hotel when Chanel contrived to be interviewed by Paul for a prospective biography. Morand was an accomplished author. His first collection of stories, *Tendres Stocks*, was published in 1921 and had an introduction by his friend Marcel Proust, so he was eminently equipped to render Chanel's monologues into prose.

Morand's notes of their conversations or, as he called them, his 'volatile pages',[15] were written up late at night on headed Badrutt's Palace notepaper. It must have been an exhausting exercise, but the pay was good and, besides, at the time he was unemployable. Desperate for work as he was, Morand was shocked by the phenomenal capacity for self-delusion that Chanel, the 'exterminating angel of nineteenth-century style',[16] exhibited:

> She had gone into voluntary exile in the Engadine, unsure whether to return to rue Cambon, and waiting to become wealthy again. She felt both trapped by the past and gripped by time regained ... black bile flowed from eyes that still sparkled, beneath arched eyebrows increasingly accentuated by eyeliner, like sculpted basalt;[17]

There was no concealing the resentment she felt at the way she was being blamed by the French state for things she had never done or consented to:

> The mystery of complexities! That's where the dark side of Chanel lies, her suffering, her taste for causing harm, her need to castigate, her pride, her strict exactitude, her sarcasm, her destructive anger, the rigidity of a character that blows hot and cold, her abusive, destructive spirit; this belle dame sans merci ... [she was] Chanel, the volcano from the Auvergne which Paris was mistaken in believing was extinct.[18]

Morand might have been an experienced diplomat, a first-hand witness of Vichy extremes, but he had never encountered a primordial force such as the one who reclined before him on a chaise longue, smoking incessantly and drinking Louis XIII cognac:

> That voice that gushed forth from her mouth like lava, those words that crackled like dried vines, her rejoinders, simultaneously crisp and snappy, a tone that grew more and more preemptory as age took its toll, a tone that was increasingly dismissive, increasingly contradictory, laying irrevocable blame ...[19]

But Chanel soon got bored with the whole process. The manuscript languished, forgotten and uncorrected, in a drawer until 1976, the year of Morand's death, when it was published as *L'Allure de Chanel* in Paris.[20]

Another writer attracted by the chance of easy money offered by a celebrity with buckets of cash to throw around for a vanity project was the Parisian-based journalist and editor Michel Déon. This time the 69-year-old Chanel seemed to take the process seriously, at least at the beginning.

In 1952, after exploring the United States by Greyhound bus and with the ghost-written memoirs of Spanish painter Salvador Dalí and three novels under his slim belt, Déon's publisher floated the idea of working with Coco Chanel on her proposed blockbuster autobiography. Why not? The 33-year-old Déon was regarded as an emerging talent, a member of a literary movement known as Les Hussards (named after Roger Nimier's 1950 novel *The Blue Hussar*) that rejected the existentialism of Jean-Paul Sartre. Chanel was already a fixture in his childhood imagination. In his autobiographical book, *Your Father's Room*, published after his death, there is the following vignette of Chanel in her pomp:

> The Duke of Westminster, the richest man in England, walked past, a cigar clamped between his teeth, in an out-at-elbow suit with corkscrewing trousers and his jacket pockets stuffed with tokens he had forgotten to cash in on his way out of the gaming room. A woman walked a step ahead of him, not turning round. She had an imperious expression and a very mobile face and wore a boater with a black ribbon. She was dripping with jewellery. Blanche said to her son, 'Look. That's Mademoiselle Chanel. Thanks to her we can cut our hair short without looking like servants.'[21]

Déon spent more than a year with Chanel, taking notes as they travelled around Europe, writing up her life story for a monthly salary to pay his rent in Paris. Angered by his long absences with Mademoiselle, Déon's girlfriend reputedly left him.

In *Pages Françaises*, published in 1999, Déon recounted a trip to the Beau-Rivage in Lausanne. He drove his sports car, with Chanel in the passenger seat, her head swathed in a sheer silk pink scarf, her liveried driver following behind in a Cadillac with two maids on the back seat, one of them clutching her famous jewellery box. Chanel talked constantly to conquer her shyness while the enormous dove-grey

Cadillac, much too big and wide for the road, slowly crawled along the promenade like a rescued beached whale on a hospital trolley. Chanel's preoccupation with the past was the same preoccupation she had tested the incredulity of Paul Morand with: the invention of a childhood she never had.

Interviewed by *The Irish Times* in 2009, Déon recalled giving Chanel his 300-page manuscript. She congratulated him on his work, then asked him to destroy it. Déon dutifully burned the sole copy. They remained friends. Chanel sent one of her classic suits to Déon's new wife, Chantal, and repeated the gift when each of their two children was born. Déon himself was the recipient of a valuable Louis XVI antique desk, which he wrote on prolifically for the next sixty years, winning the Grand Prix du Roman de l'Académie Française for *Un Taxi Mauve* in 1973. It paved the way for his election to seat 8 at the Académie Française in 1978. By then, Déon and his family had settled in Ireland, where they reared Chantal's fifty horses.

After a lifetime of writing a novel almost every year, Déon died from a pulmonary embolism at the age of 97 in 2016. From time to time before Chanel's death, he had visited rue Cambon to dine with her. There he would find her, whatever the time or day, perched on a gold chair in Atelier No. 5 snipping excess fabric from a dress worn by a model. Snip, snip, snip. The scissors cut into the silence as a long cigarette protruded from her lower lip like a quivering plank of wood. At such times, Déon knew, like everyone before him knew, that only in working did Chanel find peace: 'What Chanel really likes to do is work. Her next preference is for doing nothing. She's a great dawdler.'[22]

16

MADEMOISELLE ONLY DRINKS CHAMPAGNE

Paris on that sticky night in October 1950 was slick and wet, as if an ocean of shiny black crude oil had surged wilfully through the streets. Moving slowly, just like a sedate battleship, Chanel's chauffeur-driven Cadillac swung into rue Cambon and moored outside Maison CHANEL. 'What are we doing here?' Chanel asked her driver. It was not a question, and he knew better than to answer or even turn around. 'Take me to Rivoli,' Chanel instructed him.

Although it was just around the corner, the Cadillac, just like a turning battleship, needed to manoeuvre carefully through the narrow street and swing around into the wider rue de Rivoli. Eventually stopping outside an ornate eighteenth-century apartment building overlooking the Tuileries Garden and the Place de la Concorde, the chauffeur opened the door for Mademoiselle and her maids to get out.

Seventy-eight-year-old Misia Sert was dead. Chanel had come to pay her respects to her great friend, driving all the way from Lausanne with her maids, her luggage, a hatbox of exquisite short black wigs, and a special Goyard portmanteau of make-up.

Misia's apartment at 244 rue de Rivoli was dark and gloomy at that time of night, the mood of dilapidation exacerbated by the slowly recovering gardens of the Tuileries across the road. The last of André Le Nôtre's original double alley of bent and age-warped horse chestnut trees that had once flanked the Grande Allée from the time they were planted in 1688, had been decimated by fighting between the Germans and the *Résistance* in 1944. The denuded mall was now prone to ferocious winds that howled through the autumnal mists like wounded dogs. Some resistance was still provided by the largely intact trees along the Terrasse and Esplanade des Feuillants, the wide parallel pathways that ran alongside rue de Rivoli on the north side of the garden. Originally planted with mulberry trees by King Henry IV of France, then with orange trees after the French Revolution, there were still large ominous holes in the foliage caused by the wounds of the last few years that had not healed.

The effect might have been sobering for anyone else on that unsettled night, but Chanel, as she entered the silent building, was already high on smack she had self-administered in the Cadillac during a pit-stop on the road from Lausanne.

Misia had lived in the lavish building since 1946 when her third husband, José-Maria Sert (who had introduced both her and Chanel to smack in the 1920s),[1] had died. Previously she had resided for almost twenty years at 3 rue de Constantine, where she had maintained an artistic salon of debauched habitués that included drop-in Nazis and known French collaborators: 'At soirées after the war she invited *collaborateurs* and *résistants* on different days, but if they happened to bump into each other she left them to sort it out.'[2]

She also for a time shared the sexual favours of José-Maria's mistress and enthusiastic morphine partner, the unstable teenager Princess Roussy Mdivani, who had replaced her in 1928.

José-Maria had left all his antiques and art intact for his former wife, which added to the macabre atmosphere that night when Chanel strode into the vast boudoir with her maids, banishing everyone from the bedside vigil they had taken up beside Misia's dead body. Dispensing with the maids after they had deposited the hatbox and baskets of fresh flowers near Misia's splendid canopied Louis XIV bed, Chanel barricaded the double doors with an antique chair jammed against the handles and opened her portmanteau, arranging the bottles, brushes, and compacts on a dresser before taking off her coat and beginning work.

When a person dies, the process of decomposition begins immediately. The body changes colour. It also emits sounds and smells. Luckily, Misia's body hadn't deteriorated that much since her death a day or two ago on 15 October. It was still in the first stage, called 'autolysis', when the blood stops circulating and the body cannot receive oxygen or remove waste. The excess carbon dioxide creates an acidic environment causing the cells' membranes to rupture, one after the other, releasing enzymes that are acidic and powerful enough to eat these cells from the inside out. Misia's body had a kind of sheen to it due to these ruptured cells. Some of the top layer of skin had also started to loosen. Rigor mortis had set in, causing the muscles to stiffen. Thankfully the next stage, where the released enzymes from autolysis produces gas as they rupture, was some way off. It was important to move quickly and decisively.

First, Chanel stripped the heavy *négligée* from Misia's body and washed the corpse with soap and warm water using a sponge from a large basin she had filled from the adjoining bathroom. Misia's eyes and mouth were already closed.

Normally, when a body is prepared for viewing after death, the mortuary technician makes a small incision to reach the jugular vein and carotid artery. Forceps are then inserted into the jugular to allow the blood to drain out. At the same time, embalming solution is injected into the carotid artery. Every 20 to 30kg of body weight requires 4kg of embalming solution, largely made up of formaldehyde. But Chanel was not a mortuary technician. She was, however, an expert with cosmetics and their application. Even so, it is extremely hard to apply make-up to an un-embalmed corpse, because the skin is soft and often flabby.

Chanel was undaunted. She dyed, groomed, and curled Misia's hair, painted her nails, and again washed the body, drying it with freshly laundered towels from the bathroom. She thought about scooping up Misia's hair, flattening it and fastening it with pins for a wig from her hatbox, but decided against it, gathering it up in a white-laced chignon instead. Washing and massaging the body normally helps the corpse take on a life-like, rosy appearance, but Misia's body was severely emaciated by drugs and alcohol abuse. The once 'sloe-eyed and moon-faced, creamy-skinned and statuesque, effusively intelligent and passively carnal'[13] person in her pomp was a a wasted, skeletal scaffold of sores and scabs.

In such circumstances a technician could inject a solution via hypodermic needle to plumpen the facial features or, in cases where trauma or disease had significantly altered the appearance of the face, use wax, adhesive, and plaster to recreate the natural forms. Simply placing a wad of cotton wool in the mouth can often give a cadaver a more natural expression. Chanel improvised by pulling back Misia's jowls and loose facial skin, which she then secured, like excess fabric on a mannequin, behind her ears with dressmaker's pins.

Bottles of dark, orange juice-like liquids, compacts, and tubes of cosmetics were used to make Misia come alive once more. The many discoloured lesions on her legs and arms, hands and feet, caused by unhealed injections, were camouflaged. Towards the end she was such an addict of hardcore opiates such as heroin that she'd inject herself straight through her clothes without bothering to find a functioning vein.[4] According to the Pulitzer Prize-winning composer and lascivious Parisian diarist Ned Rorem, Misia at the end was arrested as a common junkie and never recovered from the trauma.[5]

Moisturising lotion was applied to Misia's face, lips, and hands, then primer, foundation, concealer, blush. Eye lashes were lacquered. Finally, she was dressed in some jewellery and a pre-war pink CHANEL dress.

When the doors were finally flung open and select friends and the curious like Paul Claudel were allowed in, they encountered a revitalised corpse lying in state on a bed of white Swiss flowers. Chanel attended the funeral ceremony at Notre-Dame-de-l'Assomption around the corner in rue Saint-Honoré, where the body was displayed, but did not make it to Misia's burial in the Cimetiere de Samoreau on a plot near Mallarme's grave overlooking the Seine. She returned to Lausanne in a fog of drugs and memories.

Her grand-niece Gabrielle Palasse-Labrunie always disputed this last spooky, loving episode between the two great friends,[6] much as she always denied the excessiveness of their drug abuse and rumours of a lesbian relationship spanning decades.

What was never disputed was the bond between them, especially when Misia fell on hard times after the war and Chanel was hunkered down in Switzerland, biding her time until it was safe to return to her beloved Maison. It was a bond forged, in part, on the sharing of lovers like Pierre Reverdy (Misia claimed, 'I've had only husbands, never lovers,' unlike her closest friend, Chanel, 'who had only lovers, never husbands').[7] They were 'soul sister(s)'.[8]

They were also soul junkies. Chanel's dreary days at the Beau-Rivage and Lausanne Palace, where she reputedly only drank champagne,[9] were relieved when Misia came to town on drug runs. Together, they would go on benders, forage for compliant dealers, particularly in the south of France, and shoot up several times a day.[10] They made a strange couple – two elderly, emaciated hard-core addicts: Misia almost blind, a wretched quivering stick insect, and Chanel increasingly irritated by her old friend's carefree and shameless habit of shooting up in public.

Misia's memoir of her adventures, using verbatim excerpts from a trough of documents she had hoarded throughout her life, was dictated to her amanuensis, the journalist and critic Boulos (aka Paul Ristelhueber, who supplied her with morphine and took drugs with her). Published posthumously in 1952, it included a revealing chapter on Chanel that was originally excised from the published work: 'Chanel … vetoed the essay, saying that she planned her own memoir, to which Misia retorted: "It exists already in your account books."'[11]

No doubt a deal was struck to ease that editing process, greased by cash or drugs.

Another excised episode involved a harrowing visit to Monte Carlo in mid-1949 when the pair and an impossibly handsome Swiss doctor (driving a lipstick-red Alfa Romeo Super Sport Cabriolet followed by the ubiquitous chauffeur-driven dove-grey Cadillac) conspicuously pulled up with a screech of brakes alongside the most notorious hotel on the French Riviera.

Like a garish plastic model of a grand hotel plonked on top of a luxurious sponge cake, the flamboyant Hôtel de Paris Monte-Carlo had that special aura that only places frequented by the indolent super-rich can radiate.

Old money, new money, sex money, movie-star money, money-to-burn money, crazy money, dirty money, blood money, beyond-your-wildest-dreams money, even ex-Nazi money gushed from the sumptuous colonnades and heavy gilt picture frames, dripped from the eyes of nymphs, fawns, and satyrs dotted around the walls, and drooled from the lips of marbled dolphins decorating the vast swimming pool overlooking the Mediterranean. It was a waterfall of conspicuous consumption, a torrent of luxury that belied the building's humble beginnings.

In 1856, Charles III of Monaco gave his royal assent to a couple of nouveau property speculators to build a sea-bathing facility for the treatment of various diseases in *vogue* at the time and a casino. Initially the casino was not a success due to its inaccessibility from much of Europe. Monte Carlo was still very much a provincial, sunny retreat back then. However, after several relocations, the Société des Bains de Mer took over the project and built the current Monte Carlo Casino in 1863. A year later, the 106 room Hôtel de Paris Monte-Carlo was opened adjacent to the casino and things began to happen. A trio of Riviera hotspots was completed when the Opéra de Monte-Carlo or Salle Garnier was finished in 1878, built as a miniature replica of the Paris Opera House.

And yet the principality's discovery by the rest of Europe had to wait until 1868 when a railway link to France was finally created. Then, in 1886, things really took off when the Calais-Méditerranée Express, a luxury French sleeper train, garnered international fame as the preferred mode of transport for the wealthy travelling from Calais to the French Riviera. Colloquially known as *Le Train Bleu*, it ushered in the image of opulence and risqué hedonism that was immortalised in Maurice Dekobra's 1925 bestseller, *The Madonna of the Sleeping Cars*, and Agatha Christie's 1928 novel, *The Mystery of the Blue Train*, featuring her fictional detective Hercule Poirot.

Even in 1950, a mere five years after the Principality of Monaco was liberated, the hotel still reeked of a faded grandeur and a tradition of opulence satirised by the 1934 Cole Porter song 'Anything Goes'. There was also more than a whiff of infamy as well, inflicted by recent history, which the locals tried their best to shrug off but still clung to the building like a persistent evergreen vine.

The hotel's waiters and staff who had survived the war, and re-grouped after it, preferred not to acknowledge this unavoidable episode. Their focus was on the gilded past and they were determined never to forget the heights of celebrity the Riviera's premier hotel once spawned. The fantastic parties, the intrigues, the scandals, the shootings, the vendettas, the catastrophic bankruptcies, the unbelievable excesses, the con artists and their rich 'marks' mingling with the most beautiful people on the planet together with the ugliest and most sordid like they were bosom buddies. They never forgot Who was Whom and Whom wasn't Who they said they were. It was their living and their responsibility not to. They were professionals. It was what they were paid for. They were paid to recognise the paste from the real thing, or so everyone believed. Like cockroaches, they were indestructible and as much a part of the Monte Carlo scene (perhaps even more integral and vital to it) as the luxe hotel's racy clientele.

Which is why they immediately scurried out of the hotel into the cicada-addled sun once they recognised who it was, greeting and welcoming the one person who, like them, had survived the past apparently unscathed, knew all their secrets, and embodied everything the hotel represented.

While the handsome young man driving the sports car jumped out and opened the door for the two women, porters and hotel management milled around the little group hoping to be first in line for the customary welcome tip: first to emerge was Coco Chanel, sleek, smiling, and nodding in acknowledgement of the commotion she had caused. She was followed by (gingerly to begin with) her friend Misia Sert looking frail and a little bewildered by all the attention. Chanel waved the crowd towards the Cadillac where two maids and a mountain of luggage were piled up on the back seats.

The pile was eagerly devoured.

Left alone with Misia and the young man, Chanel paused and soaked up the sensational scene, breathing in the harbour smells and the rough odour of the paving stones, squinting at the dancing light playing across the cut-glass sea, marvelling at the duck-egg blue sky. It was much as she remembered it, both before and during the war.

From 1923 onwards when she had money and prestige, Monaco was the scene of some of her greatest triumphs and (after suffering her greatest embarrassment further down the road at Juan-les-Pins) her summer sanctuary, plus everything else in between. She met Bendor here. She was accepted here. She was protected and cosseted. She gorged herself on the sun and people and easy drugs at the Monte-Carlo Beach Club, immersed herself in the Ballets de Monte-Carlo, designed swimsuits and sportswear for the 1924 ballet *Le Train Bleu* (and launched 'summer season' fashion years before anyone else had even thought of such a thing), and built her villa, La Pausa, at Roquebrune-Cap-Martin on land that once formed part of the former hunting grounds of Monaco's ruling Grimaldi family. Beyond Paris, Monaco was Chanel's favourite destination.

As in the past, she was here to celebrate and give her dear friend Misia, so down on her health and her luck, a special treat. But she couldn't help noticing, as one gold-bangled arm supported Misia while another hand gripped the wrought-iron balustrade on the gleaming hotel steps, that although everything appeared timeless, there was a sense of change in the air. The war had, like everywhere else, left an indelible mark, a crimson stain on the principality it was keen to eradicate, wash away with new thinking and new projects.

Despite its neutrality during the Second World War, the principality was fiercely coveted by both Nazi Germany and fascist Italy because of its neutrality and attractive tax and financial infrastructure. The Nazis in particular, as the war progressed, were fond of manipulating neutral countries, like Switzerland, to facilitate the procurement of foreign currency through dubious front companies created specifically for the purpose. But initially, when war was declared on 1 September 1939, there was not a hint of this future subterfuge, at least not officially. Each side played by the rules, on the surface. Communications were perfunctory but cordial. The reigning prince, 70-year-old Louis II, adopted the practice of regularly guiding his horse through the streets of his country in a French general's uniform to assure his subjects that everything was under control. Things remained calm and routine. On 5 September 300 French soldiers were stationed in Monaco for the tiny state's protection, and a plan was contemplated to evacuate the inhabitants to a refugee camp near Lodève if the situation deteriorated.

Things went rapidly downhill in May 1940 when the German army invaded the Netherlands, Belgium, and northern France. The Vichy government under Marshal Pétain was made officially responsible by the Germans for the protection of Monaco, but this scheme was aggravated and subverted by the Italian army capturing and annexing nearby Menton and Cap-Martin. Deciding in the end to avert a diplomatic confrontation with one of their few allies, after the armistice of 22 June 1940 the Germans agreed the principality would become an enclave in an Italian-occupied zone of southern France. Things changed again when the Italian government fell in September 1943 and German soldiers inevitably took the place of the Italians. The Hôtel de Paris was made the headquarters of the Gestapo, and officers were billeted at l'Hermitage. Monte Carlo's pleasure yachts were either towed away or scuttled to make room for the German navy, French-speaking propaganda programmes were broadcast on Radio Monte Carlo, and the Nazis settled in for the long haul.

The business of making money and pleasure continued and intensified. Unremarkably, the casino remained open during the German occupation as Monaco became the acknowledged centre of illegal trade and black market operations for governments and criminal gangs alike. The principality's reputation for the integrity and safety of capital deposited within its institutions (whatever its origins) was such that prominent Nazis used it to funnel substantial funds to safe havens in South America and southern Africa when the Third Reich was in its death throes.

Louis II's role in this situation was one of the reasons his successor in 1949, Prince Rainier, was keen to begin the process of change that Chanel intuitively sensed was being embraced so vigorously. On 3 September 1944, the German occupation came to an end after the principality was bombarded by Allied raids. The Allies tried to remove Louis, but he wouldn't budge, and his grandson, Rainier, was unwilling to force the issue given Louis's capacity for whipping up royalist sentiment and pro-continuity publicity. Everyone agreed Monaco's reputation for stability and financial convenience had to be maintained for the state to recover. The approach worked beautifully, and for the next several years after the war, the principality's reputation as a safe haven was enhanced. Even some Vichy Nazis were sufficiently impressed to continue to invest their dirty money in Monaco property and enjoy the lifestyle their loot afforded them.

Chanel was well aware of all this because she had used Monaco's special status throughout her exile in Switzerland, not for funnelling money to her Swiss accounts as everyone thought, but for the drugs she needed to survive. The handsome young man who had driven her and Misia from Lausanne in his lipstick-red Alfa Romeo was recruited for this purpose from the celebrated Clinique La Prairie, operated by Dr Paul Niehans. Outwardly, the all-expenses-plus-hefty-commission job was for a willing doctor to ensure the ailing Misia was properly cared for. The underlying reason, however, was to fill out and authorise pharmacy prescriptions for the two ancient druggies to get high without the usual stuffy formalities the Swiss insisted upon. The week-long booking was exactly what Chanel and Misia needed after a tumultuous eighteen months of stress, dramatic life-changing events, and acute despair.

Of the two, Misia was in the poorer physical condition. The once-celebrated impressionist muse famous for her ample décolletage was almost blind from drugs. She was a skeleton that could not move unaided, her scaly skin a mass of unhealed syringe pricks and scabs. Gone were the days when the two *monstres sacrés* of Paris, at the height of their looks and mischievousness in the 1920s and cackling tête-à-tête like a pair of fancy witches, shared a first-class sleeping car on Le Train Bleu heading to the south of France to get their holiday fix.

The blue with gold-trimmed sleeping cars were often packed with British society figures seeking to escape the British winter during the height of the season between November and April: 'The sleeping cars had only ten sleeping compartments each, with one attendant assigned to each sleeping car ... sleeping-car conductors had to speak at least three languages, and all notices were written in French, German, Italian and English.'[12]

Like the network of luxurious sleeper trains criss-crossing Europe from the 1880s to the beginning of the Second World War run by the Compagnie Internationale des Wagons-Lits (the best known being the Orient Express), the wood-panelled interiors of the Bleu were the backdrop for sumptuous meals of haute cuisine served on gold-and-blue plates with crinkled edges, the thick linen napkin at the centre of each setting folded like a vertical scallop shell in the middle of the plate to greet every black-tied diner.

And yet, the Great Depression and the inevitable devaluation of sterling in the 1930s had a knock-on effect on the volume of cashed-up British and American tourists able to afford the Riviera, reducing the size of the Bleu train to two carriages between Calais and Menton. In 1936, the death knell of its exclusivity was sounded when a new left-leaning government in France legislated paid two-week vacations for French workers and insisted that second- and third-class sleeping cars be added to the iconic train. The age of aristocratic privilege and entitlement was over. By 1938, the once magical and exotic *Le Train Bleu* was running as an ordinary night express train.

The change in fortune was mirrored in the changed situations of both Chanel and Misia after the war. The hedonistic pre-war era of no comebacks and no consequences was effectively stamped into the post-war ground like a discarded cigarette butt. No longer revered, they were forced to cope in their own way to survive. Chanel, the most loathed of the two after the war, fared the best. Misia declined at an alarming rate, despite having the best run at redemption. And yet here they were, reunited in their old luxe stamping ground.

At first Chanel insisted they share a suite with two double beds but, after a restless night when Misia (wracked with diarrhoea and cold-turkey sweats) had to visit the bathroom several times to vomit and defecate, she hired a casual nurse to take care of her in an adjoining suite.

Unlike Chanel, Misia never left the hotel. She was content to receive her morphine jabs from the handsome young Swiss doctor and luxuriate in a warm stupor of oblivion on the balcony or in bed watched over by her nurse. On the occasions when she was coaxed downstairs to sip cold consommé at the restaurant, Chanel arranged for the in-house pianist to serenade her entrance with old compositions she had inspired in her heyday, like eccentric French composer Eric Satie's 'Three Pieces in the Shape of a Pear'. Everyone knew who they were, and their arrival at the scene of former crimes, misdemeanours, and outrageous behaviours inspired a hushed reception followed by a swell of chatter among the well-heeled clients, some of whom still wore CHANEL creations from the last great shows of the 1930s.

Chanel, too, had to resort to wearing clothes that were now over ten years old but were still timeless and, with the occasional nip and tuck here and there administered ruthlessly over time by their creator, always glamorously fit for purpose.

Chanel quite enjoyed the process of redefining her old pieces. It was the only couture work she had undertaken for the past decade. It kept her hand in, but it was no substitute for the busy life she once led. Some days, as she worked on an old favourite, the memories would swell up and she would quietly cry to herself, recalling the old days when she and a few seamstresses worked tirelessly on her first creations, first at her hat store known as Chanel Modes on the ground floor of the Paris flat of her socialite lover Étienne Balsan at 21 rue Cambon in 1909; then at her first boutique at Deauville in 1912, where she began making her jersey sportswear; then at another small boutique at Biarritz in 1915; and finally the talismanic shop at 31 rue Cambon in 1918.

It was when she was putting together her outfits for this Monaco trip that she came across a pair of beach-pyjamas that triggered the most searing of memories from those early days. Searing because of the weather that day on the beach in the emerging hedonistic resort town of Juan-les-Pins on France's Côte d'Azur, and searing because it marked a defining moment in Chanel's life.

It was so hot that day in July 1918, with such a relentless unforgiving sun that people draped wet towels over their heads like giggly Arabs or cowered under priceless beach umbrellas, that the hotel was in a panic over its dwindling supply of ice for its American cocktails. But not Coco Chanel. Mademoiselle began her promenade boldly (some would say defiantly) strolling along the famous beach in a loose shirt and baggy, pyjama-style trousers. The alternative, in the day, was to strap oneself up in metres and metres of cotton and crinoline and parade under the unrelenting sun with a parasol. Not Chanel. She wasn't about to be defeated by the constraints of a costume she abhorred and didn't have in her luggage.

Heading back to the hotel, after a while she was aware of a subtle but noticeable change in the behaviour of certain guests towards her. It wasn't until she and her party of friends arrived at the casino for an evening of fun that the jaunty mood of the afternoon turned nasty, and she suffered the ignominy of being refused entry! Never had she been so embarrassed in public, ridiculed in front of incredulous friends and lovers, derided in sight of some of the wealthiest, most connected families in France. It was an outrage. She had, effectively, been cancelled. It was left up to the casino's owner, Edouard Baudoin, to deliver the coup final a few days later when he declared to cronies that Mademoiselle was barred from his establishment because she was 'living proof that one must not be merely dressed, but well dressed'.[13]

By then Chanel had packed her bags, never to return to the town where she had been mischievously accused of wearing men's pyjamas in public.

Chanel smiled as she took the soft, sheer jersey pyjama outfit (from the Hindi *paejama* meaning 'leg covering') created in Paris soon after that shattering day at the beach from its cardboard box and shook it to release the fibres from their enforced hibernation. Unsurprisingly, she was to have the last laugh when, during the next season in Biarritz, her 'beach-pyjamas' sold out, and by the mid-1920s beach-pyjamas (or 'woollen suits for the beach', as *Vogue* called them in 1931)[14] had become the fashion amongst the French Riviera elite. Chanel's 'touch' for women's needs was irresistibly proved to be correct that day. It gave her immense confidence and assured her backers her chosen fashion trajectory would be profitably rewarded over time.

Even Robert de Beauplan, the popular journalist who satirically coined the term 'Pyjamapolis' to describe the effect Chanel's simple pyjamas had on summer fashions in the Riviera, had to concede they gave:

> ... women an unprecedented look, more free, cheekier, and its relaxed attitude always remains tasteful ... It's the afternoon outfit, for visits, tea, dancing and cocktails ... There are also night pyjamas, which look like dresses from afar when you see them in casinos, until you see the person dance quickly the fox-trot and then, there's no mistaking.[15]

Chanel would have particularly enjoyed the reference to casinos in de Beauplan's description.

But how would her much-vaunted magical 'touch' be perceived today in the 1950s, she wondered to herself, after so many years kept under wraps in reluctant hibernation like the pyjamas she now held up in front of Misia? Fashion had changed so much in the interval, but had the women who once so adored her vision and judgement and mimicked her tastes so slavishly? Were their once-so-readily-influenced (some would say released) sensibilities, needs, and desires so radically altered? Of course there was only one way of finding out.

It was with a sense of exquisite vengeance, something she so enjoyed visiting on select targets, that she descended the Hôtel de Paris's marbled steps one evening escorted by her handsome young Swiss doctor (old men smelled of decay; Chanel preferred younger models and surrounded herself with them) dressed in clingy black silk pyjamas en route to the restaurant. Everything was set for a perfect evening. She and Misia had received their evening pre-dinner cocktail of drugs, and Misia was blissfully comatose upstairs. Chanel was happy, generous with her smiles. The air was warm, music tinkled like falling raindrops on glass awnings, champagne hissed from magnum bottles like ravenous vipers, there was laughter, and there was a sense of fun to be had, romance to be savoured.

But the effect was abruptly shattered.

In the crowd milling around the foot of the stairs, a man lightly bumped her shoulder and nonchalantly turned to apologise for the unwanted contact. He was a small, portly, perfectly anonymous bald man in a shiny tuxedo, one of many such men in the hotel that evening. But Chanel had to summon all her sangfroid to avoid recoiling in horror when the two of them instantly recognised each other. The bald man politely bowed and smiled. Chanel stood rooted to the spot, a hand instinctively caressing the triple strand of pearls around her neck. The bald man peeled off, disappearing into the noisy evening crowd while Chanel rigidly followed his departure with her cold dark eyes.

It was a pivotal moment.

Chanel later confided to Misia how the innocuous incident reiterated, in that split second, just how impossible her situation was. Despite all her wealth and fame, some six years after she had dramatically fled France, Chanel realised she was still eternally trapped in a no man's land of guilt and excuses, wandering like a zombie without a home. She would never be rid of the opprobrium her war connections and dalliances bestowed upon her, whatever new judicial concessions her lawyer was able to win. It was a curse she could never escape from. Not even her money could fully eradicate it. Was it worth all the risks she took all those years ago after all?

Perhaps she just should have stayed behind and rolled the dice? Many of her friends did and survived – friends like Misia and others more guilty of collaboration than she ever was. Misia agreed. It was her choice. It was too late to second guess history and, besides, this constant rehashing of previous decisions was not only pointless; it was worthless. Chanel did what she did. End of story.

Chanel and Misia flew to Paris the next day, the chauffeur-driven Cadillac, the maids, and the luggage following by road. The young doctor returned to Lausanne, and the Hôtel de Paris Monte-Carlo swallowed up Chanel's latest brush with her past infamy without a trace of it ever having happened.

17

BOTTOMS UP!

When not entertaining Misia, delivering a fictionalised version of her life to paid scribes, promenading around the lake followed by her chauffeur in a Cadillac, investing in beauty treatments at the Clinique Valmont, taking afternoon tea at the Steffen tea-room in Montreux, stopping at the Chalet-des-Enfants restaurant in the surrounding hills for a bowl of milk and a slice of flan, or exploring further ways of screwing the Wertheimers, Chanel spent her time in Switzerland rejuvenating herself with society dentist Dr Felix Valotton, rheumatologist Dr Theo de Preux for her encroaching arthritis, and ophthalmologist Professor Steig.

But it was her fixation with the seriously weird cellular therapy (also called live cell therapy) designed to arrest the ageing process practised by Swiss surgeon Dr Paul Niehans that she actively tried to hush up along with her drug abuse.

Not that Chanel had any qualms about seeking help from the medical community: 'I'm in favour of medicine. We live in an age when one needn't suffer just for the sake of a scruple.'[1]

Niehans' exclusive clinic near the town of Vevey on the northern shores of Lake Geneva was a honey pot of hope for all kinds of celebrities seeking to tap into his hocus-pocus version of the fountain of youth. Along with her drug dependency, the Niehans clinic was not something Chanel wanted the brand CHANEL to be associated with. Though there were suspicions about her use of the 'surgeon's knife' to remake her face,[2] she always put her stunning energy, superlative skin, and eternally trim figure down to good habits and a rigorously healthy discipline: 'For many decades I made it a rule to turn in before midnight. I need my eight hours' sleep, and the hours before midnight count double.'³

The cellular therapy of the kind regularly used by Chanel in Switzerland had its origins in the exploits of 72-year-old Dr Charles Edouard Brown-Sequard, who injected himself in 1889 with an organic cocktail derived from animal testicles, which he said turned him into a new man. Excited by his success, Brown-Sequard built an amazing machine with pulleys, dials, and levers that could pulverise bulls' testicles into a magical liquid designed to rejuvenate and prolong life. Uptake was slow, sabotaged by the prevailing medical establishment. The secret to the success of his venture, Brown-Sequard soon learned, wasn't the mixture itself but its clientele. If he could only get one prominent person to believe in his treatment, he would be made. But it was a long hard slog to get any kind of attention apart from ridicule.

Then along came the mysterious Dr Serge Voronoff, who became famous for injecting slices of a chimpanzee's testicle into male patients. His 'monkey-gland' treatment premiered in 1920. After being denied permission to present a paper at the French Academy of Medicine, Voronoff held a news conference with a billy goat, a ram, and an elderly gentleman. The gentleman stated he was full of transplanted goat testicles and possessed remarkable vigour as a result of Dr Voronoff's exotic procedure. He then demonstrated his new-found lust for life by doing a handstand on stage. Niehans knew Voronoff and saw him operate.

As a distinguished 49-year-old surgeon with impeccable credentials, Niehans began injecting humans with the foetuses of unborn lambs and other animals in 1931.⁴ He particularly favoured harvesting fresh cells from New Zealand black sheep and injecting them directly into his patients' buttocks. These patients included Charles de Gaulle, Chancellor Konrad Adenauer of Germany, Somerset Maugham, Noël Coward, Winston Churchill, the Duke of Windsor, Bernard Baruch, Thomas Mann, Hedda Hopper, Chanel, and Pope Pius XII who was so grateful for the relief Niehans delivered that he appointed him to the Pontifical Academy of Sciences in 1955. In 1951 Niehans reached the pinnacle of his profession when, as a last resort, he was consulted as King George VI lay dying.

The routine at Niehans' discreet and spruce Clinique La Prairie never wavered. New patients arrived for a full physical examination and extensive blood and tissue tests on a Monday, remaining at a nearby luxury hotel until Wednesday afternoon while these preliminaries were conducted and analysed. Only then were they admitted to the clinic, on Thursday mornings, and prepared for the injection programme when they received fresh foetal cells administered directly into their buttocks. (For some reason, it always had to be a Thursday.) Injected patients stayed at the clinic till the following Tuesday (to ensure there wasn't a negative reaction), then left to make way for the next wave of victims, returning reinvigorated to their country of origin.

Thursday was probably the magic day because the clinic received freshly slaughtered animal tissue from a nearby abattoir on that day. Sheep foetuses were removed, the necessary blood and tissue samples minced up, and the whole concoction pureed into a fluid for injecting affluent patients within an hour or two of the ewe's death.

For famously rich people, Niehans was the perfect guru: emphatic, confident, towering, aloof, and autocratic. He was rumoured to have Prussian royal blood coursing through his veins, and he certainly marched through his clinics as if he did not occupy the same earthly stratosphere as lesser mortals. His patients consequently adored his unwavering confidence in the efficacy of his therapy and his absolute faith in their inevitable recovery from whatever malaise they were suffering from. Little wonder he was once referred to as a 'kind of de Gaulle of medicine'[5] and it is tantalising to imagine those two supremely hedonistic behemoths, Chanel and de Gaulle, the most famous French man and woman of their day, haughtily ignoring one another in Dr Niehans' waiting room before being led away to have their French bums pricked with foetal lamb serum.

By 1948 Niehans was advocating a mishmash of offal products in his treatments: fresh livers, pancreases, kidneys, hearts, duodenums, thymus cells, and spleen cells, adding lyophilised (freeze-dried) cells in 1949 to his smorgasbord of Hannibal Lecter offerings. He wasn't too fussy about what he was treating either, administering live cell therapy to counter a variety of diseases and conditions that included anaemia, heart palpitations, specific types of diabetes, hypertension, and erectile dysfunction. He asserted he could enhance underdeveloped breasts and reduce homosexual inclinations in both men and women. He suggested the use of hypothalamus cells for conditions such as sweating, asthma, and sexual neurasthenia. Placenta cells, known for their therapeutic and rejuvenating properties, were utilised to address exhaustion following childbirth, angina, and blood pressure issues. Towards the end of his life (he died aged 89 in 1971), he announced that cell therapy helped regulate the onset of cancer, declaring, 'The rejuvenation of the sex glands is the best protection against cancer.'[6]

It probably wouldn't have mattered if his illustrious clients believed he was funnelling cat piss into their joints and muscles, so long as they felt wonderfully alive after their Thursday morning consultation. Chanel felt the same. Did it really matter if Niehans himself didn't understand or couldn't fully explain how cells from animal tissues might rejuvenate human organs? Niehans was always vague on the subject of how injected cells could travel to specific damaged organs and repair them. Cat piss or no cat piss, it worked!

Chanel's cellular treatment went into turbo-drive in 1953 when it became clear it was finally politically and judicially safer for her to return to Paris than at any other time during the past ten years of exile.

Things in France had changed, were changing. Perceptions of war activities, of actions taken to survive the war, were now different from what they had been during those first, white-hot moments after the nation was liberated in 1944. It was as if the country had taken a decisive moment to pause and reflect on what it was doing, and had been doing for so long that it had been accepted as the right thing to do, the only thing to do.

Put simply, the country was morally, spiritually, and ethically exhausted after six draining years of *épuration légale* (the wave of official trials created by the French state to purge and punish Nazi collaborators) that had begun before *Libération*. Not a day had gone by during this period without front-page coverage in French newspapers of war atrocities, degrading behaviour exercised by all levels of French society, and sadistic games played out by criminal collaborators. It was days, months, years of horror upon horror for everyone to be smeared with, whether they liked it or not.

The country was understandably sick of it. After enduring 160,287 case trials, something between 791 and 1,500 executions (depending on which historian you read), and the deprivation of citizenship handed out to 49,723 people for the crime of *indignité nationale*, which only ceased to be a criminal offence in January 1951, though people convicted of it remained unfairly deprived of their basic civic rights until August 1953), the French government and French Church felt a line had to be drawn under this self-defeating national obsession for revenge so the country could rebound and respond to new Cold War challenges:

> A total purge proved impossible while a reconstruction process, which sought to mobilize all forces available, proceeded. The amnesty of collaboration in France (1951-1953) was of this type. It was based on the idea that there was not 'a handful of the miserable and disgraceful' to be condemned, in the words of General de Gaulle in 1944.[7]

The result was the creation of Law No. 51-18 of 5 January 1951, providing amnesty for certain offences committed during the Second World War. The amnesty law, as it was called, was also a practical response to the ongoing absurdity of the French state bringing to justice former members of Pétain's Vichy regime while at the same time incorporating other members, like André Boutemy and Camille Laurens, into the government of the Fourth Republic.

Positioned as an act of national reconciliation, the law also paved the way for the election of former Pétain officials to the National Assembly (the French legislature), legitimising their re-entry into mainstream French politics. At the June 1951 legislative elections, the Union of Republican Independents (UNRI), founded by Jacques Isorni, Pétain's strident lawyer, received 288,089 votes, ensuring three officials were elected to the Assembly to overtly espouse Pétainist values and policies from the floor. They were joined by a sprinkling of far-right independents like Jacques Le Roy Ladurie, former Vichy Minister of Agriculture, to complete the partial rehabilitation of a once despised political force.

Another consequence was the growth of far-right-leaning small publishing houses such as Nouvelles Éditions Latines, Self, L'Elan,

Éditions du Conquistador, France-Empire, and A l'Enseigne du Cheval Ailé. Not only was the voice of the Vichy-inspired right wing heard unrestricted in the French Assembly, it could now be heard in the streets as well. The development reflected other ironic aspects of the French system post-*Libération* that were always evident but discreetly downplayed. Plon, the publisher of General de Gaulle for instance, also published former Vichy ministers such as Yves Bouthillier.

The 1951 amnesty law was not a complete success, but it did vividly expose the anomaly that while former collaborators under the pretext of national reconciliation were being granted amnesty, former *Résistance* fighters were still being hounded and rounded up. By 1952 a special provision for *Résistance* fighters who carried out acts with the intention of serving the cause of *Libération*, or of contributing to the *Libération* of France, was being openly considered by the Assembly. The push for a total amnesty was unstoppable and a second amnesty law (Law No. 53-681) supplementing the 1951 law came into effect on 6 August 1953.

Coincidentally, Chanel began sowing the seeds of her possible return to haute couture around this time.

The amnesty laws of 1951 and 1953 were the decisive chain of events that allowed her to believe she could return. Without this change in direction and attitude of the French state, Chanel would still be languishing in exile as a gilded canary in a sparkling, gilded cage stuffed with boring treats. At the age of 70, she had the chance to be once more at the epicentre of the work she loved, the work she craved, before that chance evaporated due to the inevitable caprices of changing governments, time, fashion, and receding reputation: 'She lived for her work, and the passion that she brought to it was the secret of her appeal, an elixir washing over [and] away the bitterness of exile and forced inactivity.'[8]

The timing was right for other reasons as well.

People important to her life story, one way or another, were dying: Vera Bate in 1948, Schellenberg in 1952, and Bendor in 1953, after which Chanel sold La Pausa, their love nest in Roquebrune-Cap-Martin. And besides, Baron von Dincklage (still described by her circle as merely a former 'German tennis player')[9] was gone too. Assured by her ever-faithful and well-connected lawyer, René de Chambrun, that the official tide had officially turned in her favour, Chanel considered her options. There was nothing now to keep her away. Nothing to prevent her returning Maison CHANEL to its former glories in the wake of the seemingly unstoppable Christian Dior and his frilly, frothy 'New Look' that violated all her design values.

Of course, she still needed a trigger to maintain control of the narrative.

There are many apocryphal stories about Chanel chomping at the bit to return to haute couture, of her ripping up taffeta curtains to make dresses for friends (like Marie-Hélène de Rothschild) who she thought were dressed hideously. But the fact is she knew exactly what to do to make her comeback a reality. And it wasn't putting on a histrionic show for friends at parties.

In the late summer of 1953 her old adversary Pierre Wertheimer provided this trigger for her when he was summoned to the Beau-Rivage to (at least on the surface) explain No. 5's lagging sales. Chanel knew the perfume business was running out of steam and something was needed to galvanise and reinvigorate the brand. She had an idea. It would take money of course, money she did not have. All she had was her genius and her tenacity, her capacity for hard work, and, of course, the name, the magical name that conjured up a whole raft of exotic financial possibilities.

Pierre was enchanted, maybe even mesmerised. On offer was something akin to The Beatles re-forming after a decade of retirement. Expectations of a mountain of money and blanket publicity were too tantalising to refuse. Timing is everything, and by the end of the interview, a delighted and numb Pierre had not only agreed to fund her return to rue Cambon to 'save' the business but also cover all her expenses.

Whipping up the necessary publicity was comparatively easy with so many willing acolytes and collaborators in the fashion business on hand to help. All Chanel had to do was take them, one by one, into her confidence – just like the old days. Most prominent among the willing was probably Irish-born Carmel Snow of *Harper's Bazaar*.

The waspish Mrs Snow had been Harper's editor-in-chief since 1934 after formerly being fashion editor with *Vogue*. Her instincts were said to be infallible, but she was also renowned for dozing off at fashion shows, though this was probably the result of her famous liquid lunches: 'Waiters knew she would eschew food (unless jellied consommé counts as food) for a three-martini lunch, the first drink gulped down while the following two were sipped slowly with her characteristic elegance.'[10]

On 12 February 1947, at Dior's famous first show introducing his label, she stoically endured the freezing conditions of the austere surroundings bolt-upright in her usual front-row seat: '[The 90-piece] show over, the stunned audience remained mute until Carmel stood up and loudly baptized the collection, "Your dresses have such a new look!"'[11]

The 'New Look' moniker stuck and stuck to her as the leading herald of France's post-war fashion rejuvenation.

Carmel's personal look was tailored Cristóbal Balenciaga suits and pale-blue curled hair, finished off with a string of sea-island pearls. By the end of the Spanish designer's celebrated first show in 1937, she was championing him so enthusiastically that Harper's entire Paris issue was devoted to his collection. She was totally smitten with Balenciaga, believing they were both in love, though Balenciaga was gay and had a long-standing relationship with the Franco-Polish millionaire Władzio Jaworowski d'Attainville (who helped fund his fashion business) as well as the occasional dalliance with his milliner. Everyone knew except Mrs Snow, but no one dared tell her, such was the power and influence she wielded throughout the world of fashion.

Chanel dangled the tantalising possibility of her return before Carmel Snow soon after the deal with Pierre Wertheimer was struck, writing to her in the autumn of 1953: 'I thought it would be fun to work again ... you know I might one day create a new style adapted to today's living ... I feel that this time has come.'[12]

Of course, the sensational news spread as only fashion gossip spreads: fast and loose. She either received effusive congratulations or stony silence from her designer peers. Chanel was such a polarising figure throughout her career, the uneven reaction wasn't unexpected. She didn't care. She never cared. The only couturier she ever admired was Balenciaga.

Things began to move. A momentum had been created that was unstoppable, inevitable. On 21 December 1953, *The New York Times* announced Chanel's first show after a squillion years (actually fifteen) would occur on Friday, 5 February 1954 in Paris.

Meanwhile the dusty, deserted workrooms on the second floor of Maison CHANEL at rue Cambon were swept and re-painted. Structurally, the place had changed little from the 1930s: 'No. 31, Rue Cambon looks neither like a museum, a bar, nor a revue. It looks what it is, a shop—de luxe and glassy, but still a shop. Upstairs and behind the glass scenes it is a rabbit warren of corkscrew staircases, labyrinthine corridors, and sodden doors.'[13]

In tandem with the restoration, Mademoiselle's former staff were reassembled from *maisons* around the capital, where they had sought sanctuary after she closed her business in 1939. They had forgiven but not forgotten her. Madame Lucie, once Chanel's chef de *cabinet*, left her own shop at 18 rue Royale and brought with her over thirty ex-Maison CHANEL staff from the 1920s and '30s. The troop included the formidable Manon Ligeour, who had started with Chanel at the age of 13 and worked her way up to become a distinguished premier.

And then, in swept Mademoiselle herself, gold bangles jangling, '... a spare spruce sparrow voluble and vital as a woodpecker',[14] with a Camel cigarette drooping from her mouth, looking as if all the dangerous manoeuvres and deceptions of the past ten years had merely been a series of unhappy dreams.

18

FIASCO

Rising like a medieval monastery out of the long grass at Pantin, a commune on the suburban fringes of Paris, is the Patrimoine, the holy sepulchre of Maison CHANEL.

While 31 rue Cambon, where Chanel founded her fashion business in 1910, might be Chanel's shrine, the Patrimoine is where her legacy is protected, carefully maintained, strictly controlled, and meticulously preserved ... much like the way Chanel approached the conservation of her mind, body, and story during her life.

The Patrimoine building (the word literally means 'heritage') is a dead ringer for the Aubazine orphanage that shaped Chanel's aesthetic and which she tried to strangle into obscurity. The interior has been described as like a:

> Chanel No 5 box exploded to engulf entire floors. The whole place is coloured black and white: the rolling storage lockers, familiar from photographs of archival spaces and usually cranked by hand, are here sleekly automated, their exteriors lacquered a glossy black. Inside, clothes are temperature controlled and veiled in specially tailored, semi-transparent white covers, protected from the elements and one another. Before a garment is permitted into this inner sanctum, it is subjected to a biblical 40 days and nights in a hermetically sealed space to eradicate any pestilence inside its fibres.[1]

The Patrimoine's archives of clothing, paper, and financial accounts of Chanel's beauty and perfume businesses amount to more than 100,000 items, presided over by twenty conservators in black-and-white

CHANEL outfits moving noiselessly through the corridors like nuns. Visits are a rare privilege. Generally, access is given to new CHANEL staff as part of their induction process and to long-standing, deep-spending haute couture clients (known as 'The Club') who spend time within the Holy of Holies soaking in the history of their clothes' creator and then, sufficiently lubricated with the CHANEL ethos, are presumably chauffeur-driven back to rue Cambon for the commissioning of new pieces to add to their own collections.

The oldest, most sacred item in the Patrimoine is a blouse from 1916 made six years after Chanel inaugurated her hat business, CHANEL Modes, at 21 rue Cambon (the earliest labels feature that address prior to Chanel's relocation to 31 rue Cambon in 1918). The CHANEL conservators consider this blouse their *Mona Lisa*, the Holy Grail of all the sacred relics they have been entrusted to preserve. It is a pliable silk jersey, a soft material that Chanel controversially stole from Edwardian men's undergarments, as used by her English boyfriend, Boy Capel. Even in the 1930s this garment was famous in the fashion world and was described as 'a cobalt tricot sailor frock that might have been worn, at least in masquerade, by the French navy.'[2]

Back then and today, this one garment, created over 100 years ago, is precious because it single-handedly symbolises Chanel's uncompromising devotion to freedom and simplicity, a line of design and construction she rigorously pursued throughout her life.

Even her first hats embodied this addictive, captivating simplicity that was so different from the contrasting feather-embellished, wide-brimmed designs produced by contemporary milliners in *vogue* at the time. The starkness of this new direction was enthusiastically embraced by Chanel's growing clientele and was the catalyst in the establishment of a second store on rue Gontaut-Biron in the fashionable resort town of Deauville, where she began to diversify into uncomplicated garments purged of the intricate embellishments and stifling, emasculating intricacies of the period:

> Women were full of gussets, garters, corsets, whalebones, plackets, false hair, and brassieres ... Chanel began turning out matrons and débutantes on whom unornamented, workmanlike, though expensive, gowns and glass jewelry were exciting, chic, and becoming ...

at any rate mondaine Parisian women breathed freely and were at ease for the first time in French history.[3]

It is hard to imagine now, but Chanel's charming convent-inspired simplicity was perceived as subversive and dangerous when her clothes first appeared. They exuded a feeling of freedom and *Libération*, independence, and a free expression of that spirit: dangerous things for early twentieth-century bourgeoise French women to embrace. But, by the early 1930s, the revolution in French tastes and fashion she inspired was well underway, prompting Janet Flanner in 1931 to famously write in *The New Yorker* that Chanel 'has put the apache's sweater into the Ritz, utilised the ditch-digger's scarf, made chic the white collars and cuffs of the waitress, and put queens into mechanics' tunics'.[4]

When Chanel died on 10 January 1971, Maison CHANEL had zero examples of her past work apart from what was being prepared for the February show and the contents of Mademoiselle's wardrobe. The exquisite clothes of the greatest fashion figure of the twentieth century had been pragmatically scattered throughout the world without a single thought as to their historical importance and value. Even now, some fifty years after her death, and despite the immense volume of artefacts contained with the Patrimoine, only around 600 pieces from Chanel's forty-six-year working life as a couturière have been collected and held in the vaults.

The idea of capturing and preserving the handmade products of Maison CHANEL bearing the touch of its *maîtresse* had not yet formed. Historically, in common with most other fashion houses, Maison CHANEL did not see the point in preserving its collections. Quite the opposite, in fact. The stigma of leftovers from previous shows cluttering up a thriving Maison's studio was quickly dealt with to ward off any lingering bad luck or scent of failure. The prevailing custom was that outfits modelled at the Maison's fashion shows were sold off after a negotiated discount to clients or discreet friends of the house. In some cases, they were even given away.

On Saturday 2 December 1978, Christie's in London staged Chanel's last fashion show of pieces bearing her personal touch when it auctioned a collection that had been assembled by her former assistant, Lilian Grumbach. It included items from Chanel's own wardrobe: forty-three pieces of costume jewellery and sixty-seven suits, dresses, shoes, and accessories in total.

Nobody knew it at the time, but it was the start of an ensuing mania for vintage clothes, especially haute couture vintage.

The bidding was frenzied that evening. Though pitched as a chic party by the auctioneers, decorum soon went out the window according to *The New York Times*. After a champagne reception, the stylish audience filled three rooms in a demonstration of Chanel's pulling power:

> It was also a demonstration of the discomforts people will endure in the search for glamour. A few times, the presale party became almost frightening as people trampled for position near the countesses and the television cameras. One woman was thrown with some force against a wall as a man shoved his way into the main floodlit room where 'the action' was ... Hundreds of expensively dressed people sloshed champagne and studied each other for signs of beautifulness as they elbowed through the high-ceilinged old sales rooms.[5]

With the exception of a bodice Chanel designed for herself in 1930, all the clothes in the auction dated from the years after her comeback show in 1954. The Oslo Museum paid the highest price: US$4,800 for a tweed jacket and skirt bordered with braid and bright-pink silk that Chanel often wore. The Smithsonian in Washington bought a glen-plaid suit and a midnight-blue handbag (one of eight sold) stitched with the initials 'CC' that contained an atomiser of CHANEL No. 22. The price was US$800. The V&A Museum nabbed a black-and-white suit accompanied by a straw boater hat. The Geneva jewellers Xoilan took away US$16,000 of costume jewellery that included an oval filigree brooch said to have been Chanel's favourite piece for US$2,000. The Baroness de Rothschild bought the only sample on sale of Chanel's famous little black dress (from Chanel's winter 1960 collection), a short silk chiffon dress with spaghetti straps for US$3,000. Two of the white cotton smocks that Chanel wore while working were bought by British museums for US$1,170 and US$741. British interior designer John Sidderley bought two tunics at US$975 and US$682 for his wife's collection.

Christie's claimed the sale total was US$133,877. However, this figure also included US$20,280 of items that were bought by the auction house because they did not reach the reserve price. More than one-quarter of the suits and dresses in the collection were not sold. Among these were the last two suits that she made for herself and another suit that she wore when the Duke and Duchess of Windsor dined with her.

Maison CHANEL bought nothing and wasn't even present at the sale. That all changed in 1983 when the Patrimoine was founded and began reassembling Maison CHANEL's past. The catalyst was Karl Lagerfeld's first collection for the house that year that was inspired and based on Chanel's rangy designs of the 1930s.

If the 1916 jersey cobalt tricot sailor frock is the Patrimoine's Mona Lisa, then the few pieces they have squirrelled away from Chanel's sensational comeback show of 5 February 1954 are its Turin Shroud. These clothes represent the resurrection of Maison CHANEL from the black hole of the brand's sixteen-year period of inactivity when most people in the fashion world thought it was dead and buried. Even so, Chanel's much hyped 5 February 1954 comeback collection was almost an extinction event in itself. Almost.

Initially, it was viewed by the majority of critics and witnesses as a disaster.

After so many excruciating years of controversy, mayhem, and life-threatening danger, the Maison, the brand, and its 71-year-old creator were unexpectedly teetering on the knife edge of irrelevance and failure once again. And once again, Chanel had only herself to blame for organising such a rushed, hastily put-together, sparse show after so many years away. Instinctively she knew, like most of Paris knew, that after what seemed like an eternity (actually fifteen years) of enforced inactivity she might have lost her touch, and her first show in well over a decade wasn't going to be a wholly convincing vindication of her mad scramble to return to the epicentre of haute couture action.[6] Rather than postpone or cancel, Mademoiselle decided to roll the dice on her life once more, as she had always done. But the strain was telling. On the night before her comeback show, she became ill with severe stomach cramps and nausea.[7]

The collection she presented the next day was called N°5 (what else?) and comprised only thirty pieces, some of which had actually been taken out of a cheap cardboard box of outfits dating from the 1930s in a desperate attempt to make up a meaningful number.[8] Ironically, no one present noticed the difference between these clothes and the new ones that were presented. What everyone did notice was that Chanel's basic style had not varied since the 1930s.

The select audience inside the atelier on rue Cambon was mesmerised. Every seat was taken on that chilly, overcast day. All 200 guests turned up, on time, causing a scramble for the best seats to view what, for many, was a historical event. European, French, American, and British critics were either jammed into corners or huddled uncomfortably on the cold floor, some at the feet of their rivals and sworn enemies of only a few years ago.

From America, there were the heavy hitters like Bettina Ballard for *Vogue*, Carmel Snow for *Harper's Bazaar*, and Sally Kirkland for *Life* magazine. Of course, the Parisian editors from *Vogue, Elle, Paris Match*, and *Marie Claire* were all there, as were newspaper editors from *L'Oracle, Combat, Figaro*, and the rest. Most importantly for Chanel were the buyers from most of the big American and British stores. They were allocated optimum seats but, in accordance with universal fashion tradition, their reservation cards were switched by fashion hounds in the hustle and bustle generated by the early arrivals to less advantageous spots at the back.[9]

For two hours, guests stewed in uncomfortable silence watching a parade of well-known Chanel staples: tweed suits and neat blouses. Meanwhile, Mademoiselle had managed to drag herself out of bed. Throughout the tense proceedings she watched from her usual position, crouched at the top of the winding iron staircase, looking down at everything and everyone from her favourite spot above the fray. She was implacable. Calm. Probably fortified by a dose of friendly morphine or two. On the stroke of 12, the models sauntered out to start the défilé. Chanel had taught them to glide with imperiously stretched necks, hips thrust out, one hand cradling a simple white card with the outfit's number handwritten on it.

The first outfit to make its way into the full glare of the atelier to open her show was a collarless box jacket suit in navy wool jersey simply called 5 (Chanel detested the prevailing custom of giving names to her clothes and had abandoned the conceit long before) worn by a long-legged brunette model.[10] It was complemented by a creamy cotton blouse buttoned down to the skirt (to prevent it riding up) with a ribbon tied at the collar that resembled an exaggerated men's bow tie Chanel had worn at the time of her first collection delivered before the advent of the First World War.

Her friend Charles-Roux described the mood in the room: '[It] resembled that of a courtroom in the final minutes before a verdict.'[11]

Like her clothes, the stage on which they appeared were similarly stripped down, left bereft of all adornment: no music or flowers; no programme was handed out. It had the feel of what it was: a snapshot of a *maison* gathering itself with as much dignity as it could muster after a decade or more on the run.

It took a while for it all to sink in – a sharp intake of breath, a pause before the storm. When the verdicts eventually poured in, it was like an avalanche of bad news. The French attitude, most probably coloured by the notorious abandonment of her business and her country, plus her well-known collaborationist activities during the war, was to be expected:

> Michel Déon, member of the French Academy, was at the opening. He published an article in Les Nouvelles littéraires: 'The French press were atrocious in their vulgarity, meanness, and stupidity. They drubbed away at her age (71) assuring everyone that she had learned nothing in the fifteen years of silence. We watched the mannequins file by in icy silence' ... The looks on the faces of the press and buyers showed skepticism. Her collection was nothing like the current 'New Look'. As Janet Wallach puts it: 'Chanel was seen as the antichrist.' There were grimaces and snickers breaking the icy silence in the room. Life magazine was courteous and American *Vogue* applauded. *Vogue* saying: 'The Chanel look, as specific as [water], meant a combination of youth, comfort, jersey, pearls, of luxury hidden away.'[12]

The prevailing French media view was that Chanel's 'look' was mired in the past, which it certainly was based on the evidence on show. L'Aurore thought the clothes had 'the figure of 1930 – no breasts, no waist, no hips'.[13]

Le Monde relished using the word 'fiasco' in its splenetic review. Even *Le Figaro* wrote condescendingly: 'It was really quite touching. One could have thought oneself back in 1925.'[14]

And the plummy, cocky reviewer for Britain's *Daily Mail* tried to be funny: 'It was a fashion show for grandmothers, but I must say I had always thought of Grandma as more elegant than that.'[15] The paper also dubbed it 'a fiasco'.[16]

On the other side of the ledger, the magazines *Elle*, *Paris Match*, and *Marie Claire* were more sympathetic, taking a more balanced view, not exactly enthusiastic, but not exactly desiring to stick a knife into the venerable scary monster that filled the room at rue Cambon. The American press generally saw it as the re-emergence of sturdy simplicity after a decade of the froths and frills of the New Look.

But there was some good news, mostly from the American side. A four-page spread of the February designs appeared in the 1 March 1954 issue of *Life* magazine. The accompanying article noted the repetition of style over nearly thirty years: 'Chanel has lost none of her skill. Her styles hark back to her best of the '30s—lace evening dresses that have plenty of elegant dash and easy-fitting suits that are refreshing after the "poured-on" look of some styles.'[17]

Following the disappointment of the February show and sensing another chance for salvation, Maison CHANEL went all out for another shoot, this time for the March issue of American *Vogue*. The elegant, enigmatic face of CHANEL throughout the 1950s, Marie-Hélène Arnaud, was photographed by Henry Clarke. Arnaud wore three carefully selected outfits:

> ... a red dress with a V-neck pared [sic] with ropes of pearls, a tiered seersucker evening gown, and a jersey suit, navy-blue, mid-calf, slightly padded square-shouldered cardigan jacket, with patch pockets, sleeves that unbuttoned back showing crisp white cuffs, together with a muslin blouse sporting a perky collar and bow at the neck. The blouse stayed in place with tabs that buttoned onto the waistline of the A-line skirt.[18]

Bettina Ballard, fashion editor of *Vogue*, bought the jersey suit for herself. It was a good omen. American orders for the clothes Arnaud modelled poured in. By the second and third collections after the much-vaunted return, the negative tide had well and truly turned. *Life* admitted she had miscalculated with her initial 1954 offering but now 'she is influencing everything. At 71 she is bringing in more than a style—a revolution.'[19]

The Maison's perseverance had paid off. But it was another close-run thing in the life of Mademoiselle Coco Chanel. In interviews after her post-war success was secured, she was described as a 'formidable charmer [with] the unquenchable vitality of a twenty year old'[20] and a personality that was 'snappy, feisty and forthright'.[21] But in the immediate aftermath of her February 1954 show, things were not that rosy.

While Chanel was alone at the rue Cambon atelier, with no one around but still working, her old jousting partner Pierre Wertheimer, who had financed her disastrous return, visited her. The question of what to do naturally came up. True to form, Chanel was working on her next collection, busily snipping the hem of some tweedy fabric. She shrugged. She was not ready to concede defeat in the contest of life.

'You know, I want to go on, go on and win,' she told him.

'You're right,' he said. 'You're right to go on.'[22]

On the strength of this determination to succeed, Pierre negotiated a new deal with Chanel: the Wertheimers would finance the Maison's headquarters on rue Cambon, the remuneration of her staff, any expenses associated with her collections, her personal expenditures, and all her taxes for the duration of her life in exchange for total ownership of the brand. In the absence of official Chanel heirs, they would also receive her perfume royalty payments on her death. Several years later, the Wertheimers acquired the remaining 20 per cent of Maison CHANEL.

The most extraordinary person of the twentieth century had won everything she could possibly win in her lifetime, including a crucial amount of privacy and deception that was necessary to sustain the sumptuous façade of her life. She had achieved it all on her own exhilarating terms, in her own exhilarating way, through all the good and dangerous times of her life.

And Mademoiselle kept on winning in the never-ending procession of skirmishes, battles, and wars her life embodied. Even after death, she remained victorious. As she once told Paul Morand: 'I have never known failure ... I have succeeded totally in everything I have undertaken.'[23]

POSTSCRIPT: SHADOWS DEEP AND LONG

All over France, especially in the little villages and towns where the pockmarks of bullets fired in anger still remain on ancient churches and railway stations, people gather to honour French *Résistance* fighters who died to liberate their country from the Nazis.

It is D-Day, 6 June, and I am in the village of Savonnières on the glassy river Cher between Tours and the Renaissance Château de Villandry. The village square is bathed in warm late-afternoon sunshine. After the midday speeches and laughter and silent tears had come lunch *en plein air* (in the open air), when the villagers set a vast array of homemade dishes on giant trestle tables covered in red-and-white checkered tablecloths, the entire picnic banquet shimmering under a sagging network of triangular French flags pegged like washing to lines of string.

But now, after plenty of local Touraine wine and the luxury of a summery afternoon nap, the few *Résistance* survivors remaining in the village and the families of those that either could not make it or who had died, had gathered in front of the local *mairie* on deck chairs and other plastic outdoor furniture for a final gathering of cakes and coffee before everyone peeled away for another year.

Many of the women went from table to table, carrying another round of homemade desserts to share with friends and strangers. As each dessert was passed around, people became more and more talkative, and yet, strangely, no one spoke about the war or recalled past exploits, good or bad. It was as if there was a secret and silent communion between the survivors and the families of those who had passed away that transcended the need for speech because they knew that speech somehow tended to devalue, tended to minimise the deeds of the past. Instead, as children in shorts and soiled T-shirts wheeled about playing tag or flirted with strangers, parents sipped their drinks, musing about this or that mundane domestic issue, and the elderly chewed their gums cocooned in thought; the talk was about how the weather was unusually warm for this time of year: not a cloud or drop of rain in sight. A hat to shade the face was exactly what was needed on a day like today. If only they had thought of it.

There were still plenty of leftovers from the feast of family recipes saved from the earlier banquet now covered in tinfoil and sheets of glistening plastic, plus of course lots of bread and cheese. But nobody was that interested in eating except the children, who skimmed the cream off the tops of fruit trifles with their fingers and stuffed the remains of flaky *saucisse en croûte apéro* (sausage rolls) into their pockets.

One old veteran, however, nudged me in the ribs and then gestured with his wizened head at another creased and gnarled individual dozing in a wheelchair opposite us. 'See that old bastard?' he said in impeccable English. 'He saved my life once.'

I nodded and sipped my coffee. 'When was that?'

'A few years ago when I fell over in my garden and he saw me.'

And that was the extent of my conversations on a day that had been set aside across the world to commemorate the tremendous outpouring of heroism under fire that even touched on the subject of death.

My friend Henri shrugged when I casually brought it up at his bar the next day. 'The French don't like to talk about it because there is much bullshit around it,' he explained. 'People say they are *Résistance* when they were not and …' he shrugged again, '… how do you know? The government say they have all the names but that is bullshit too. No one knows. Not even the people in the *Résistance* know.' He tapped his head. 'Memory is a trick many people in France use to get away with murder.' He folded his dishcloth and went to serve someone else.

I learned there were not that many things the French didn't like talking about, but the subject of the *Résistance*, and collaborators, was one of them. They had no qualms about pointing out bullet-riddled buildings that saw action during the *Libération*, or which mansions in the best streets served as the headquarters of the Gestapo, the SS, or where the town's Jews were held and interrogated. They spoke candidly about the origins of street names that were associated with appeaser politicians, left/right-wing martyrs, even parts of their town that had to be razed, bulldozed into extinction because no one wanted to live there on account of their association with some heinous massacre or wartime tragedy. But to talk about actual figures, actual people who they knew were *Résistance* or who they thought were collaborators was rare. Maybe they were reticent to discuss such things in front of strangers, or foreigners like me, while in the company of family and people they grew up with, they were more relaxed speaking about such things?

That was probably true because, as I learned in the five years my family and I lived in France, if you were not French, you always felt there was this diaphanous but solid wall of familiarity that existed between you and any French friends you made. Sometimes it was overt and you could see and feel it hovering there in front of you or around you like a rigid curtain, but at other times it didn't drop until you wandered into a moment or tossed off a phrase and then snap (a click of the fingers) and a mask would spread across the face of the person you were having a joke with and you knew you had inadvertently crossed a line or wandered into territory you were excluded from entering on account of your nationality and upbringing.

Maybe this isn't just a French thing. Maybe this is a normal thing all over the world with certain subjects you feel are taboo in certain countries. Maybe, but unlike Germany and Japan (the war), and the United Kingdom and the United States (race), I never felt this phobia was as real or as pervasive as the moral dilemma created by the behaviour of some French citizens during the Second World War.

Take, for example, my other friend Gérard, whom I played tennis with two, three times a week and who invited my wife and I to numerous dinner parties at his place. I always felt each interaction was a kind of casual test that, if I somehow passed by whatever it was I said or how I reacted, I'd be permitted into a different area of intimacy and familiarity. It wasn't a big deal, and I never felt intimidated by it, but I'd be disingenuous if I said it wasn't there or it didn't exist. It was only after five years of friendship, when my family and I were leaving the country to return home, that Gérard paid me the ultimate compliment after a long, well-lubricated lunch by saying, 'Mon ami, I know I can trust you with this thing I have on my back, my family has on the back. You know, there are some places in this town I cannot go because of what we did in the past, you know?'

I nodded.

He shrugged. 'Nothing can change that but there are many families like this here.'

'What do you do?' I asked.

Another shrug but this time with a laugh and a slap on my shoulder as if I'd supplied him with the punchline of a gag. 'Only thing I can do, never go there.'

I didn't realise the reality of this serious sentiment, wrapped in a light-hearted crust, until I was halfway through writing this book, and then it occurred to me that, along with the excruciating pain of memory, there is also the pain of suppression.

In France, the pain of suppression is diluted by physically avoiding its origin. For many, it seems like the only way to survive it. That and a kind of ambivalence or numbness, call it what you will, a quintessentially French quality best expressed in the opening lines of *L'Étranger*, the most devastatingly beautiful novel ever written in any language, begun and finished by the outsider Albert Camus as the Nazis approached Paris in 1940: '*Aujourd'hui Maman est morte. Ou peut-être hier, je ne sais pas.*' (My mother died today. Or maybe yesterday, I don't know.)[1]

The scars run deep. They always will. Like the shadows on that long-ago afternoon on the banks of the Cher that ran away into the night, they get deeper and longer with time. Who am I, a comfortable and well-fed foreigner, to judge what is normal and what is not in circumstances, situations I have no direct or indirect experience of? That is my dilemma as a historian, as a writer, as a husband, as a father, as a son, and a brother. As a friend. It is the inconvenient truth of my life and profession. It is the load I cannot shake off my back.

So then, what do I as an outsider personally think about the actions and activities of the one person in France's Second World War narrative that no one in France wants to talk about? I believe Chanel collaborated with the Nazis for four reasons: initially to rescue her nephew, André Palasse, from internment; secondly, to win back control of her perfume business from the Wertheimers; thirdly, because she had to justify her privileged status in Nazi-controlled Paris and earn her keep; and fourthly, because she could not get out of the arrangement she and her lover had so cosily negotiated with the Nazi hierarchy. It was convenient for Chanel to play along, go along, keep going with the arrangement, because the alternative was too hideous to contemplate: losing everything she had worked and scraped and schemed for – ending up a loser.

She was dependent on the Nazis for so many critical things: drugs, money, food, safety, status, all the things she could not, would not, live without. As previously expressed, she was a survivor and was adept at surviving whatever her life threw at her through a dynamic mix of wits, guile, and an absolute determination to win with whatever it took to win. Every day under the Nazis was a test, an examination of survival. She didn't need haute couture to survive. She needed haute couture to live, a different thing altogether.

Was she ashamed about this? In any way remorseful? Embarrassed she had survived when so many had not? As the record of her interview with MI6's Malcolm Muggeridge and the extreme lengths she went to in order to deceive and suppress the truth with her money shows, she was none of these things. She was defiant, witheringly, defensively, imperiously so. Muggeridge was struck by her immense reservoir of strength, not steely strength, but bottomless, fathomless, infinite reserves of raw determination and the conviction that whatever she did was the right thing for her to do. Distasteful? Certainly, but necessary. Chanel was clever. Some might call it peasant cunning, and there is no doubt she had that, but she also had something else, a ruthless cleverness that made her almost invincible, almost untouchable, formidable. In describing this quality, I am reminded of how Jean Cocteau, a similar 'monster', was reputed to have described her: 'She looks at you tenderly, nods her head, and you're condemned to death!'[2]

Am I condemning her? Do I think she is guilty of willingly committing unspeakable acts during a war? Do I like her? Do I admire her?

Do you?

ACKNOWLEDGEMENTS

To my wife for her unwavering support throughout this journey.

To my agent, Andrew Lownie, for believing in the project, shaping the initial story, and championing it tirelessly.

To my editor at The History Press, Claire Hartley, for bringing out the best in me, providing insightful, constructive suggestions throughout, and turning my incomplete drafts into a proper book.

To my friends Gérard Durand (de Brinon family) and Henri Couraud, whom I first met in the Touraine during the early 2000s, and their willingness to share sensitive family correspondence concerning the activities, both good and bad, of relatives engaged in surviving the Second World War by any means possible.

To the archivists at both the Centre historique des archives, département de l'armée de terre at Vincennes and the Centre de Recherches des Archives Nationales in Paris for their patience in putting up with my impossible French and pedantic probing.

To my friends and colleagues at the Royal Scots Club in Edinburgh, where this book was mostly written, for enduring endless lectures on the subject when we really should have been watching rugby, drinking the excellent house beer, or just browsing the papers.

To my fellow cricket coaches and players at George Herriot's School for taking my mind off things whenever I reached a dead end.

And to my readers who have stuck by me, my sincere and heartfelt *merci*.

NOTES

Timeline of Key Events
1 Charles-Roux, E., *L'irreguliere: Ou, Mon Itineraire Chanel* (Grasset, 1974) pp. 536–537
2 Mazzeo, T., *The Secret of Chanel No. 5* (HarperCollins, 2010) p. 150

Introduction: Atelier No. 5
1 Cocteau, J., *Théâtre: Les Monstres sacrés. La Machine à écrire. Renaud et Armide. L'Aigle à deux tête* (Gallimard, 1962)
2 Herald, G.W., 'The life and times of the amazing COCO CHANEL', *The Australian Women's Weekly*, 13 January 1965
3 Flanner, J., '31, rue Cambon: Coco Chanel's Revolutionary Style', *The New Yorker*, 14 March 1931
4 Picardie, J., *Coco Chanel: The Legend and the Life* (HarperCollins, 2010) p. 188
5 Capote, T., *Portraits and Observations* (Random House, 2007) p. 220
6 web.archive.org/web/20240129095119/http://lastyeargirl.blogspot.com/2013/05/the-world-of-carmel-snow.html
7 20 July 1969 interview with journalist and TV presenter Micheline Sandrel, available on YouTube in two parts via French TV archives institute INA
8 Anderson, A., 'Coco Chanel – Her Re-Entry', *Classic Chicago Magazine*, 17 January 2021
9 Flanner, '31, rue Cambon'
10 Herald, 'The life and times of the amazing COCO CHANEL'
11 Flanner, '31, rue Cambon'
12 www.newyorksocialdiary.com/my-love-affair-with-chanel-part-iii
13 Ibid., part ii
14 Choderlos de Laclos, P., *Les Liaisons Dangereuses* (Penguin Books, 2007)
15 Hampton, C., *Les Liaisons Dangereuses* from the novel by Choderlos de Laclos (Faber & Faber, 1985)
16 www.newyorksocialdiary.com/my-love-affair-with-chanel-part-ii
17 Picardie, *Coco Chanel*
18 www.areaofdesign.com/coco-chanel
19 Delay, C., *Chanel Solitaire*, translated by Barbara Bray (Collins, 1973), p. 190
20 Ibid., p. 191
21 www.areaofdesign.com/coco-chanel
22 Ibid.
23 www.10magazine.com/chanel-speaking-in-code
24 Picardie, *Coco Chanel*, p. 272
25 www.newyorksocialdiary.com/my-love-affair-with-chanel-part-iii

26 Flanner, '31, rue Cambon'
27 Wilson, A., 'Coco Chanel's other life', *Tatler*, 22 May 2017
28 Capote, *Portraits and Observations*, p. 221
29 Reed, R., 'Coco Chapel's Clothes and Jewelry Are Auctioned in London', *The New York Times*, 4 December 1978
30 Ibid.
31 Barchfield, J., 'New book claims Coco Chanel was anti-Semite and Nazi spy', *The Associated Press*, 17 August 2011
32 McAuley, J., 'The Exchange: Coco Chanel and the Nazi Party', *The New Yorker*, 31 August 2011
33 www.chanel-muggeridge.co.uk
34 William Ewart Gladstone as quoted in *The Spectator*, Volumes 168–169 (1942) p. 182, 'Duty of a Prime Minister'
35 Muggeridge, M., *Chronicles of Wasted Time Part 2: The Infernal Grove* (Fontana Books, 1981) p. 248

Chapter 1

1 www.thelandofdesire.com/2020/01/16/coco-chanel
2 www.messynessychic.com/2017/10/31/the-27-inch-dolls-that-saved-post-war-paris-as-the-fashion-capital
3 Étiève-Cartwright, B., 'French Fashion during the German Occupation', *World History Encyclopedia* (online), 2 October 2024
4 Ibid.
5 Gildea, R., *Marianne in Chains* (Pan Macmillan, 2002) Introduction
6 www.theparisreview.org/blog/2016/09/19/paris-camuss-notebooks
7 King, D., *Death in the City of Light: The Serial Killer of Nazi-Occupied Paris* (Crown, 2011)
8 'Paul Collette, the man who shot Pierre Laval and Marcel Deat, is expected to be condemned and executed early this week, the Vichy correspondent of the Basler Nachrichten said today', *The New York Times*, 1 September 1941, p. 6
9 Pascal, J., 'Vichy's shame', *The Guardian*, 11 May 2002
10 www.smithsonianmag.com/history/vichy-government-france-world-war-ii-willingly-collaborated-nazis-180967160/
11 Gildea, *Marianne in Chains*, Introduction
12 Lot 1, ADOLF HITLER'S FUHRER ORDER TO PREPARE DEFENSES FOR D-DAY (www.alexautographs.com/auction-lot/adolf-hitler-s-fuhrer-order-to-prepare-defenses-f_4FF4826953)
13 www.iwm.org.uk/history/the-german-response-to-d-day
14 Ibid.
15 Venohr, W., *Stauffenberg, Symbol of Resistance: The Man Who Almost Killed Hitler* (Frontline Books, 2019)
16 Mazzeo, T.J., *The Hotel on Place Vendôme: Life, Death, and Betrayal at the Hotel Ritz in Paris* (HarperCollins, 2014) Chapter 7
17 First published in French during the 1960s as *From Sevastopol to Paris: A soldier among the soldiers*
18 Named after the Roman Emperor Nero, who, according to legend, orchestrated the Great Fire of Rome in AD 64
19 Randall, C., 'General "spared Paris by disobeying Führer"', *The Daily Telegraph*, 24 August 2004
20 Melvin, J., 'Nazi general didn't save Paris: historian', *The Local*, 25 August 2014
21 Ibid.

22 Ibid.
23 Kladstrup, D., *Wine and War: The French, the Nazis, and the Battle for France's Greatest Treasure* (Broadway Books, 2002) p. 275
24 Melvin, 'Nazi general didn't save Paris'

Chapter 2
1 Mazzeo, *The Hotel on Place Vendôme*, Chapter 8
2 www.thelandofdesire.com/2020/02/27/french-resistance
3 Ibid.
4 Ibid.
5 Argyle, R., *The Paris Game: Charles de Gaulle, the Liberation of Paris, and the Gamble that Won France* (Dundurn, 2014) pp. 215–223
6 www.nationalww2museum.org/war/articles/first-lieutenant-levitt-c-beck-jr
7 Argyle, *The Paris Game*
8 Cobb, M., *Eleven Days in August: The Liberation of Paris in 1944* (Simon & Schuster, 2013) p. 287
9 Ibid.
10 www.lithub.com/on-hitlers-last-desperate-plan-to-destroy-paris
11 Ibid.
12 Muggeridge, M., *Chronicles of Wasted Time Part 2*, pp. 249–250
13 www.lithub.com
14 Muggeridge, *Chronicles of Wasted Time Part 2*, pp. 249–250
15 Ibid., p. 250
16 Millington, C., *France in the Second World War: Collaboration, Resistance, Holocaust, Empire* (Bloomsbury Publishing, 2020) pp. 148–152
17 Antony Beevor, 'An ugly carnival', *The Guardian*, 5 June 2009
18 Brook, T., 'Collaboration in the History of Wartime East Asia', *The Asia-Pacific Journal*, 2 July 2008
19 Millington, *France in the Second World War*, p. 57
20 Mah, A., 'This Picture Tells a Tragic Story of What Happened to Women After D-Day', *Time*, 6 June 2018
21 Millington, *France in the Second World War*, p. 150
22 Judt, T., *Postwar: A History of Europe Since 1945* (Pimlico, 2007) p. 46
23 Norwell Smith, G., *The Oxford History of World Cinema* (Oxford University Press, 1997) p. 347

Chapter 3
1 Muggeridge, *Chronicles of Wasted Time Part 2*, p. 267
2 Ibid.
3 Flanner, J., '31, rue Cambon: Coco Chanel's revolutionary style', *The New Yorker*, 14 March 1931
4 Vaughan, H., *Sleeping with the Enemy* (Vintage Books, 2012) p. 147
5 www.newyorksocialdiary.com/my-love-affair-with-chanel-part-iii
6 Vaughan, *Sleeping with the Enemy*, p. 148
7 Ibid.
8 Muggeridge, *Chronicles of Wasted Time Part 2*, p. 267
9 Ibid., p. 268
10 Ibid.
11 Charles-Roux, E., *Chanel*, translated by Nancy Amphoux (Alfred A. Knopf, 1975) p. 318

12 Muggeridge, *Chronicles of Wasted Time Part 2*, p. 267
13 Madsen, A., *Coco Chanel: A Biography* (Bloomsbury 2009) p. 3
14 Flanner, '31, rue Cambon'
15 To encourage the look, she invented a new type of brassiere that suppressed the bust as much as possible

Chapter 4
1 Picardie, J., 'The secret life of Coco Chanel', *The Daily Telegraph*, 5 September 2010
2 Ibid.
3 Ibid.
4 Wilson, B., 'Why are you so fat?', *London Review of Books*, Vol. 32 No. 1, 7 January 2010
5 Ibid.
6 Delay, C., *Chanel Solitaire*, translated by Barbara Bray (Collins, 1973) p. 150
7 Vaughan, H., *Sleeping with the Enemy* (Vintage Books, 2012) p. 31
8 Flanner, '31, rue Cambon'
9 www.messynessychic.com/2012/04/03/coco-chanel-was-definitely-a-nazi
10 Herald, G.W., 'The life and times of the amazing COCO CHANEL', *The Australian Women's Weekly*, 13 January 1965, pp. 23–30
11 Ibid.
12 Flanner, '31, rue Cambon'
13 Morand, P., *L'Allure de Chanel* (Hermann, 1996) p. 166
14 Delay, *Chanel Solitaire*, p. 172
15 www.thejc.com/lifestyle/features/how-far-did-the-uk-aristocracy-s-love-of-the-nazis-really-go
16 www.thelandofdesire.com/2020/01/16/coco-chanel
17 Vaughan, *Sleeping with the Enemy*, p. 111
18 National Trust, Chartwell
19 Ridley, G., *Bend'Or, Duke of Westminster: A Personal Memoir* (Quartet Books, 1986) p. 135
20 Vaughan, *Sleeping with the Enemy*, p. 45
21 Herald, 'The life and times of the amazing COCO CHANEL'
22 Muhlstein, A., 'The Cut of Coco', *The New York Review*, 9 October 2014
23 Muggeridge, M., *Chronicles of Wasted Time Part 2*, pp. 238–239
24 Ibid.
25 Ibid., pp. 239–240

Chapter 5
1 Seaton, J., *Pinkoes and Traitors: The BBC and the Nation, 1974–1987* (Profile Books, 2015) p. 225
2 Trevor-Roper, H., *The Wartime Journals*, edited by Richard Davenport-Hines (I.B. Tauris, 2012) p. 239
3 Ibid. p. 215
4 Holt, T., *The Deceivers: Allied Military Deception in the Second World War* (Skyhorse, 2007) p. 332
5 Camus, A., *The Fall* (Penguin Classics, 1990)
6 Mahoney, D.J., 'Rediscovering St. Mugg', *The Catholic Thing* (online), 13 October 2010
7 www.chanel-muggeridge.co.uk
8 Hastings, M., 'Smoke and Mirrors', *The New York Review*, 27 September 2018
9 Muggeridge, M., *Chronicles of Wasted Time Part 2*, pp. 267–268
10 Ibid.

11 Ibid., pp. 267–269
12 Ibid., p. 267
13 www.chanel-muggeridge.co.uk
14 Ibid.
15 Ibid.
16 www.chanel-muggeridge.co.uk
17 Ibid.
18 Ibid.
19 Ibid.
20 Ibid.

Chapter 6
1 Picardie, J., 'The secret life of Coco Chanel', *The Daily Telegraph*, 5 September 2010
2 www.10magazine.com/chanel-speaking-in-code
3 Fishman, S., 'Grand Delusions: The Unintended Consequences of Vichy France's Prisoner of War Propaganda', *Journal of Contemporary History*, 1991, pp. 229–254
4 www.thelandofdesire.com/2020/01/16/coco-chanel
5 Abescat, B. and Stavridès, Y., 'Behind the Chanel Empire … The Fabulous Story of the Wertheimers', *l'Express*, 2005
6 www.newyorksocialdiary.com/my-love-affair-with-chanel-part-iii
7 Pascal, J., 'Vichy's shame', *The Guardian*, 11 May 2002
8 www.bbc.co.uk/history/worldwars/genocide/jewish_deportation_01.shtml
9 Pascal, 'Vichy's shame'
10 Ibid.
11 Ibid.
12 de Rochemont, R., 'The French Underground', *Life*, 24 August 1942
13 everything.explained.today/German_military_administration_in_occupied_France_during_World_War_II/
14 www.you-books.com/book/L-Chaney/Coco-Chanel-An-Intimate-Life
15 Vaughan, H., *Sleeping with the Enemy* (Vintage Books, 2012) p. 142
16 Mitchell, A., *In Nazi Paris: The History of an Occupation, 1940–1944* (Berghahn Books, 2010) p. 13
17 Rosbottom, R.C., *When Paris Went Dark* (Little, Brown, 2014) p. 18
18 everything.explained.today/German_military_administration_in_occupied_France_during_World_War_II/
19 www.chanel-muggeridge.co.uk

Chapter 7
1 'Coco Chanel Biography Claims She Was a Nazi Spy', *The Hollywood Reporter*, 16 August 2011
2 Vaughan, H., 'Sleeping with the Enemy: Coco Chanel's Secret War', *The New York Times*, 2 September 2011
3 Lloyd, C., www.aspectsofhistory.com/rationing-and-the-black-market-in-paris-during-the-war
4 Ibid.
5 Centre historique des archives, département de l'armée de terre (archives du 2eme Bureau, Army Intelligence) 7NN 2717
6 CARAN Z/6/672 Justice file greffe 5559
7 Ibid.
8 Charles-Roux, *Chanel*, p. 321

9 Vaughan citing a *Services Spéciaux* file on Bedaux, p. 152
10 Vaughan quoted by Andy Walker, *BBC Today*, BBC Radio Four, 20 August 2011
11 Vaughan, p. 164
12 Ibid., pp. 164–165
13 Archives de la Préfecture de Police, Paris: Série BA 1990
14 Muggeridge, M., *Chronicles of Wasted Time Part 2*, p. 270
15 www.chanel-muggeridge.co.uk
16 Ibid.
17 Ibid.
18 Trevor-Roper, H., *The Wartime Journals*, pp. 214–215
19 www.chanel-muggeridge.co.uk
20 Ibid.

Chapter 8
1 Muggeridge, M., *Chronicles of Wasted Time Part 2*, p. 254
2 Centre de Recherches des Archives Nationales F/7/14939
3 Thurman, J., 'Scenes from a Marriage', *The New Yorker*, 15 May 2005
4 Series 7NN 2ème Bureau: 2145-2973
5 Series F/7/Police 14713-15332
6 Series BA, DB, GA
7 areaofdesign.com/coco-chanel/#biography
8 Ibid.
9 Beevor, A. and Cooper, A., *Paris After the Libération* (Penguin Books, 2007) p. 134
10 www.messynessychic.com/2015/10/08/inside-the-paris-department-store-where-nazis-shopped-for-stolen-jewish-goods/
11 Gensburger, S., *Witnessing the Robbing of the Jews*, translated by Jonathan Hensher and Elisabeth Fourmont (Indiana University Press, 2015)
12 www.chanel-muggeridge.co.uk
13 Ibid.
14 Ibid.
15 Abescat, B. and Stavridès, Y., *L'Express*, 11 July 2005, p. 1
16 18 August 1940
17 Maurus, V., 'No. 5, l éternel parfum de femme', *Le Monde*, 20 April 1997, p. 9
18 Gold, M.J., *Crossroads Marseilles, 1940* (Doubleday, 1980)
19 Mortimer, G., 'The Glamorous American Socialite Who Saved Thousands from the Nazis', www.historynet.com, 12 December 2022
20 US National Archives, APA letter, 25 March 1941
21 US National Archives, OSS Personnel Name File, Thomas, Entry 168 A, Box 2
22 Berman, P. and Sawaya, Z., 'Chanel Lost Her Most Precious Asset', *Forbes*, 21 April 1989
23 Hondelatte, C., *Hondelatte Raconte* podcast, 'Coco Chanel: Coco la collabo' (Europe 1, 27 August 2020)
24 Charles-Roux, E., *Chanel*, p. 320

Chapter 9
1 *Le Soir*, 2 August 1940
2 Kraft, P. and Ledard, C., 'From Rallet N°1 to Chanel N°5 versus Mademoiselle Chanel N°1', *Perfumer & Flavorist*, Volume 32, October 2007
3 www.snopes.com/news/2017/03/06/coco-chanel-nazi-spy
4 Munday, A.H., 'Remembering French Collaboration and Resistance during Vichy France during the Vel' d'Hiv Roundup', *Grand Valley Journal of History*, Volume 4, 2015

5 Ibid.
6 Hondelatte, C., *Hondelatte Raconte* podcast, 'Coco Chanel: Coco la collabo' (Europe 1, 27 August 2020)
7 Anderson, C., 'Coco Chanel – Her Re-Entry', *Classic Chicago Magazine*, 17 January 2021
8 www.chanel-muggeridge.co.uk
9 Contessa Isabella Vacani von Fechtmann to Rhonda Garelick, Garelick, R., *Mademoiselle: Coco Chanel and the Pulse of History* (Random House, 2014) p. 533
10 Pascal, J., 'Vichy's shame', *The Guardian*, 11 May 2002
11 www.theguardian.com/business/2023/dec/29/loreal-heiress-and-board-member-francoise-bettencourt-meyers-is-first-woman-to-amass-100bn-fortune

Chapter 10
1 Vaughan, H., *Sleeping with the Enemy* (Vintage Books, 2012) p. 209
2 Ibid., p. 237
3 Vaughan, H., 'Sleeping with the Enemy: Coco Chanel's Secret War', *The New York Times*, 2 September 2011
4 Garelick, R.K., *Mademoiselle*, p. 351
5 Berma and Sawaya, 'How Chanel Lost Her Most Precious Asset'
6 www.kafkaesqueblog.com/2014/01/24/coco-chanel-nazi-collaborator-spy
7 Gilbert, M., *Winston S. Churchill: Volume 7 1941–1945* (Heinemann, 1986) p. 943
8 Schellenberg, W., *The Labyrinth* (Harper Brothers, 1956) p. 8
9 Doerries, R., *Hitler's Last Chief of Foreign Intelligence: Allied Interrogations of Walter Schellenberg* (Frank Case Publishers, 2003) p. 164
10 US National Archives, 'Final Report', Schellenberg file,65; OSS file, XE001752, Box 195,65
11 www.chanel-muggeridge.co.uk
12 OSS Schellenberg file
13 Doerries, R., *Hitler's Intelligence Chief, Walter Schellenberg* (Enigma Books, 2009) p. 240
14 OSS Schellenberg file
15 The Sir Winston Churchill Archive Trust, CHAR 2/255, Bate
16 OSS Schellenberg file
17 Goni, U., *The Real Odessa* (Granta Books, 2002) p. 241
18 OSS Schellenberg file
19 www.chanel-muggeridge.co.uk
20 Ibid.
21 Ibid.
22 Ibid.

Chapter 11
1 Churchill Archive Trust, Chartwell, CHAR 20/198 A
2 Ibid.
3 www.chanel-muggeridge.co.uk
4 Churchill Archive, Chartwell, CHAR 20,198
5 Ibid.
6 Muggeridge, M., *Chronicles of Wasted Time Part 2*, p. 269
7 Picardie, J., 'An intimate portrait of Gabrielle Chanel: the woman at the vanguard of modernist fashion', *Harper's Bazaar*, 9 September 2023
8 Vaughan, H., *Sleeping with the Enemy*, p. 210; Higham, C., *The Duchess of Windsor* (John Wiley & Sons, 2005) pp. 359–362
9 Madsen, A., *Chanel: A Woman of Her Own* (Owl Books, 1990) p. 262

10 Morand, P., *The Allure of Chanel* (Pushkin Press, 2008) p. 178
11 Cooper, D. (Viscount Norwich), *The Duff Cooper Diaries 1915–1951*, edited by John Julius Norwich, (Weidenfeld & Nicholson 2005) p. 319
12 Ibid., p. 323
13 Vaughan, *Sleeping with the Enemy*, p. 207
14 Cooper, *The Duff Cooper Diaries*, p. 320
15 Ibid., p. 295
16 Muggeridge, *Chronicles of Wasted Time Part 2*, p. 510
17 Cooper, *The Duff Cooper Diaries*, Introduction xiii
18 Guillaume Pollack/Private/Archive reference number: SHD/GR 16 P 118851
19 Ibid.
20 Cartner-Morley, J., 'Coco Chanel exhibition reveals fashion designer was part of French resistance', *The Guardian*, 9 September 2023
21 Pollack, G., *The silent army: History of resistance networks in France 1940-1945* (Editions Tallandier, 2022)
22 www.france24.com/en/europe/20231127-historian-debunks-claims-that-coco-chanel-served-in-the-french-resistance
23 Ibid.
24 Ibid.
25 www.france24.com/en/europe/20231127-historian-debunks-claims-that-coco-chanel-served-in-the-french-resistance
26 Ibid.
27 Charles-Roux, *Chanel*, p. 346
28 www.poetryfoundation.org
29 Reverdy, P., letter to Louis Thomas, reprinted in *Pierre Reverdy* (Culturesfrance, 2006) p. 64
30 Vaughan, *Sleeping with the Enemy*, p. 204
31 www.harpersbazaar.com/uk/fashion/fashion-news/a45019860/gabrielle-chanel-october-2023

Chapter 12
1 Charles-Roux, E., *L'irreguliere: Ou, Mon Itineraire Chanel* (Grasset, 1974) pp. 536–537
2 Vaughan, *Sleeping with the Enemy* p. 204
3 Ibid., p. 210
4 Ibid., p. 277
5 Ibid., p. 210
6 Vaughan, H., 'Sleeping With the Enemy: Coco Chanel's Secret War', *The New York Times*, 2 September 2011
7 Berman, P. and Sawaya, Z., 'How Chanel Lost Her Most Precious Asset', *Forbes*, 21 April 1989
8 Garelick, R., *Mademoiselle*, p. 351
9 www.thundersaidenergy.com/2022/03/03/oil-and-war-ten-conclusions-from-wwii
10 Ibid.
11 web.archive.org/web/20250207011106/http://www.history.army.mil:80/books/wwii/civaff/ch32.htm

Chapter 13
1 www.aspectsofhistory.com/rationing-and-the-black-market-in-paris-during-the-war
2 Aziz, P., *Tu trahiras sans vergogne: Historie deux 'collabos' du 93, rue Lauriston Bonny et Lafont* (Fayard, 1969)

3   Othen, C., *The King of Nazi Paris* (Biteback, 2020)
4   Boudard, A., *L'Étrange Monsieur Joseph* (Pocket, 1998) p. 152
5   Aziz, *Tu trahiras sans vergogne*, p. 44
6   Doyle, P 'The forgotten story of the … France football captain who murdered for Hitler', *The Guardian*, 16 November 2009
7   Ibid.
8   Aziz, *Tu trahiras sans vergogne*, p. 74
9   Doyle, 'The forgotten story of the…France football captain who murdered for Hitler'
10 Based on de Brinon and Couraud family correspondence dealing with the exploits of relatives on the periphery of organised crime during the period in question
11 www.memoiresdeguerre.com/article-girier-rene-dit-rene-la-canne-43712871.html
12 Girier R., *Chienne de vie* (André Martel 1952); la Canne, R., *I draw my bow* (The Round Table, 1977); la Canne, R. and Baillon, J-C., *You can't know* (Londreys, 1988)
13 Shakespeare, N., *Ian Fleming: The Complete Man* (Harvill Secker, 2023) p. 111

Chapter 14

1   Dear, I. and Foot, M., *The Oxford Companion to World War II* (Oxford University Press, 2005) p. 321
2   Ibid.
3   Footitt, H., *War and Libération in France: Living with the Liberators* (Palgrave, 2004)
4   Beevor, A. and Cooper, A., *Paris After the Libération 1944–1949* (Penguin, 2007) Chapter 15
5   Ibid.
6   *The New York Times*, 16 May 1990, Section C, p. 8
7   Sebba, A., 'Post-War France and the Petite Théâtre de la Mode', *The Telegraph*, 29 June 2016
8   Ibid.
9   Ibid.
10 '*Qui qu'a vu Coco*' (Who Has Seen Coco?), French ballad
11 Flanner, J., '31, rue Cambon: Coco Chanel's revolutionary style', *The New Yorker*, 14 March 1931

Chapter 15

1   Thomas, D., 'The Power Behind The Cologne', *The New York Times*, 24 February 2002
2   Garelick, R., *Mademoiselle*, p. 363
3   Berman, P. and Sawaya, Z., 'How Chanel Lost Her Most Precious Asset', *Forbes*, 21 April 1989
4   Garelick, *Mademoiselle*, p. 364
5   www.messynessychic.com/2012/04/03/coco-chanel-was-definitely-a-nazi
6   Vaughan, H., *Sleeping with the Enemy*, p.xix
7   Centre d'accueil et de recherche des Archives nationales (CARAN) Z/6/672 greffe 5559
8   Vaughan, H., 'Sleeping with the Enemy: Coco Chanel's Secret War', *The New York Times*, 2 September 2011
9   COGA was also used to support von Dincklage long after his relationship with Chanel ended in the early 1950s, funding his last years on an island off the coast of Spain
10 Phyllis Berman and Zina Sawaya, 'How Chanel Lost Her Most Precious Asset', *Forbes Magazine*, 21 April 1989
11 CARAN Z/6/672 greffe 5559
12 CARAN Z/6/672 greffe 5559

13 British National Archives, Kew: KV2/159 Ledebur file
14 Flanner, J., '31, rue Cambon: Coco Chanel's revolutionary style', *The New Yorker*, 14 March 1931
15 Morand, P., *The Allure of Chanel*, translated by Euan Cameron (Pushkin Press, 2008) Preface
16 Ibid.
17 Ibid.
18 Ibid.
19 Ibid.
20 Morand, *The Allure of Chanel*, Preface
21 Déon, M., *Your Father's Room*, translated by Julian Evans (Gallic Books, 2017) p. 36
22 Flanner, '31, rue Cambon'

Chapter 16
1 James, C., 'Misia and All Paris' (review of *Misia* by Arthur Gold and Robert Fizdale), *London Review of Books*, 1980
2 Ibid.
3 Rorem, N., 'Mistress of the Arts', *The Washington Post*, 2 February 1980
4 James, 'Misia and All Paris'
5 Rorem, 'Mistress of the Arts'
6 Garelick, R., *Mademoiselle*, p. 532
7 Rorem, 'Mistress of the Arts'
8 Vaughan, H., *Sleeping with the Enemy*, p. 109
9 www.swissinfo.ch/eng/culture/how-coco-chanel-spent-her-exile-in-switzerland
10 McNicoll, T., 'Misia, Queen of Paris at the Musee D'Orsay', *Newsweek*, 18 June 2012
11 Rorem, 'Mistress of the Arts'
12 Martin, A., 'Blue Train reveries: the Paris-to-Nice sleeper', *The Observer*, 12 February 2017
13 Parkinson, Justin, 'When pyjamas ruled the fashion world', *BBC News Magazine*, 31 January 2016)
14 Parkinson, J., BBC News Magazine, 31 January 2016
15 Ibid.

Chapter 17
1 Chanel to Delay, Delay, C., *Chanel Solitaire*, p. 152
2 Picardie, J., *Coco Chanel: The Legend and the Life* (HarperCollins, 2010) p. 328
3 Herald, G.W., 'The life and times of the amazing COCO CHANEL', *The Australian Women's Weekly*, 13 January 1965, pp. 23–30
4 'Obituary of Dr. Paul Niehans', *The New York Times*, 4 September 1971
5 Ferris, P., 'The Fountain of Youth' (updated), *The New York Times*, 2 December 1973
6 Ibid.
7 Gacon, S., 'Amnesty: Practices of political forgetting in Europe during the Modern Period', *Encyclopédie d'Histoire Numérique de l'Europe*
8 Anderson, C., 'Coco Chanel – Her Re-Entry'
9 Transcript of an interview with René de Chambrun for the BBC documentary *Reputations*, broadcast on BBC Four, 29 January 2009
10 Rogers, R., 'Wild Irish Women: Carmel Snow, the Fashionista', *Irish America*, October/November 2017
11 Ibid.

12 Galante, P., *Mademoiselle Chanel* (Henry Regency Company, 1973) pp. 204–209
13 Flanner, J., '31, rue Cambon: Coco Chanel's revolutionary style', *The New Yorker*, 14 March 1931
14 Capote, T., *Portraits and Observations* (Random House, 2007) p. 220

Chapter 18

1 Fury, A., 'The Radical History and Philosophy of Coco Chanel', *AnOther Magazine*, 22 September 2023, Autumn/Winter Issue
2 Flanner, J., '31, rue Cambon: Coco Chanel's revolutionary style', *The New Yorker*, 14 March 1931
3 Ibid.
4 Ibid.
5 Reed, R., 'Coco Chapel's Clothes and Jewelry Are Auctioned in London', *The New York Times*, 4 December 1978
6 Anderson, C., 'Coco Chanel – Her Re-Entry'
7 Herald, G.W., 'The life and times of the amazing COCO CHANEL'
8 Ibid.
9 'What Chanel Storm is About: She Takes a Chance on a Comeback', *Life*, 1 March 1954, p. 49
10 'Chanel a La Page? "But No!"', *Los Angeles Times*, 6 February 1954
11 Anderson, 'Coco Chanel – Her Re-Entry'
12 Ibid.
13 Fury, 'The Radical History and Philosophy of Coco Chanel'
14 Herald, 'The life and times of the amazing COCO CHANEL'
15 Ibid.
16 Anderson, 'Coco Chanel – Her Re-Entry'
17 'What Chanel Storm is About: She Takes a Chance on a Comeback', *Life*
18 Anderson, Coco Chanel – Her Re-Entry'
19 Ibid.
20 Ibid.
21 Ibid.
22 Thomas, D., 'The Power Behind the Cologne', *The New York Times*, 24 February 2002
23 Morand, P., The Allure of Chanel, translated by Euan Cameron (Pushkin Press, 2008) p. 174

Postscript

1 Camus, A., *The Outsider*, translated Sandra Smith (Penguin Modern Classics, 2013). Smith's translation is based on a recording of Camus reading his work aloud on French radio in 1954
2 Galante, P., *Mademoiselle Chanel*, p. 260

SELECT BIBLIOGRAPHY

Archival source materials comprising public and personal collections, interviews, and correspondence with subject matter experts, family members with access to family records, and relevant contemporary witnesses

France
Archives de la Préfecture de Police, Paris
Archives de la ville de Sanary-sur-Mer
Archives departmentalise du Var
Bibliotheque Nationale de France, Mitterand and Richelieu
Cabinet du Minster de l'Intérieur, Mission des Archives Nationales
Centre d'Accueil et de Recherche des Archives Nationales
Centre de Recherches des Archives Nationales (CARAN)
Centre historique des archives, département de l'armée de terre (archives du 2eme Bureau, Army Intelligence) (CHADAT)
Couraud family
de Brinon family records
Dr Guillaume Pollack
Services Speciaux

Britain
British Library Newspaper Library, London
British Library, London
National Archives, Kew
The Sir Winston Churchill Archive Trust, Chartwell

United States
Henry Ransom Center, University of Texas, Austin
Unites States Department of State, Washington
United States Holocaust Memorial Museum, Washington
US National Archives and Records Administration, Maryland

Germany and Switzerland
Archives of German Foreign Office, German Embassy, Paris
Bundesarchiv, Berlin
Bundesarchiv-Militararchiv, Freiburg
Landesarchiv, Berlin State Archives
Swiss Federal and Cantonal Archives, Bern

Collections
Brooklyn Museum Costume Collection at The Metropolitan Museum of Art
Patrimoine, France
The Metropolitan Museum of Art, New York
Victoria & Albert Museum

Contemporary Internet Sources

www.10magazine.com/chanel-speaking-in-code
www.alexautographs.com/auction-lot/adolf-hitler-s-fuhrer-order-to-prepare-defenses-f_4FF4826953
annesebba.com/journalism/in-the-world-of-fashion-the-war-was-just-beginning-in-1944-post-war-france-and-the-petit-theatre-de-la-mode
www.areaofdesign.com/coco-chanel
www.aspectsofhistory.com/rationing-and-the-black-market-in-paris-during-the-war
www.atlasobscura.com
www.bbc.co.uk
www.bbc.co.uk/history/worldwars/genocide/jewish_deportation_01.shtml
www.chanel-muggeridge.co.uk
www.chanel.com
www.christies.com
www.cnn.com
www.dailymail.co.uk
www.etoile.co.uk
everything.explained.today/German_military_administration_in_occupied_France_during_World_War_II
www.express.co.uk
www.france24.com/en/europe/20231127-historian-debunks-claims-that-coco-chanel-served-in-the-french-resistance
www.grosvenor.com
www.harpersbazaar.com/uk/fashion/fashion-news/a45019860/gabrielle-chanel-october-2023
www.history.army.mil/
www.historyextra.com
www.iwm.org.uk/history/the-german-response-to-d-day
www.kafkaesqueblog.com/2014/01/24/coco-chanel-nazi-collaborator-spy
www.lastyeargirl.blogspot.com/2013/05/the-world-of-carmel-snow
www.lithub.com/on-hitlers-last-desperate-plan-to-destroy-paris
www.memoiresdeguerre.com/article-girier-rene-dit-rene-la-canne
www.messynessychic.com
www.mylondon.news
www.nationalarchives.gov.uk
www.nationalww2museum.org/war/articles/first-lieutenant-levitt-c-beck-jr
www.newyorksocialdiary.com/my-love-affair-with-chanel-part-ii & iii
www.poetryfoundation.org
www.smithsonianmag.com/history/vichy-government-france-world-war-ii-willingly-collaborated-nazis-180967160
www.snopes.com/news/2017/03/06/coco-chanel-nazi-spy
www.sorbonne-universite.fr/en/university/history-and-heritage/archives
www.swissinfo.ch/eng/culture/how-coco-chanel-spent-her-exile-in-switzerland
www.thebeaumonde.org

www.theglampad.com
www.theguardian.com
www.thejc.com/lifestyle/features/how-far-did-the-uk-aristocracy-s-love-of-the-nazis-really-go
www.thelandofdesire.com/2020/01/16/coco-chanel
www.thenationalnews.com
www.theparisreview.org/blog/2016/09/19/paris-camuss-notebooks
www.thesun.co.uk
www.thundersaidenergy.com/2022/03/03/oil-and-war-ten-conclusions-from-wwii
www.time.com
www.townandcountrymag.com
www.u-paris.fr/en/2019/12
www.victorianweb.org

Newspapers, Magazines, Television Programs, Podcasts and Videos

Parliamentary Debates (Hansard); *The Architectural Digest*; *International Business Times*; *Professional Security Magazine* (Online); *The Guardian*; *The Washington Post*; *Vanity Fair*; *The New York Times*; *Financial Times*; *Daily Mail*; *Times Literary Supplement*; *The Melbourne Age*; *The Rake*; *Harper's Bazaar*; *Time*; *The Independent*; BBC America; *History Today*; New York Daily News; *Journal of British Studies*; *Manchester Guardian*, *Royalty Magazine*, *Daily Telegraph* (UK*)*; *The Sydney Morning Herald*; *Launceston Daily Telegraph*; BBC Timewatch; YouTube, Reuters; United Press International; *Los Angeles Times*; *Daily Express* (UK); *Town & Country Magazine*; *The Wall Street Journal*; *The Canberra Times*; *Vogue*, *Le Soir*

Articles

Abescat, B. and Stavridès, Y., 'Behind the Chanel Empire ... The Fabulous Story of the Wertheimers', *l'Express*, 2005

Anderson, C., 'Coco Chanel – Her Re-Entry', *Classic Chicago Magazine*, 17 January 2021

Barchfield, J., 'New book claims Coco Chanel was anti-Semite and Nazi spy', *The Associated Press*, 17 August 2011

Berman, P. and Sewaya, Z., 'The Billionaires Behind Chanel', *Forbes*, 3 April 1989

Berman. P. and Sawaya, Z., 'How Chanel Lost Her Most Precious Asset', *Forbes*, 21 April 1989

Brook, T., 'Collaboration in the History of Wartime East Asia', *The Asia-Pacific Journal*, 2 July 2008

Cartner-Morley, J., 'Coco Chanel exhibition reveals fashion designer was part of French resistance', *The Guardian*, 9 September 2023

de Rochemont, R., 'The French Underground', *Life*, 24 August 1942

Doyle, P., 'The forgotten story of the...France football captain who murdered for Hitler', *The Guardian*, 16 November 2009

Étiève-Cartwright, B., 'French Fashion during the German Occupation', *World History Encyclopedia*, 2 October 2024

Ferris, P., 'The Fountain of Youth' (updated), *The New York Times*, 2 December 1973

Fishman, S., 'Grand Delusions: The Unintended Consequences of Vichy France's Prisoner of War Propaganda', *Journal of Contemporary History*, 1991

Flanner, J., '31, rue Cambon: Coco Chanel's revolutionary style', *The New Yorker*, 14 March 1931

SELECT BIBLIOGRAPHY

Fury, A., 'The Radical History and Philosophy of Coco Chanel', *AnOther Magazine*, Autumn/Winter issue, 22 September 2023

Gacon, S., 'Amnesty: Practices of political forgetting in Europe during the Modern Period', *Encyclopédie d'Histoire Numérique de l'Europe*

George, C., 'Critics Scoffed but Women Bought: Coco Chanel's Comeback Fashions Reflect the Desires of the 1950s American Woman', *The Forum: Journal of History*, Volume 3: Issue 1, Article 13, 2011

Gladstone, W.E., as quoted in *The Spectator*, Vols 168–169 (1942) p. 182, 'Duty of a Prime Minister'

Hastings, M., 'Smoke and Mirrors', *The New York Review*, 27 September 2018

Herald, G.W., 'The life and times of the amazing COCO CHANEL', *The Australian Women's Weekly*, 13 January 1965

Hondelatte C., *Hondelatte Raconte* podcast: 'Coco Chanel: Coco la collabo' (Europe 1, 27 August 2020)

Interview with René de Chambrun for the BBC documentary *Reputations*, broadcast on BBC Four, 29 January 2009

James, C., 'Misia and All Paris', review of *Misia* by Arthur Gold and Robert Fizdale, *London Review of Books*, 1980

Kraft, P. and Ledard, C., 'From Rallet N°1 to Chanel N°5 versus Mademoiselle Chanel N°1', *Perfumer & Flavorist*, Vol. 32, October 2007

Lewis, D., 'Ned Rorem, Composer Known for Both His Music and His Diaries, Dies at 99', *The New York Times*, 18 November 2022

Mah, A., 'This Picture Tells a Tragic Story of What Happened to Women After D-Day', *Time*, 6 June 2018

Mahoney, D.J., 'Rediscovering St. Mugg', *The Catholic Thing*, 13 October 2010

Martin, A., 'Blue Train reveries: the Paris-to-Nice sleeper', *The Observer*, 12 February 2017

Maurus, V., 'No. 5, l éternel parfum de femme', *Le Monde*, 20 April 1997

McAuley, J., 'The Exchange: Coco Chanel and the Nazi Party', *The New Yorker*, 31 August 2011

McNicoll, T., 'Misia, Queen of Paris, at the Musee D'Orsay', *Newsweek*, 18 June 2012

Melvin, J., 'Nazi general didn't save Paris: historian', *The Local*, 25 August 2014

Mortimer, G., 'The Glamorous American Socialite Who Saved Thousands from the Nazis', www.historynet.com, 12 December 2022

Muhlstein, A., 'The Cut of Coco', *The New York Review*, 9 October 2014

Munday, A.H., 'Remembering French Collaboration and Resistance during Vichy France during the Vel' d'Hiv Roundup', *Grand Valley Journal of History*, Vol. 4, 2015

Parkinson, J., 'When pyjamas ruled the fashion world', *BBC News Magazine*, 31 January 2016

Pascal, J., 'Vichy's shame', *The Guardian*, 11 May 2002

Picardie, J., 'An intimate portrait of Gabrielle Chanel: the woman at the vanguard of modernist fashion', *Harper's Bazaar*, 9 September 2023

Picardie, J., 'The secret life of Coco Chanel', *The Daily Telegraph*, 5 September 2010

Randall, C., 'General "spared Paris by disobeying Fuhrer"', *The Daily Telegraph*, 24 August 2004

Reed, R., 'Coco Chanel's Clothes and Jewelry Are Auctioned in London', *The New York Times*, 4 December 1978

Reverdy, P., letter to Louis Thomas (reprinted in *Pierre Reverdy*: Cultures Frances 2006)

Rogers, R., 'Wild Irish Women: Carmel Snow, the Fashionista', *Irish America Magazine*, October/November 2017

Rorem, N., 'Mistress of the Arts', *The Washington Post*, 2 February 1980

Taylor, D., 'When the OSS Meant Business for Spies', www.medium.com, 30 March 2018
Thomas, D., 'The Power Behind the Cologne', *The New York Times*, 24 February 2002
Thurman, J., 'Scenes From a Marriage', *The New Yorker*, 15 May 2005
[Unknown], 'Chanel a La Page? "But No!"', *Los Angeles Times*, 6 February 1954
[Unknown], 'Chanel Criticizes Sack Look', *Los Angeles Times*, 9 September 1957
[Unknown], 'Dior, Chanel Aim at Budget Trade', *Los Angeles Times*, 18 June 1957
[Unknown], 'Foreign News: Feeneesh?', *Time*, 15 February 1954
[Unknown], 'French Designer Griffe Makes Most of the Tunic', *Los Angeles Times*, 3 August 1950
[Unknown], 'H Hour, H Line', *Newsweek*, 9 August 1954
[Unknown], 'Just a Simple Little Dressmaker', *Life*, 19 August 1957
[Unknown], 'Serene Elegance and Taste Mark Coco Chanel Collection', *Los Angeles Times*, 31 July 1956
[Unknown], 'Spring Clothes Deserve Medals', *New York Times*, 20 March 1957
[Unknown], 'The Strong Ones', *The New Yorker*, 28 September 1957
[Unknown], 'What Chanel Storm is About: She Takes a Chance on A Comeback', *Life*, 1 March 1954
[Unknown], 'Obituary of Dr. Paul Niehans', *The New York Times*, 4 September 1971
[Unknown], 'Paul Collette, the man who shot Pierre Laval and Marcel Deat, is expected to be condemned and executed early this week, the Vichy correspondent of the Basler Nachrichten said today', *The New York Times*, 1 September 1941, p. 6
Vaughan H., quoted by Andy Walker, BBC Today, BBC Radio 4, 20 August 2011
Vaughan, H., 'Sleeping with the Enemy: Coco Chanel's Secret War', *The New York Times*, 2 September 2011
Wilson, A., 'Coco Chanel's other life', *Tatler*, 22 May 2017
Wilson, B., 'Why are you so fat?', *London Review of Books*, Vol. 32, No. 1, 7 January 2010

Secondary Materials

Argyle, R., *The Paris Game: Charles de Gaulle, the Liberation of Paris, and the Gamble that Won France* (DunDurn Press, 2014)
Auda, G., *Les belles années du 'milieu', 1940–1944: le grand banditisme dans la machine répressive allemande en France* (Éditions Michalon, 2013)
Aziz, P., *In the service of the enemy: the French Gestapo in the provinces 1940-1944* (Fayard, 1972)
Aziz, P., *Tu trahiras sans vergogne: historie deux "collabos" du 93, rue Lauriston Bonny et Lafont* (Fayard, 1969)
Baillén, C., *Chanel Solitaire*, translated by Barbara Bray (William Collins Sons & Co. Ltd, 1973)
Beevor, A. and Cooper, A., *Paris After the Libération* (Penguin Books, 2007)
Belot, R., *Les Resistants* (Larousse, 2006)
Bergère, M., *Economic cleansing in France during the Liberation* (Presses universitaires de Rennes, 2008)
Berlière, J-M., *Polices des temps noirs: France, 1939–1944* (Perrin, 2018)
Bott, D., *Chanel: Collections and Creations* (Thames & Hudson, 2007)
Boudard, A., *L'étranger Monsieur Joseph* (Pocket, 1998)
Briand, L., *Alexandre Villaplane, captain of 'les Bleus' and Nazi officer* (Plein Jour, 2022)
Camus, A., *The Fall* (Penguin Classics, 1990)
la Canne, R., *I draw my bow* (The Round Table, 1977)
la Canne, R. and Baillon, J-C., *You can't know* (Londreys, 1988)
Capote, T., *Portraits and Observations* (Random House, 2007)

SELECT BIBLIOGRAPHY

Chaney, L., *Coco Chanel: An Intimate Life* (Penguin, 2011)
Charles-Roux, E., *L'irreguliere: Ou, Mon Itineraire Chanel* (Grasset, 1974)
Charles-Roux, E., *Chanel* (Jonathan Cape, 1976)
Charles-Roux, E., *Chanel: Her Life, Her World and the Woman Behind the Legend She Herself Created*, trans. Nancy Amphoux (Alfred A. Knopf, 1975)
Charles-Roux, E., *Chanel and Her World: Friends, Fashion, and Fame* (Vendome Press, 2005)
Cobb, M., *The Resistance: the French fight against the Nazis* (Pocket Books, 2009)
Cobb, M., *Eleven days in August: the liberation of Paris in 1944* (Simon & Schuster, 2013)
Cocteau, J., *Théâtre: Les Monstres sacrés. La Machine à écrire. Renaud et Armide. L'Aigle à deux tête* (Gallimard, 1962)
Collingham, E., *The Taste of War: World War II and the Battle for Food* (Penguin Press, 2012)
Collins, L. and Lapierre, D., *Is Paris Burning?* (Penguin Books, 1965)
Combeau, Y., *Histoire de Paris* (Presses Universitaires de France, 2013)
Cooper, D. (Viscount Norwich), *The Duff Cooper Diaries 1915-1951*, edited by John Julius Norwich (Weidenfeld & Nicholson, 2005)
de Courcy, A., *Chanel's Riviera: Glamour, Decadence, and Survival in Peace and War, 1930–1944* (St Martin's Press, 2020)
Cullen, O. and Burks, C.K. (eds), *V&A Gabrielle Chanel exhibition book* (V&A Publications, 2023)
Davis, M., *Classic Chic: Music, Fashion and Modernism* (University of California Press, 2006)
Dank, M., *The French Against the French: Collaboration and Resistance* (J.B. Lippincott Company, 1974)
Dear, I. and Foot, M., *The Oxford Companion to World War II* (Oxford University Press, 2005)
Delarue, J., *Smuggling and crime under the Occupation* (Fayard, 1993)
Delay, C., *Chanel Solitaire*, translated by Barbara Bray (Collins, 1973)
De la Haye, A. and Tobin, S., *Chanel: The Couturiere at Work* (Victoria & Albert Museum, 1994)
Déon, M., *Your Father's Room*, translated by Julian Evans (Gallic Books, 2017)
Doerries, R., *Hitler's Last Chief of Foreign Intelligence: Allied Interrogations of Walter Schellenberg* (Frank Case Publishers, 2003)
Doerries, R., *Hitler's Intelligence Chief, Walter Schellenberg* (Enigma Books, 2009)
Drake, D., *Paris at War: 1939–1944* (Belknap Press, 2015)
Eder, C., *Countesses of the Gestapo* (Grasset, 2006)
Fiemeyer, I., *Intimate Chanel* (Flammarion, 2011)
Fiemeyer, I., *CHANEL: The Enigma* (Flammarion, 2019)
Footitt, H., *War and Libération in France: Living with the Liberators* (Palgrave, 2004)
Frame, A., *Toto & Coco: Spies, seduction and the fight for survival* (Kelvin House, 2020)
Galante, P., *Mademoiselle Chanel* (Henry Regency Company, 1973)
Garelick, R., *Mademoiselle: Coco Chanel and the Pulse of History* (Picador, 2016)
Gassend, J-L., *Operation Dragoon: Autopsy of a Battle, the Allied Liberation of the French Riviera* (Schiffer Publishing, 2014)
Gensburger, S., *Witnessing the Robbing of the Jews*, translated by Jonathan Hensher and Elisabeth Fourmont (Indiana University Press, 2015)
Gilbert, M., *Winston S. Churchill: Volume 7 1941-1945* (Heinemann, 1986)
Gildea, R., *Fighters in the shadows: a new history of the French resistance* (Allen & Unwin, 2015)
Gildea, R., *Marianne in Chains* (Pan Macmillan UK, 2002)
Glass, C., *Americans in Paris: Life and Death under Nazi Occupation 1940-44* (HarperPress, 2009)
Gold, M.J., *Crossroads Marseilles, 1940* (Doubleday, 1980)

Girier, R., *Chienne de vie* (André Martel, 1952)
Haedrich, M., *Coco Chanel: Her Life, Her Secrets* (Little Brown, 1972)
Hampton, C., *Les Liaisons Dangereuses* from the novel by Choderlos de Laclos (Faber & Faber, 1985)
Higham, C., *The Duchess of Windsor* (John Wiley & Sons, 2005)
Holt, T., *The Deceivers: Allied Military Deception in the Second World War* (Skyhorse, 2007)
Hunter, I., *Malcolm Muggeridge: A Life* (Collins, 1980)
Ingrams, R., *Muggeridge: The Biography* (HarperCollins, 1995)
Jacquemard, S., *The Bonny-Lafont gang* (Fleuve noir, 1992)
Judt, T., *Postwar: A History of Europe Since 1945* (Pimlico, 2007)
Kedward, H., and Wood, N., *The Liberation of France: Image and Event* (Berg Publishers, 1995)
Keegan, J., *Six Armies in Normandy: From D-Day to the Liberation of Paris June 6th–August 25th, 1944* (Pimlico Military Classics, 2011)
King, D., *Death in the City of Light: The Serial Killer of Nazi-Occupied Paris* (Crown, 2011)
Kladstrup, D., *Wine and War: The French, the Nazis, and the Battle for France's Greatest Treasure* (Broadway Books, 2002)
Knight, F., *The French Resistance 1940–44* (Lawrence and Wishart, 1975)
Madsen, A., *Coco Chanel: A Biography* (Bloomsbury Publishing Lives of Women, 2009)
Madsen, A., *Chanel: A Woman of Her Own* (Henry Holt and Company, 2013)
Madsen, A., *Chanel: A Woman of Her Own* (Owl Books, 1990)
Mazzeo, T.J., *The Secret of Chanel No. 5* (HarperCollins, 2010)
Mazzeo, T.J., *The Hotel on Place Vendome: Life, Death, and Betrayal at the Hotel Ritz in Paris* (HarperCollins, 2014)
McCrum, R., *Wodehouse, A Life* (W.W. Norton, 2004)
Millington, C., *France in the Second World War: Collaboration, Resistance, Holocaust, Empire* (Bloomsbury Publishing, 2020)
Miniac, J-F., *Major criminal cases in the Doubs* (De Borée, 2009)
Mitchell, A., *In Nazi Paris: The History of an Occupation, 1940-1944* (Berghahn Books, 2010)
Morand, P., *L'Allure de Chanel* (Hermann, 1996)
Morand, P., *The Allure of Chanel*, translated by Euan Cameron (Pushkin Press, 2008)
Muggeridge, M., *Chronicles of Wasted Time Part 2: The Infernal Grove* (Fontana Books, 1981)
Nicholas, L., *The Rape of Europa: The Fate of Europe's Treasures in the Third Reich and the Second World War* (Paperpac, 1994)
Othen, C., *The King of Nazi Paris* (Biteback, 2020)
Penaud, G., *Inspector Pierre Bonny: The Fallen Policeman of the French Gestapo of 93, rue Lauriston* (Harmattan, 2011)
Picardie, J., *Coco Chanel: The Legend and the Life* (HarperCollins, 2010)
Pollack, G., *The silent army: History of resistance networks in France 1940–1945* (Editions Tallandier, 2022)
Porch, D., *The French Secret Services: From the Dreyfus Affair to the Gulf War* (Farrar Straus & Giroux, 1995)
Ray, R., *Rapprochement with France in the service of Hitler? Otto Abetz and German policy towards France 1930–1942* (Oldenbourg, 2000)
Reverdy, P., *Selected poems Pierre Reverdy: a bilingual edition*, translated by Kenneth Rexroth (Jonathan Cape, 1973)
Ridley, G., *Bend'Or, Duke of Westminster: A Personal Memoir* (Quartet Books, 1986)
Rolli, P., *The North African Phalange in the Dordogne: the story of an alliance between the underworld and the Gestapo, 15 March–19 August 1944* (Éditions l'Histoire en Partage, 2013)

Rosbottom, R.C., *When Paris Went Dark* (Little Brown, 2014)
Sapiro, G., *The French Writers' War 1940–1953* (Duke University Press, 2014)
Schellenberg, W., *The Labyrinth* (Harper Brothers, 1956)
Schoenbrun, D., *Soldiers of the Night: The Story of the French Resistance* (Dutton, 1980)
Seaton, J., *Pinkoes and Traitors: The BBC and the Nation, 1974–1987* (Profile Books, 2015)
Sebba, A., *Les Parisiennes; How the Women of Paris lived, loved and died in the 1940s* (Weidenfeld & Nicolson, 2016)
Shakespeare, N., *Ian Fleming: The Complete Man* (Harvill Secker, 2023)
Simon, L., *Coco Chanel* (Reaktion Books, 2011)
Smith, J-E., *The Liberation of Paris: How Eisenhower, De Gaulle, and Von Choltitz Saved the City of Light* (Simon & Schuster, 2019)
Smith, N., *Churchill on the Riviera: Winston Churchill, Wendy Reves, and the Villa La Pausa Built by Coco Chanel* (Biblio Publishing, 2017)
Smith, G.N., *The Oxford History of World Cinema* (Oxford University Press, 1997)
Sweets, J., *The Politics of Resistance in France, 1940–1944: A History of the Mouvements Unis de la Résistance* (Northern Illinois University, 1976)
Thornton, W., *The Liberation of Paris* (Harcourt, Brace, and World, 1962)
Trevor-Roper, H., *The Wartime Journals*, edited by Richard Davenport-Hines (I.B. Tauris, 2012)
Vaughan, H., *Sleeping with the Enemy* (Vintage Books, 2012)
Venohr, W., *Stauffenberg. Symbol of Resistance: The Man Who Almost Killed Hitler* (Frontline Books, 2019)
Wallach, J., *Chanel: Her Style and Her Life* (N. Talese, 1998)
Wieviorka, O., *The French Resistance*, translated by Jane Marie Todd (Belknap Press, 2016)
Wolfe, G., *Malcolm Muggeridge: A Biography* (Hodder & Stoughton, 1995)
Zaloga, S., *Liberation of Paris 1944: Patton's Race for the Seine* (Osprey, 2012)

INDEX

2nd Armoured Division (2e DB), French 46–7
2nd SS Panzer Division, German 172
4th Infantry Division, US 47

The Allure of Chanel (Paul Morand) 116
Americans, hostility to 174–5
Amiot, Felix (aircraft manufacturer) 106–7, 109–10, 114–17
amnesty laws 211–2
Angelina (Parisian patisserie) 19
Arletty (actress) 52
Arnaud, Marie-Hélène (model) 223
Atelier No. 5 13
Aubert, Angèle (CC's right-hand woman) 81
auction of CC's work 218–20
Auzello, Blanche (*Résistance* member) 41–4
Auzello, Claude (Hôtel Ritz manager) 41–2

Balenciaga, Cristóbal (designer) 214
Balsan, Étienne (CC's lover) 57, 80
Bate, Vera (CC's friend) 102, 212
Beauplan, Robert de (journalist) 204
Beaux, Ernest (perfumer) 62, 114–15
Bedaux, Fern (CC's neighbour) 93
Bendor *see* Westminster, 2nd Duke of ('Bendor')
betrayal 41–2
The Bettencourt Affair (Tom Sancton) 118
Bettencourt family (L'Oréal) 119
black marketeers 50
Blanke, Dr Kurt (lawyer) 116
bob cut hair fashion 60
Bonny, Pierre (corrupt police officer) 34, 164–8
Bourbon-Archeambault 85

Bourjois & Cie 62–3, 107
Bousquet, Marie-Louise (socialite) 81–2
Brandl, Hermann 'Otto' (*Abwehr* officer) 165
Brinon, Fernand, Marquis de 172
Brooke, Field Marshal Sir Alan 139
Brown-Sequard, Dr Charles Edouard (cellular therapist) 208
Buchenwald concentration camp 46
Buisson, Émile (gangster) 169
bureaux d'achats 91

Cambon, rue (CC's salon) 20
Camus, Albert (novelist) 32
Capa, Robert (photographer) 48
Capel, Arthur 'Boy' (CC's lover) 58–9, 65, 79
Capote, Truman (novelist) 24
Case, Margaret (fashion editor) 64
casualties 174
Céline (CC's maid) 20–2
cellular therapy 207–10
Centre de Recherches des Archives Nationales 102
Cercle Européen 177
Chambre Syndicale de la Couture 30
Chambrun, Josée 'Chérie-chérie' de (CC's friend) 84
Chambrun, René de (CC's lawyer) 84–5, 181–4
Chanel, Gabrielle 'Coco'
  acquires property 64
  alleged membership of *Résistance* 150–2
  appearance 13–14
  appears before Court of Justice, Paris 185–8
  aversion to bad odours 61–2

INDEX

birth 57
calls maid, Céline, Jeanne 20
and cellular therapy 207–10
close relationship with Churchill,
 exaggerated 142–7
closes down Maison CHANEL 79–80
comeback show, 1954 220–4
confusion over date of FFI
 interrogation 148–50
court order issued for her return to
 Paris 183–5
crops hair 60–1
Déon's (destroyed) biography
 written 190–1
diet 65
and drugs 20–2, 81, 84, 93–4
and Elsa Schiaparelli 63–4
escapes to Switzerland 157–73
and Étienne Balsan 57
fetish about number 5 14–15
first haute couture collection 59
given *Abwehr* agent number and code
 name 95
gives out No. 5 perfume free on
 liberation of Paris 56
in Hollywood 64–5
interrogated by *Les Fifis* 99–104,
 113–14, 119–20
interviewed by Malcolm Muggeridge
 71–7, 95–8, 104–6, 116–17, 143–5
links with *Le Milieu* 162–9
meets Malcolm Muggeridge 53–7
meets with SS General
 Schellenberg 140–1
in Monaco 196–206
money, affection for 23–4
money banked in Switzerland 170
Morand's biography written 188–9
moves into 31 rue Cambon 59
moves to Vichy 82–5
opens first shop 59
and Operation *Modellhut* 142–7
origin of 'Coco' nickname 58
personal car 158–60
prepares Misia Sert's body for
 viewing 193–5
relationship with Wertheimers 63
released from FFI interrogation
 137–9, 150–6
relies on Sedol 20–2

relinquishes perfume rights 182
resurrects Maison CHANEL
 213–15, 220–4
reunited with Spatz 183
sleepwalking 20
smoking 16
stays in Corbères-Abères 80–1
sues Wertheimers 181–2
suite at Hôtel Ritz 20
in Switzerland 178–80
told to leave France after FFI
 interrogation 156–9
travels to Madrid with Vera
 Lombardi 141–2
visits Spain 94
wardrobe, personal 14
wears beach-pyjamas in Monte
 Carlo 203–4
and the Wertheimer brothers 62–3, 93,
 104–6, 113–14
writes to Carmel Snow 214
death 22, 218
Chanel, Julia-Berthe (CC's sister) 78
CHANEL No. 5 invented 62–3
Charles-Roux, Edmonde (CC's friend) 67,
 112, 153
Charles-Roux, François (CC's friend) 56
Chirac, President Jacques 35
Choltitz, General Dietrich von 39–40,
 46–7, 49
Christie's of London (auctioneers) 218–19
Chronicles of Wasted Time (Malcolm
 Muggeridge) 56
Churchill, Prime Minister Winston
 66–7, 137–50
clothing restrictions during
 occupation 30–1
Coco (musical) 19
Cocteau, Jean (artist) 52, 66
COGA trust fund 184–5
collaboration defined 50–2
collections of CC's work assembled
 217–19
Collette, Paul (resistance fighter) 35
Combat newspaper 48
conclusion 229
Corbères-Abères 80–1
Corrèze, Jacques (war criminal) 119
corruption 91–2
Coty, François (perfumer) 30

Couraud, Raymond (French Foreign Legionnaire) 111–12
criminal gangs 162–9
Cullen, Oriole (exhibition curator) 22, 150–1

Dali, Salvador (artist) 64
Dardenne, Lionel (historian) 39–40
Davenport, Miriam (student) 110–11
D-Day invasion 36–7
de Gaulle, General Charles 45–6, 208–9
Déat, Marcel (collaborationist) 35
Delay, Claude (CC's friend) 20–2
demarcation line between French Zones 82
Déon, Michel (author) 190–1
Der Deutsche Wegleiter für Paris 86–7
Dincklage, Baron Hans Günther von ('Spatz') 88–90, 92–3, 98, 101, 140–1, 182–3, 212
Directorat-General des Etudes et Recherches (DOER) *see* Services Speciaux, French
Domenger, Germaine (CC's maid) 52, 137
drug traffic 163–4
Dubois, André-Louis (Vichy official) 84
Duff Cooper, Ambassador Alfred 137–8, 148–50, 156–7

épuration sauvage (wild purge) of Paris 49–52
Eric (French *Résistance* network) 151–2
exodus from Paris 30–2

fashion industry revival 176–8
Les Fifis see French Forces of the Interior (FFI)
Fleury-Marié, Jacqueline (*Résistance* member) 44–5
formula, Chanel No. 5 62–3, 107–9
Francs-tireurs et Partisans (FTP) 45, 156
French Forces of the Interior (FFI) 45–6, 49, 52, 99–103
Fresnes prison 42–6
Fry, Varian (journalist) 110–11
fuel, shortage of 160–1
furniture, Germans loot Jews' 103–14

Gabrielle Chanel: Fashion Manifesto (V&A Museum) 150–2
Gang des Tractions Avant (GTA) 162–9

German garrison in France 36–7
Girier, René (gangster) 168–9
Gold, Mary Jane (Couraud's girlfriend) 110–11
Goldwyn, Samuel (film producer) 64–5
Göring, Reich Marshal Hermann 29, 55
Grosvenor, Hugh 'Bendor' *see* Westminster, 2nd Duke of ('Bendor')
Grumbach, Lilou (CC's secretary) 21–3, 218
Guevara y Sotomayor, Don Armando de *see* Thomas, Herbert Gregory (US president of Chanel)
Guide Aryien 87

Hankey, Henry (British diplomat) 146
Hauteclocque, General Philippe François Marie Leclerc de 153
Herald, George W. (journalist) 13
Hitler, Adolf 38–9, 48
Hôtel de Paris, Monte-Carlo 196–8, 200

indignité nationale crime 52, 155, 211
Iribe, Paul (CC's lover) 103
Is Paris Burning? (Dietrich von Choltitz) 39–40

Jews, reprisals against 115–16

Kharmayeff, Lily (*Résistance* member) 41–3
Kluge, General Günther von 38
Knowles, Isée St John (CC's biographer) 26
Kraft, Dr Philip (Givaudan chemist) 114

La Cagoule anti-semitic outfit 118–19
La Pausa villa, Roquebrune-Cap-Martin 64, 66, 80, 199, 212
Lafont, Henri (gangster) 34, 164–8
L'Allure de Chanel (Paul Morand) 65, 188–9
Lanvin, Jeanne (couturière) 29, 177
Larcher (CC's driver) 81–2, 87
Laval, Pierre (collaborationist) 35, 82, 84
Le Chagrin et la Pitie film 49
Le Milieu (French criminal society) 162–9
Le Témoin journal 103
Le Train Bleu 197, 201–2
Leclercq, Judge Fernand 185–6, 188
Ledebur-Wicheln, Count Joseph von (*Abwehr* agent) 93, 187
Legion of French Volunteers Against Bolshevism 35

INDEX

Lelong, Lucien (couturier) 30
Léon (CC's butler) 52
Lerner, Alan (lyricist) 18–9
Les Françaises, les Français et l'Épuration (François Rouquet and Fabrice Virgili) 49–50
Lévitan department store 103–4
L'Humanité newspaper 48
Lifar, Serge (Ukrainian dancer) 154
Ligeour, Manon (Chanel premier) 215
Limouse, Roger (artist) 26
Lombardi, Colonel Alberto 102–3, 142
Lombardi (Bate), Vera (CC's friend) 141–6
L'Oréal company 118–19
Louis II of Monaco, Prince 199–200
Loutrel, Pierre (gangster) 168
Luizet, Charles (Prefect of Police) 148

Macron, President Emmanuel 35–6
Mademoiselle Chanel (rogue fragrances) 114–15
Madoux, Georges (Maison CHANEL director) 80–1, 115
Madsen, Axel (biographer) 148
Maginot Line 79
Manon (chief seamstress) 81
Marianne in Chains (Robert Gildea) 31
Maryhill Museum of Art, Washington 176–7
Mdivani, Princess Roussy 193
Meier, Frank (Hôtel Ritz barman) 38–9
Meurice, Hôtel 38, 40
Maison Chanel, rue Cambon 20
Mironnet, François (CC's butler) 21
Mitterrand, President François 118–19
Modellhut, Operation 142–7
Molyneux, Edward (designer) 29
Monaco 196–200
Montand, Yves (singer) 87
Morand, Paul (author) 188–9
Moser, First Lieutenant Joseph Frank 'Joe' 46
Moulin, Jean (prefect) 31
Muggeridge, Major Malcolm 59, 67–77, 149
   character 69–70
   meets CC 53–7
   interviews CC 71–7, 95–8, 106–7, 116–17, 143–5
   affair 71–4

Mul family (No 5 ingredient suppliers) 109
Museum of Decorative Arts, Paris 176

'New Look' 214
New Yorker magazine 17
Niebuhr, Hermann (Dr Henri) 92–3, 186
Niehans, Dr Paul (cellular therapist) 207–10

Palasse, André (CC's nephew) 78–9, 92–3, 95, 185–6
Palasse-Labrunie, Gabrielle (CC's great-niece) 26, 74, 137, 156–7
Paris
   under occupation 85–7
   exodus from 30–2
   uprising 45–8
   liberated 29, 48–9
Pascal, Julia (historian) 82–3
'Pat Line' escape route 171
The Patrimoine building 216–7, 220
Patton, General George 159
Perfumer & Flavorist magazine 114
Pétain, Maréchal Philippe (Head of Vichy State) 7, 50, 83–4
Petiot, Marcel André Henri Félix 'Dr Satan' (serial killer) 32–4
Philby, Kim (double-agent) 70
Piaf, Edith (singer) 87
Pierrot le Fou (Crazy Pete) 168
Pinkoes and Traitors (Jean Seaton) 69
Pollack, Dr Guillaume (historian) 151–2
premiers (*atelier* heads) 14
pyjamas, beach 203–4

Rallet No.1 perfume 114
Raphael, Frederick (novelist) 70
rationing in occupied France 90–2
Ravensbruck concentration camp 44–5
Reverdy, Pierre (CC's lover) 153–8, 195
Ritz, Hôtel 20, 38–9, 54–5
Robespierre, Maximilien 50
Rochas, Marcel (collaborator) 177
Rogers, Jackie (model) 17–18, 23
Rol-Tanguy, Colonel Henri (FFI) 45, 47
Roquebrune-Cap-Martin 64, 66, 80, 199, 212
Rosbottom, Ronald C. (writer) 86
Rouff, Maggy (collaborator) 177
Rundstedt, Field Marshal Gerd von 36, 38

Schellenberg, SS General Walter 140–2, 144–5, 184–5, 212
Schiaparelli, Elsa (designer) 20, 29, 63–4
Schillinger, Hans (Spatz's companion) 182–3
Schueller, Eugène (L'Oréal creator) 118–19
Serre, Judge Roger 183, 185
Sert, José-Maria (muralist) 193
Sert, Misia (CC's friend) 20, 84, 192–206
Service du Travail Obligatoire (STO) 86
Services Speciaux, French 56–7, 69–72
show, CC's 1954 comeback 220–4
Sleeping with the Enemy: Coco Chanel's Secret War (Hal Vaughan) 25
Snow, Carmel (*Harper's Bazaar* editor) 64, 213–14
Spatz *see* Dincklage, Baron Hans Günther von ('Spatz')
Stauffenberg, Oberst Claus von 38
Streitz, Robert (*Résistance* supporter) 80
Stülpnagel, General Carl-Heinrich von 38–9
Swanson, Gloria (film star) 65
Switzerland, hotel life in 178–80

Théâtre de la Mode 176–8
Thomas, Herbert Gregory (US president of Chanel) 107–12
Trevor-Roper, Hugh (historian) 69, 97

Tu trahiras sans vergogne (Philippe Aziz) 164, 166

Vaufreland, Baron Louis de (traitor) 92–4, 116, 154, 156, 185–7
Vaughan, Hal (author) 25–6
Versailles 35
Vichy town 82–4
Villaplane, Alex (footballer/criminal) 34, 164–8
vintage clothing mania 219
Voronoff, Dr Serge (cellular therapist) 208

Wallace, Brian (diplomat) 94
Wertenbaker, Charles Christian (correspondent) 48–9
Wertheimer, Jacques (Pierre Wertheimer's son) 109–11
Wertheimer, Paul and Pierre (manufacturers) 62–3, 93, 104–17, 213–14, 224
Westminster, 2nd Duke of ('Bendor') 65–6, 80, 156–8, 212
When Paris Went Dark (Ronald C. Rosbottom) 86
Witnessing the Robbing of the Jews (Sarah Gensburger) 104
Wodehouse, P. G. (writer) 71, 148
wood-fired gas generators 161

By the same author

978 1 80399 438 3

Geneva, April 1987. The staid Swiss town is awash with limousines, journalists and minor European aristocracy. They are all focused on one place: Sotheby's auction house, which is preparing to host the 'auction of the century' – that of the late Duchess of Windsor's jewellery collection.

But where did this treasure trove come from? And was it ever really the Duchess' at all?

You may also enjoy ...

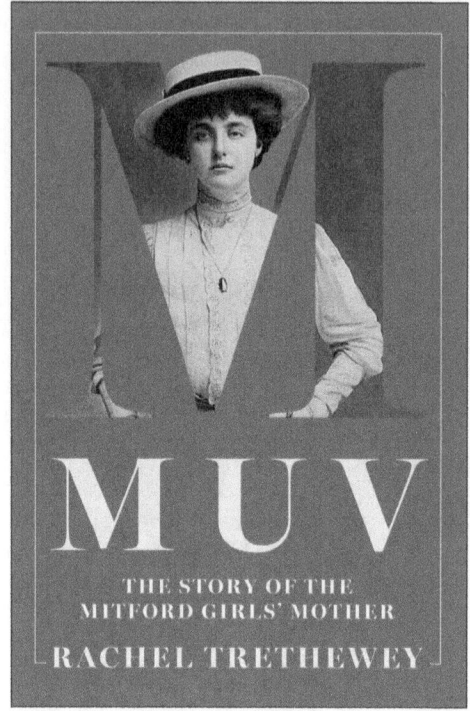

978 1 80399 780 3

Nancy, Pamela, Diana, Unity, Jessica, Deborah: these are the flamboyant Mitford Girls, the Bright Young Things who defined their era. The trials, tribulations and outrageous escapades of these six controversial sisters continue to fascinate us. Yet what about the seventh and arguably most vital Mitford woman of them all – their mother?

The destination for history
www.thehistorypress.co.uk